The Personal
Communication Process

The Personal
Communication Process

John R. Wenburg
University of Nebraska

William W. Wilmot
University of Montana

John Wiley & Sons, Inc.
New York London Sydney Toronto

Library of Congress Cataloging in Publication Data:

Wenburg, John.
   The personal communication process.

   1. Communication—Psychological aspects. I. Title.

BF637.C45W4   808.5   72-7469

ISBN 0-471-93364-3

Printed in the United States of America

10 9 8 7 6 5 4 3 2

For our 2 C's and 4 J's
through whom we perceive things of consequence

Preface

We believe that the central concern in introductory communication courses should be the communication theory that is derived from the study of communication in all the arenas (intrapersonal, interpersonal, small group, public speaking, and mass media). An understanding of the variables of the communication process, per se, makes one a more capable observer and participant in all communication encounters. Most introductory textbooks have treated communication as an interactive process. We, however, view communication as a transactional phenomenon.

Because this book deals with these principal elements in the personal communication process, we feel that it is appropriate for various types of introductory courses. For example, an instructor who teaches communication with a particular focal point, such as interpersonal communication or public speaking, will find that the book gives the student a meaningful context for that perspective of communication. Furthermore, the exercises at the end of each chapter provide the necessary linkage between understanding and specific oral applications. Also, we believe the instructor who blends public speaking and interpersonal communication or deals exclusively with theory will find the book useful as well. We have attempted to blend the behavioral study of communication with traditional contributions. The subject matter is treated descriptively; yet it is balanced with traditional insights.

We believe that if one internalizes the transactional perspective he will begin to understand better his own communication behavior and the communication behavior of others. Again, increased understanding is a prerequisite to more effective participation.

John R. Wenburg
William W. Wilmot

Acknowledgments

Book writing (like all forms of communication) is a process. The actual beginning and end of this process cannot be identified. We can, however, recognize many individuals who had significant inputs at various stages of this process. Several early teachers were influential as they led us to experience the joys of inquiry. Among them are Jerome Davies, Richard Fox, Elbert W. Harrington, Harold M. Jordan, Patrick O. Marsh, and C. Fred Phelps. Our professors to whom we are most indebted for our conceptual approach to communication are William B. Lashbrook, James C. McCroskey, Gerald R. Miller, C. David Mortensen, and Kenneth K. Sereno. Two colleagues deserve special credit for their influence as personal friends, graduate school peers, and professional models—Edward M. Brodaken and Stephen W. King.

The present content of the book was directly affected by the conscientious contributions of our reviewers. Among those who provided valuable insight during early review stages were Daniel P. Millar of Central Michigan University, Linda Putnam of Normandale State Junior College, and Malcolm O. Sillars of the University of Massachusetts. Those reviewers who followed the project from conception to completion and deserve special credit are James L. Golden of Ohio State University, William B. Lashbrook of Illinois State University and Gerald R. Miller of Michigan State University. Also, C. David Mortensen of the University of Wisconsin provided us with significant encouragement and advice in his dual role of friend and counselor during the dark days of early writing before the book was contracted.

Robert C. Morgan of McGraw Hill Publishing Co. supplied us with the necessary initial incentive to tackle the project. We thank Jerry M. Anderson of Central Michigan University for exercising his intellectual and administrative skills in making it possible for us to be together in a working relationship. Without his appreciation for the difficulties in writing a book, this project would not have been possible. Fred H. Bess gave us constant friendship and professional encouragement. Special acknowledgment is also given to Joe Foltz and the rest of EJ's gang.

Charney Wilmot typed numerous working drafts for us to polish so that Ellie Wiles could expertly type the entire manuscript. Just as a book cannot be written without initial inspiration and typing assistance, the necessary facilities must be present for it to reach fruition. We thank the Department of Speech and Dramatic Arts at Central Michigan University for providing those facilities.

Numerous other colleagues and friends have been kind enough to "lend us their ears" and react to our ideas. We owe a *special* debt to our Speech 241 students and our graduate students at Central Michigan University. They gleefully endured the constant references to "our book" and openly criticized those ideas that were in need of refinement.

We thank our editor, Thomas O. Gay, for his insightful analysis and faith. More than any other individual, he directly influenced the completion of this project.

In the academic world of knowledge consumption and generation, parental influence and support are often overlooked. For perspective and confidence, we thank our parents, Mr. and Mrs. Floyd A. Wenburg and Mr. and Mrs. H. W. (Wally) Wilmot.

JRW
WWW

Contents

Part I.   Conceptions of Oral Communication   1

     Chapter 1.   The Nature of Communication   3

         A.   Communication is Personal   3
         B.   Communication is a Process   4
         C.   Communication is Transactional   4
         D.   Communication Defined   5
         E.   "A Sound of Thunder"   7

     Chapter 2.   Communication Arenas   19

         A.   Intrapersonal Communication   20
         B.   Interpersonal Communication   22
         C.   Small Group Communication   29
         D.   Public Speaking   38
         E.   Mass Communication   40

     Chapter 3.   Communication Models   44

         A.   The Process of Conceptualization   45
         B.   Models of Communication   47
         C.   Functions of Models   61
         D.   Shortcomings of Models   62

     Chapter 4.   Ethical Considerations in Communication   65

         A.   An Historical Perspective   66
         B.   Views of Ethics   68
         C.   Choice of Ethical Approaches   71

D.   Application of Ethics to Communication   73
E.   "A Lie is Always a Lie"   74

Part II.   The Exchange of Ideas Through Oral Communication   79

Chapter 5.   Message Mainstays: Verbal Elements   81

A.   The Nature of Language   81
B.   Language Acquisition   84
C.   General Semantics   90
D.   The Dynamics of Language   93

Chapter 6.   The Language of Nonverbal Communication   96

A.   Axioms of Communication   99
B.   Nonverbal Codes   105
C.   Selected Research Findings   106
D.   A Challenge   108

Chapter 7.   Selectivity in Communication   111

A.   Selective Attention   111
B.   Selective Perception   113
C.   Selective Exposure   120
D.   Selective Retention   123

Chapter 8.   Feedback: The Essence of Transaction   126

A.   The Nature of Feedback   126
B.   The Human Need for Feedback   128
C.   Sources of Feedback   132
D.   Effects of Feedback   133
E.   Costs of Feedback   134

Part III.   Constituent Elements of Oral Communication   137

Chapter 9.   The Sender's Influence: Source Credibility   139

A.   Source Credibility Defined   140
B.   Dynamics of Credibility   140
C.   Dimensions of Credibility   144
D.   Enhancing Credibility   151

Chapter 10. Message Construction: Advice for
Verbal Encoding 156

    A. Message Adaptation 157
    B. Message Discrepancy 159
    C. Types of Appeals 160
    D. Message Organization 166
    E. Related Message Variables 168

Chapter 11. Processing Messages: The Role of Decoding 171

    A. Personality Variables 172
    B. The Theory of Ego-Involvement 175
    C. Cognitive Consistency Theories 177

Part IV. The Effects of Oral Communnication 191

Chapter 12. Receiver Modification: The Impact on
Decoders 193

    A. Changes in Behavior and Attitude 194
    B. The Persistence of Effects 202
    C. Resisting Persuasive Attempts 203

Chapter 13. Source Modification: The Impact on
Encoders 207

    A. Encoding for Self-Understanding 208
    B. Encoding to Understand Others 212
    C. Encoding Effects and Rewards 213
    D. Eavesdropping 214

Chapter 14. Personal Modification: The Impact of
Self-Disclosure 217

    A. Intrapersonal Self-Disclosure 218
    B. Interpersonal Self-Disclosure 219
    C. Benefits of Self-Disclosure 220
    D. Risks of Self-Disclosure 220
    E. Social Norms Working Against
       Self-Disclosure 222
    F. Self-Disclosure and Roles 225
    G. Self-Disclosure and Life 227

Index 231

The Personal
Communication Process

Part I ▶ Conceptions of Oral Communication

Chapter 1 ▶ The Nature of Communication

Objectives

On completion of this chapter you should be able to:
1. Realize that communication is personal.
2. Conceptualize the notion of "process."
3. Understand communication as a form of process.
4. Distinguish between communication transaction and interaction.
5. Define communication.

Today is the first day of the rest of your life. Realization of this truth is both frightening and exciting. It is frightening because it suggests a future termination date. It is exciting because it compels you to realize that life is a process; each second you live is affected by those seconds that came before and affects all that come after. And, each second is unique, unlike all the rest. Each second is significant because if it did not exist, all the rest would be different. All of life is a process, a very personal process. One of the most prominent aspects of life is *communication,* which is also a *very personal process.*

COMMUNICATION IS PERSONAL

Communication is personal because, as you will learn in later chapters, it is impossible to separate "self" from the process. How you receive (decode) or construct (encode) messages is strongly influenced by who you are. Since there are no two individuals who are identical in experiences, thoughts, feelings, and desires, no two individuals interpret various communication stimuli identically. As you read these pages, you will interpret our message differently from everyone else who reads these pages. The differences may be slight at times, but they do exist. Reliance on "self" is inherent in communication. Thus, without question, *the process is personal.*

COMMUNICATION IS A PROCESS

The concept of process is not new. In the sixth century B.C., Heraclitus stated that "A man can never step in the same river twice; the man is different and so is the river." As we stated at the beginning of this chapter, "Today is the first day of the rest of your life." Therefore, this hour is the hour that begins the rest of your life. But, so is this minute, this second, this millisecond, this . . . . Try to stop the process of life for a moment and say, "*Now* the rest begins." The "Now" that you identified is gone; you cannot identify it because it continually changes. It is extremely difficult to discuss the process nature of life or communication (or anything else, for that matter). We do not have the necessary language to analyze and represent the process adequately. In order to discuss the aging process of life, for example, we use "years." We then subdivide this unit of time into months, weeks, days, hours, minutes, seconds, and milliseconds. But try as we might, we are still using static concepts—stable, unchanging, discrete concepts—to discuss a process. Communication, just like you, is continually changing.[1]

COMMUNICATION IS TRANSACTIONAL

In speech communication, we used to view communication as a static event. We thought of it in these terms: "The speaker speaks, the message travels to an audience, the audience listens, and, perhaps, behaves accordingly." Realizing that such a static view was an inadequate description of the interchange that exists in actual communication, we began viewing communication as an "interaction" process. A communicator acts (sends some communication stimuli, spoken or unspoken), a receiver listens and reacts, the communicator

[1] The writing of this book, too, was a process. Its present form is dependent on when we wrote it. If we had written it earlier, or later, it would be different than it now is.

then reacts to the reaction, and so on. But this view of communication is also an inadequate description of the dynamics of the communication process.

We prefer to view communication as a "transactional" process. All persons are engaged in sending (encoding) and receiving (decoding) messages *simultaneously*. Each person is constantly *sharing* in the encoding and decoding process, and each person is *affecting* the other.

In this book, for purposes of description, we use static labels such as sources, receivers, and messages. But keep in mind that communication is a process—a personal, transactional process. If you understand the process nature of personal communication transactions, you will be able to interpret what we are saying more accurately.

COMMUNICATION DEFINED

One can now say, "OK, so communication is a personal transactional process. Now, what is it?" Notice that no one has presented *the* definition of communication. Since there are many divergent views on this subject, we will frame our own definition. However, we do not maintain that it is the best definition or the correct one. Nevertheless, it serves our purpose.

Most attempts to define communication are either source oriented or receiver oriented. Source-oriented definitions emphasize the role of the *sender* in a communication transaction, while receiver-oriented definitions stress the role of the *message recipient*.

An example of a source-oriented definition that highlights the encoding process is given by G. R. Miller. Miller suggests that communication takes place when a source transmits a message to a receiver (s) with *conscious intent* to affect the receiver's behavior.[2] The distinguishing characteristic of Miller's definition is "conscious intent." In other words, communication is purposeful. It takes place when one attempts to influence another through a message. The message may consist of either verbal or nonverbal symbols or both. The element of "message" in the definition eliminates coercion or forced compliance. Obviously, Miller does not argue that "all communication" is only that type of persuasive communication that meets the requirements of his definition. His definition is an attempt to place boundaries on the type of communication that is of central concern to the speech scholar, and as such, it has a great deal of utility. The criterion of conscious intent, however, makes

[2] Gerald R. Miller, "On Defining Communication: Another Stab," *Journal of Communication* (1966), *26*, 88–99.

this a source-oriented definition. The definition identifies communication as "attempted purposeful persuasion" on the part of a source.

S. S. Stevens has given a useful definition of communication, which we label as "receiver oriented." According to Stevens, communication is the discriminatory response of an organism to a stimulus.[3] This definition is much more inclusive than Miller's definition. Many instances of both human and animal exchange that are excluded from the Miller perspective can qualify as communication under this definition. Imagine, if you can, a young coed, who most peers (and elders) classify as "sexy." During an exam, this young coed needs to sharpen a pencil. To fulfill this need, she, in her extremely short skirt, walks to the front of the room, where the pencil sharpener is located. She is deeply engrossed in thinking about the exam and is unaware of the impact she is having on the students who are observing her journey to the pencil sharpener. She is not intentionally interrupting their chains of thought, but they are interrupted. Is she communicating to them? According to the Miller definition, she is not. She is a source; she is sending a message to receivers and she is affecting their behavior. But, at least according to her, she is in all honesty, not consciously intending to do so. But, *is* she communicating? According to the Stevens definition, she is. She is a stimulus and she is generating discriminatory responses among individual organisms.

This kind of "affective behavior" is communication within the receiver-oriented definition; but according to the source-oriented definition, although the behavior might be exciting and interesting, it is not communication. To many people, the Stevens-type definition is too all-inclusive, while to others, it is too exclusive. Some contend that a furnace's response to a thermostat reading is communication. These people contend that communication is *any* response to *any* stimulus, not just discriminatory responses of organisms. Some people feel that the Miller-type definition is too restrictive, while others believe that it successfully establishes meaningful boundaries for the type of persuasive communication that is of primary concern to the study of the personal communication process.

Conflicting opinions about communication have existed for a long time and the issue will not be resolved in the near future. The main requirement of a definition of communication is that it must be helpful to you. If a certain definition helps you to gain an insight into the communication process, by all means, use it.

The preceding definitions view communication as interaction. The Miller definition, which requires **discrete encoding behavior**, and the

[3] S. S. Stevens, "Introduction: A Definition of Communication," *The Journal of the Acoustical Society of America*, (November 1950), *XXII*, 689.

Stevens definition, which requires *discrete decoding behavior*, both lead us to visualize communication as a series of actions and reactions. Again, we prefer to view communication as a transaction. The encoding and decoding elements of communication are not discrete, in our opinion. They are *spontaneous* and *simultaneous* within an individual and among individuals linked in a communication event.

For our purposes, we define communication as an "attempt to get meaning." When any organism (human or animal; referred to as a source or receiver), "attempts to get meaning," communication is taking place. Although we may not be consciously aware of our "attempt" to get meaning, whenever we interpret stimuli in order to better cope with our environment, we are engaged in a personal communication transaction. We do not argue that "mechanical" communication is not communication, we simply are not concerned with it here. We are concerned with communication among or within organisms, primarily human. Our focus is on the personal (unique within each individual), transactional (simultaneous encoding and decoding behaviors within each individual and among individuals), communication process. It is an *attempt to get meaning*.

"Attempt" means *any effort*. The effort may or may not be intentional. "To get" means *to acquire*. "Meaning" is another word for *understanding*. Stated another way, communication is any effort to acquire understanding.

Thus, communication (attempt to get meaning), is a personal, transactional process. It is "personal" because the meaning or understanding that we acquire differs with each of us. It is "transactional" because in our attempts to acquire meaning or understanding, we simultaneously give off signals that may be perceived by others. It is a "process" because we are always attempting, intentionally or otherwise, to understand. Furthermore, where the process begins or ends cannot be determined; the process is affected by all that has happened previously and it affects all that follows.

The notion of "process" is often difficult to appreciate and internalize. The following short story helps dramatize the real essence of process.

A SOUND OF THUNDER
Ray Bradbury

The sign on the wall seemed to quaver under a film of sliding warm water. Eckels felt his eyelids blink over his stare, and the sign burned in this momentary darkness:

TIME SAFARI, INC.

SAFARIS TO ANY YEAR IN THE PAST.
YOU NAME THE ANIMAL.
WE TAKE YOU THERE.
YOU SHOOT IT.

A warm phlegm gathered in Eckels' throat; he swallowed and pushed it down. The muscles around his mouth formed a smile as he put his hand slowly out upon the air, and in that hand waved a check for ten thousand dollars to the man behind the desk.

"Does this safari guarantee I come back alive?"

"We guarantee nothing," said the official, "except the dinosaurs." He turned. "This is Mr. Travis, your Safari Guide in the Past. He'll tell you what and where to shoot. If he says no shooting, no shooting. If you disobey instructions, there's a stiff penalty of another ten thousand dollars, plus possible government action, on your return."

Eckels glanced across the vast office at a mass and tangle, a snaking and humming of wires and steel boxes, at an aurora that flickered now orange, now silver, now blue. There was a sound like a gigantic bonfire burning all of Time, all the years and all the parchment calendars, all the hours piled high and set aflame.

A touch of the hand and this burning would, on the instant, beautifully reverse itself. Eckels remembered the wording in the advertisements to the letter. Out of chars and ashes, out of dust and coals, like golden salamanders, the old years, the green years, might leap; roses sweeten the air, white hair turn Irish-black, wrinkles vanish; all, everything fly back to seed, flee death, rush down to their beginnings, suns rise in western skies and set in glorious easts, moons eat themselves opposite to the custom, all and everything cupping one in another like Chinese boxes, rabbits into hats, all and everything returning to the fresh death, the seed death, the green death, to the time before the beginning. A touch of a hand might do it, the merest touch of a hand.

"Unbelievable." Eckels breathed, the light of the Machine on his thin face. "A real Time Machine." He shook his head. "Makes you think. If the election had gone badly yesterday, I might be here now running away from the results. Thank God Keith won. He'll make a fine President of the United States."

"Yes," said the man behind the desk. "We're lucky. If Deutscher had gotten in, we'd have the worst kind of dictatorship. There's an anti-everything man for you, a militarist, anti-Christ, anti-human, anti-intellectual. People called us up, you know, joking but not joking. Said if Deutscher became President they wanted to go live in 1492. Of course it's not our business to conduct Escapes, but to form Safaris. Anyway, Keith's President now. All you got to worry about is—"

"Shooting my dinosaur," Eckels finished it for him.

"A Tyrannosaurus rex. The Tyrant Lizard, the most incredible monster in history. Sign this release. Anything happens to you, we're not responsible. Those dinosaurs are hungry."

Eckels flushed angrily. "Trying to scare me!"

"Frankly, yes. We don't want anyone going who'll panic at the first shot. Six Safari leaders were killed last year, and a dozen hunters. We're here to give you the severest thrill a real hunter ever asked for. Traveling you back sixty million years to bag the biggest game in all of Time. Your personal check's still there. Tear it up."

Mr. Eckels looked at the check. His fingers twitched.

"Good luck," said the man behind the desk. "Mr. Travis, he's all yours."

They moved silently across the room, taking their guns with them, toward the Machine, toward the silver metal and the roaring light.

First a day and then a night and then a day and then a night, then it was day-night-day-night. A week, a month, a year, a decade! A.D. 2055. A.D. 2019. 1999! 1957! Gone! The Machine roared.

They put on their oxygen helmets and tested the intercoms.

Eckels swayed on the padded seat, his face pale, his jaw stiff. He felt the trembling in his arms and he looked down and found his hands tight on the new rifle. There were four other men in the Machine. Travis, the Safari Leader, his assistant, Lesperance, and two other hunters, Billings and Kramer. They sat looking at each other, and the years blazed around them.

"Can these guns get a dinosaur cold?" Eckels felt his mouth saying.

"If you hit them right," said Travis on the helmet radio. "Some dinosaurs have two brains, one in the head, another far down the spinal column. We stay away from those. That's stretching luck. Put your first two shots into the eyes, if you can, blind them, and go back into the brain."

The Machine howled. Time was a film run backward. Suns fled and ten million moons fled after them. "Think," said Eckels. "Every hunter that ever lived would envy us today. This makes Africa seem like Illinois."

The Machine slowed; its scream fell to a murmur. The Machine stopped.

The sun stopped in the sky.

The fog that had enveloped the Machine blew away and they were in an old time, a very old time indeed, three hunters and two Safari Heads with their blue metal guns across their knees.

"Christ isn't born yet," said Travis. "Moses has not gone to the mountains to talk with God. The Pyramids are still in the earth, waiting to be cut out and put up. Remember that. Alexander, Caesar, Napoleon, Hitler—none of them exists."

The man nodded.

"That"—Mr. Travis pointed—"is the jungle of sixty million two thousand and fifty-five years before President Keith."

He indicated a metal path that struck off into green wilderness, over streaming swamp, among giant ferns and palms.

"And that," he said, "is the Path, laid by Time Safari for your use.

It floats six inches above the earth. Doesn't touch so much as one grass blade, flower, or tree. It's an anti-gravity metal. Its purpose is to keep you from touching this world of the past in any way. Stay on the Path. Don't go off it. I repeat. Don't go off. For any reason! If you fall off, there's a penalty. And don't shoot any animal we don't okay.''

''Why?'' asked Eckels.

They sat in the ancient wilderness. Far birds' cries blew on a wind, and the smell of tar and an old salt sea, moist grasses, and flowers the color of blood.

''We don't want to change the Future. We don't belong here in the Past. The government doesn't like us here. We have to pay big graft to keep our franchise. A Time Machine is finicky business. Not knowing it, we might kill an important animal, a small bird, a roach, a flower even, thus destroying an important link in a growing species.''

''That's not clear,'' said Eckels.

''All right,'' Travis continued, ''say we accidentally kill one mouse here. That means all the future families of this one particular mouse are destroyed, right?''

''Right.''

''And all the families of the families of the families of that one mouse! With a stamp of your foot, you annihilate first one, then a dozen, then a thousand, a million, a billion possible mice!''

''So they're dead,'' said Eckels. ''So what?''

''So what?'' Travis snorted quietly. ''Well, what about the foxes that'll need those mice to survive? For want of ten mice, a fox dies. For want of ten foxes a lion starves. For want of a lion, all manner of insects, vultures, infinite billions of life forms are thrown into chaos and destruction. Eventually it all boils down to this: fifty-nine million years later, a caveman, one of a dozen on the entire world, goes hunting wild boar or saber-toothed tiger for food. But you, friend, have stepped on all the tigers in that region. By stepping on one single mouse. So the caveman starves. And the caveman, please note, is not just any expendable man, no! He is an entire future nation. From his loins would have sprung ten sons. From their loins one hundred sons, and thus onward to a civilization. Destroy this one man, and you destroy a race, a people, an entire history of life. It is comparable to slaying some of Adam's grandchildren. The stomp of your foot, on one mouse, could start an earthquake, the effects of which could shake our earth and destinies down through Time, to their very foundations. With the death of that one caveman, a billion others yet unborn are throttled in the womb. Perhaps Rome never rises on its seven hills. Perhaps Europe is forever a dark forest, and only Asia waxes healthy and teeming. Step on a mouse and you crush the Pyramids. Step on a mouse and you leave your print, like a Grand Canyon, across Eternity. Queen Elizabeth might never be born, Washington might not cross the Delaware, there might never be a United States at all. So be careful. Stay on the Path. Never step off!''

"I see," said Eckels. "Then it wouldn't pay for us even to touch the grass?"

"Correct. Crushing certain plants could add up infinitesimally. A little error here would multiply in sixty million years, all out of proportion. Of course maybe our theory is wrong. Maybe Time can't be changed by us. Or maybe it can be changed only in little subtle ways. A dead mouse here makes an insect imbalance there, a population disproportion later, a bad harvest further on, a depression, mass starvation, and finally, a change in social temperament in far-flung countries. Something much more subtle, like that. Perhaps only a soft breath, a whisper, a hair, pollen on the air, such a slight, slight change that unless you looked close you wouldn't see it. Who knows? Who really can say he knows? We don't know. We're guessing. But until we do know for certain whether our messing around in Time can make a big roar or a little rustle in history, we're being careful. This Machine, this Path, your clothing and bodies, were sterilized, as you know, before the journey. We wear these oxygen helmets so we can't introduce our bacteria into an ancient atmosphere."

"How do we know which animals to shoot?"

"They're marked with red paint," said Travis. "Today, before our journey, we sent Lesperance here back with the Machine. He came to this particular era and followed certain animals."

"Studying them?"

"Right," said Lesperance. "I track them through their entire existence, noting which of them lives longest. Very few. How many times they mate. Not often. Life's short. When I find one that's going to die when a tree falls on him, or one that drowns in a tar pit, I note the exact hour, minute, and second. I shoot a paint bomb. It leaves a red patch on his side. We can't miss it. Then I correlate our arrival in the Past so that we meet the Monster not more than two minutes before he would have died anyway. This way, we kill only animals with no future, that are never going to mate again. You see how careful we are?"

"But if you come back this morning in Time," said Eckels eagerly, "you must've bumped into us, our Safari! How did it turn out? Was it successful? Did all of us get through—alive?"

Travis and Lesperance gave each other a look.

"That'd be a paradox," said the latter. "Time doesn't permit that sort of mess—a man meeting himself. When such occasions threaten, Time steps aside. Like an airplane hitting an air pocket. You felt the Machine jump just before we stopped? That was us passing ourselves on the way back to the Future. We saw nothing. There's no way of telling if this expedition was a success, if we got our monster, or whether all of us—meaning you, Mr. Eckels—got out alive."

Eckels smiled palely.

"Cut that," said Travis sharply. "Everyone on his feet!"

They were ready to leave the Machine.

The jungle was high and the jungle was broad and the jungle was the entire world forever and forever. Sounds like music and sounds like flying tents filled the sky, and those were pterodactyls soaring with cavernous gray wings, gigantic bats of delirium and night fever. Eckels, balanced on the narrow Path, aimed his rifle playfully.

"Stop that!" said Travis. "Don't even aim for fun, blast you! If your guns should go off—"

Eckels flushed. "Where's our Tyrannosaurus?"

Lesperance checked his wristwatch. "Up ahead. We'll bisect his trail in sixty seconds. Look for the red paint! Don't shoot till we give the word. Stay on the Path. Stay on the Path!"

They moved forward in the wind of morning.

"Strange," murmured Eckels. "Up ahead, sixty million years, Election Day over. Keith made President. Everyone celebrating. And here we are, a million years lost, and they don't exist. The things we worried about for months, a lifetime, not even born or thought of yet."

"Safety catches off, everyone!" ordered Travis. "You, first shot, Eckels. Second, Billings, Third, Kramer."

"I've hunted tiger, wild boar, buffalo, elephant, but now, this is it," said Eckels. "I'm shaking like a kid."

"Ah," said Travis.

Everyone stopped.

Travis raised his hand. "Ahead," he whispered. "In the mist. There he is. There's His Royal Majesty now."

The jungle was wide and full of twitterings, rustlings, murmurs, and sighs.

Suddenly it all ceased, as if someone had shut a door.

Silence.

A sound of thunder.

Out of the mist, one hundred yards away, came Tyrannosaurus rex.

"It," whispered Eckels. "It . . . ."

"Sh!"

It came on great oiled, resilient, striding legs. It towered thirty feet above half of the trees, a great evil god, folding its delicate watchmaker's claws close to its oily reptilian chest. Each lower leg was a piston, a thousand pounds of white bone, sunk in thick ropes of muscle, sheathed over in a gleam of pebbled skin like the mail of a terrible warrior. Each thigh was a ton of meat, ivory, and steel mesh. And from the great breathing cage of the upper body those two delicate arms dangled out front, arms with hands which might pick up and examine men like toys, while the snake neck coiled. And the head itself, a ton of sculptured stone, lifted easily upon the sky. Its mouth gaped, exposing a fence of teeth like daggers. Its eyes rolled, ostrich eggs, empty of all expression save hunger. It closed its mouth in a death grin. It ran, its pelvic bones crushing aside trees and bushes, its taloned feet clawing damp earth, leaving prints six inches deep wherever it settled its weight.

It ran with a gliding ballet step, far too poised and balanced for its ten tons. It moved into a sunlit area warily, its beautifully reptilian hands feeling the air.

"Why, why," Eckels twitched his mouth. "It could reach up and grab the moon."

"Sh!" Travis jerked angrily. "He hasn't seen us yet."

"It can't be killed," Eckels pronounced this verdict quietly, as if there could be no argument. He had weighed the evidence and this was his considered opinion. The rifle in his hands seemed a cap gun. "We were fools to come. This is impossible."

"Shut up!" hissed Travis.

"Nightmare."

"Turn around," commanded Travis. "Walk quietly to the Machine. We'll remit half your fee."

"I didn't realize it would be this big," said Eckels. "I miscalculated, that's all. And now I want out."

"It sees us!"

"There's the red paint on its chest!"

The Tyrant Lizard raised itself. Its armored flesh glittered like a thousand green coins. The coins, crusted with slime, steamed. In the slime, tiny insects wriggled, so that the entire body seemed to twitch and undulate, even while the monster itself did not move. It exhaled. The stink of raw flesh blew down the wilderness.

"Get me out of here," said Eckels. "It was never like this before. I was always sure I'd come through alive. I had good guides, good safaris, and safety. This time, I figured wrong. I've met my match and admit it. This is too much for me to get hold of."

"Don't run," said Lesperance. "Turn around. Hide in the Machine."

"Yes." Eckels seemed to be numb. He looked at his feet as if trying to make them move. He gave a grunt of helplessness.

"Eckels!"

He took a few steps, blinking, shuffling.

"Not that way!"

The Monster, at the first motion, lunged forward with a terrible scream. It covered one hundred yards in six seconds. The rifles jerked up and blazed fire. A windstorm from the beast's mouth engulfed them in the stench of slime and old blood. The Monster roared, teeth glittering with sun.

The rifles cracked again. Their sound was lost in shriek and lizard thunder. The great level of the reptile's tail swung up, lashed sideways. Trees exploded in clouds of leaf and branch. The Monster twitched its jeweler's hands down to fondle at the men, to twist them in half, to crush them like berries, to cram them into its teeth and its screaming throat. Its boulderstone eyes leveled with the men. They saw themselves mirrored. They fired at the metallic eyelids and the blazing black iris.

Like a stone idol, like a mountain avalanche, Tyrannosaurus fell. Thundering, it clutched trees, pulled them with it. It wrenched and tore the metal Path. The men flung themselves back and away. The body hit, ten tons of cold flesh and stone. The guns fired. The Monster lashed its armored tail, twitched its snake jaws, and lay still. A fount of blood spurted from its throat. Somewhere inside, a sac of fluids burst. Sickening gushes drenched the hunters. They stood, red and glistening.

The thunder faded.

The jungle was silent. After the avalanche, a green peace. After the nightmare, morning.

Billings and Kramer sat on the pathway and threw up. Travis and Lesperance stood with smoking rifles, cursing steadily.

In the Time Machine, on his face, Eckels lay shivering. He had found his way back to the Path, climbed into the Machine.

Travis came walking, glanced at Eckels, took cotton gauze from a metal box, and returned to the others, who were sitting on the Path.

"Clean up."

They wiped the blood from their helmets. They began to curse too. The Monster lay, a hill of solid flesh. Within, you could hear the sighs and murmurs as the furthest chambers of it died, the organs malfunctioning, liquids running a final instant from pocket to sac to spleen, everything shutting off, closing up forever. It was like standing by a wrecked locomotive or a steam shovel at quitting time, all valves being released or levered tight. Bones cracked; the tonnage of its own flesh, off balance, dead weight, snapped the delicate forearms, caught underneath. The meat settled, quivering.

Another cracking sound. Overhead, a gigantic tree branch broke from its heavy mooring, fell. It crashed upon the dead beast with finality.

"There." Lesperance checked his watch. "Right on time. That's the giant tree that was scheduled to fall and kill this animal originally." He glanced at the two hunters. "You want the trophy picture?"

"What?"

"We can't take a trophy back to the Future. The body has to stay right here where it would have died originally, so the insects, birds, and bacteria can get at it, as they were intended to. Everything in balance. The body stays. But we can take a picture of you standing near it."

The two men tried to think, but gave up, shaking their heads.

They let themselves be led along the metal Path. They sank wearily into the Machine cushions. They gazed back at the ruined Monster, the stagnating mound, where already strange reptilian birds and golden insects were busy at the steaming armor.

A sound on the floor of the Time Machine stiffened them. Eckels sat there, shivering.

"I'm sorry," he said at last.

"Get up!" cried Travis.

Eckels got up.

"Go out on that Path alone," said Travis. He had his rifle pointed. "You're not coming back in the Machine. We're leaving you here!"

Lesperance seized Travis's arm. "Wait—"

"Stay out of this!" Travis shook his hand away. "This fool nearly killed us. But it isn't that so much, no. It's his shoes! Look at them! He ran off the Path. That ruins us! We'll forfeit! Thousands of dollars of insurance! We guarantee no one leaves the Path. He left it. Oh, the fool! I'll have to report to the government. They might revoke our license to travel. Who knows what he's done to Time, to History!"

"Take it easy, all he did was kick up some dirt."

"How do we know?" cried Travis. "We don't know anything! It's all a mystery! Get out of here, Eckels!"

Eckels fumbled his shirt. "I'll pay anything. A hundred thousand dollars!"

Travis glared at Eckels' checkbook and spat. "Go out there. The Monster's next to the Path. Stick your arms up to your elbows in his mouth. Then you can come back with us."

"That's unreasonable!"

"The Monster's dead, you idiot. The bullets! The bullets can't be left behind. They don't belong in the Past; they might change anything. Here's my knife. Dig them out!"

The jungle was alive again, full of the old tremorings and bird cries. Eckels turned slowly to regard the primeval garbage dump, that hill of nightmares and terror. After a long time, like a sleepwalker he shuffled out along the Path.

He returned, shuddering, five minutes later, his arms soaked and red to the elbows. He held out his hands. Each held a number of steel bullets. Then he fell. He lay where he fell, not moving.

"You didn't have to make him do that," said Lesperance.

"Didn't I? It's too early to tell." Travis nudged the still body. "He'll live. Next time he won't go hunting game like this. Okay." He jerked his thumb wearily at Lesperance. "Switch on. Let's go home."

1492. 1776. 1812.

They cleaned their hands and faces. They changed their caking shirts and pants. Eckels was up and around again, not speaking. Travis glared at him for a full ten minutes.

"Don't look at me," cried Eckels. "I haven't done anything."

"Who can tell?"

"Just ran off the Path, that's all, a little mud on my shoes—what do you want me to do—get down and pray?"

"We might need it. I'm warning you, Eckels, I might kill you yet. I've got my gun ready."

"I'm innocent. I've done nothing!"

1999. 2000. 2055.

The Machine stopped.

"Get out," said Travis.

The room was there as they had left it. But not the same as they had left it. The same man sat behind the same desk. But the same man did not quite sit behind the same desk.

Travis looked around swiftly. "Everything okay here?" he snapped.

"Fine. Welcome home!"

Travis did not relax. He seemed to be looking through the one high window.

"Okay, Eckels, get out. Don't ever come back."

Eckels could not move.

"You heard me," said Travis. "What're you staring at?"

Eckels stood smelling of the air, and there was a thing to the air, a chemical taint so subtle, so slight, that only a faint cry of his sublimal senses warned him it was there. The colors, white, gray, blue, orange, in the wall, in the furniture, in the sky beyond the window, were . . . were . . . . And there was a feel. His flesh twitched. His hands twitched. He stood drinking the oddness with the pores of his body. Somewhere, someone must have been screaming one of those whistles that only a dog can hear. His body screamed silence in return. Beyond this room, beyond this wall, beyond this man who was not quite the same man seated at this desk that was not quite the same desk . . . lay an entire world of streets and people. What sort of world it was now, there was no telling. He could feel them moving there, beyond the walls, almost, like so many chess pieces blown in a dry wind . . . .

But the immediate thing was the sign painted on the office wall, the same sign he had read earlier today on first entering.

Somehow, the sign had changed:

TYME SEFARI INC.

SEFARIS TU ANY YEER EN THE PAST.

YU NAIM THE ANIMALL.

WEE TAEKYUTHAIR.

YU SHOOT ITT.

Eckels felt himself fall into a chair. He fumbled crazily at the thick slime on his boots. He held up a clod of dirt, trembling, "No, it can't be. Not a little thing like that. No!"

Embedded in the mud, glistening green and gold and black, was a butterfly, very beautiful and very dead.

"Not a little thing like that! Not a butterfly!" cried Eckels.

It fell to the floor, an exquisite thing, a small thing that could upset balances and knock down a line of small dominoes and then big dominoes and then gigantic dominoes, all down the years across Time. Eckels' mind whirled. It couldn't change things. Killing one butterfly couldn't be that important! Could it?

His face was cold. His mouth trembled, asking: "Who—Who won the presidential election yesterday?"

The man behind the desk laughed. "You joking? You know very well. Deutscher, of course! Who else? Not that fool weakling Keith. We got an iron man now, a man with guts!" The official stopped. "What's wrong?"

Eckels moaned. He dropped to his knees. He scrabbled at the golden butterfly with shaking fingers. "Can't we," he pleaded to the world, to himself, to the officials, to the Machine, "can't we take it back, can't we make it alive again? Can't we start over? Can't we—"

He did not move. Eyes shut, he waited, shivering. He heard Travis breathe loud in the room; he heard Travis shift his rifle, click the safety catch, and raise the weapon.

There was a sound of thunder.[4]

Although one can argue that this story describes process as "interaction" rather than "transaction," the notion that a process is "on-going" is vividly captured. We believe that small, seemingly inconsequential, happenings in a communication transaction can have dramatic impacts on the future, too. For example, two men were talking with each other (over a few beers) and one of them asked the other, "Do you respect my wife?" The second man replied "Respect her? No—why?" The first man became angry immediately, "You don't respect my wife. Why, you *!= + * !" The men were immediately in a violent, verbal confrontation. Although the battle remained verbal rather than physical, the future of their entire relationship was certainly affected. The conflict centered around the word "respect." The man who asked the initial question defined respect as "think well of." The other man defined respect as "feeling someone is superior." One little word in the process affected their future relationship. We do not have a time machine to use so that we can go back and see what would have happened if the first man would have selected a different word. We are confident, however, that if a different word had been used, the consequences would have been altered. Again, communication is a process—a personal transactional process.

Exercises

1. Present a brief speech to the class about your own experiences where an initial event significantly altered a later event.
2. Divide into small groups within the class. Relate to your group as nearly as you can recall, the step-by-step process you went through in deciding to attend this particular college. What communication transactions with others had the most influence on your decision? Why?

[4] Ray Bradbury, "A Sound of Thunder," reprinted from *R is for Rocket*, Doubleday, New York, 1952.

3. Within the same group, discuss your outlook on college. Is it, or do you expect it to be fun? Hard work? Do you feel a part of the college? Detail the communication transactions that gave rise to your feelings.
4. Construct your own definition of communication and compare it to the Wenburg-Wilmot definition. Hold onto your definition and at the end of the course see if your view of communication is still captured by it.

Suggested Readings

Larry L. Barker and Robert J. Kibler (Eds.), *Speech Communication Behavior: Perspectives and Principles,* Prentice-Hall, Englewood Cliffs, 1971.

Dean C. Barnlund, *Interpersonal Communication: Survey and Studies,* Houghton Mifflin, Boston, 1968.

David K. Berlo, *The Process of Communication,* Holt, Rinehart and Winston, New York, 1960.

Howard H. Martin and Kenneth Andersen, *Speech Communication: Analysis and Readings,* Allyn and Bacon, Boston, 1968.

Terry A. Welden and Huber W. Ellingsworth, *Effective Speech—Communication: Theory in Action,* Scott, Foresman, Glenview, 1970.

Chapter **2** ▶ *Communication*
Arenas

Objectives

On completion of this chapter you should be able to:
1. View intrapersonal communication as the basis of all human communication transactions.
2. Understand why communication transactions are complicated by the presence of additional persons.
3. Explain the basic interpersonal needs.
4. Understand the importance and effects of your own group memberships on yourself.
5. Specify the importance of group cohesion, norms, and leadership functions.
6. Describe the interpersonal nature of public speaking.
7. Explain why mass communication is an interaction rather than a transaction.

You experience the personal process of communication in a variety of settings. These arenas range from sitting alone and thinking to participating in a mass communication event. Although we feel that all communication is ultimately a process of intrapersonal communication, in order to understand human communication behavior it is helpful to visualize it in all its various arenas. The arenas of intrapersonal, interpersonal, small group, public speaking, and mass media communication are not mutually exclusive, and the distinctions among them are not clear-cut. Actually, the arenas are more alike than different.[1] But,

[1] William D. Brooks expresses this same notion in *Speech Communication,* Wm. C. Brown, Dubuque, 1971, p. 12.

so that you can realize the various applications of concepts presented later in this book, we offer some detailed information on the arenas.

INTRAPERSONAL COMMUNICATION

Intrapersonal communication is communication with oneself. Within this arena, one receives signals that represent one's own feelings or sensations.[2] These signals, or cues, arise from various sources. If, for example, you are sitting alone and thinking or reflecting, you are receiving cues about the internal, physical state of your body. These *private cues* may be verbal or nonverbal, and are unique to you. They are not experienced in the same way by anyone else.

The *public cues* you receive inform you about your immediate environment. Situational factors such as temperature, noise, and recognition of a pretty flower are examples of this type of signal.[3] If you are using symbols that are not words (making a peace sign or other symbols with your hand), these are *behavioral nonverbal cues* that impinge on your thinking process.[4] And, if you are talking to yourself, or writing a poem for yourself, then you are producing and responding to *behavioral verbal cues*. Of course, in a particular intrapersonal event, all the cues do not occur with equal frequency. In some cases, cues of a particular type may be missing entirely. For instance, awareness of private cues, such as intense pain, may preclude perception of public cues; or exposure to violent public cues, such as a roaring fire in a building, may rule out awareness of private cues.

The distinguishing characteristic of the intrapersonal arena is that you are the *only* participant. Messages originate and end within you.[5] Since you cannot check your perceptions with someone else, all message meanings are determined from your own perspective. You cannot get outside of yourself to acquire meanings; they all come from within you.

Even though intrapersonal communication is exclusively personal, since you are the only participant, your message meanings can be "corrected" or changed. For example, a man stationed in Germany during the Cold War era, had a dream in which he visualized himself

---

[2] Jurgen Reusch and Gregory Bateson, *Communication: The Social Matrix of Psychiatry,* W. W. Norton, New York, 1968, p. 278.

[3] Ibid., p. 278.

[4] Frank E. X. Dance, ed., *Human Communication Theory,* Holt, Rinehart and Winston, New York, 1967, p. 298.

[5] Ruesch and Bateson, p. 278 (cited in footnote 2).

waking up during the night and then casually walking over to his window to look outside. While he was viewing the night scene, there was a sudden flash of light. Immediately following, a gigantic mushroom cloud began to form. He was convinced that a disaster was in the making and that thousands of people, including himself, would immediately die. He then awakened from his dream; but even with the realization that the disaster he had so vividly perceived was just a figment of his imagination, the dream had a significant long-term impact on his life. From that point on, he abhorred war and actively campaigned for peace. It was through communication within the intrapersonal arena that he changed from his neutral position on the justifiability of wars. His intrapersonal communication experience led him to the definite conclusion that all wars are futile, wasteful, and cannot be justified. The issue was not new to him because he had read many books and talked with many people about it. It was not until he communicated with himself, however, that he made his decision to become one of the early antiwar campaigners.

Other dramatic examples of intrapersonal communication are easily constructed. Walter Mitty, for instance, relied heavily on communication within the intrapersonal arena to maintain his mental balance (or imbalance). He transformed himself into a bold, adventurous person by using intrapersonal communication. Most types of inner speech, such as deep personal meditation, are forms of intrapersonal communication that are important to our lives.

Ultimately, *all* communication responses take place within a person as he reacts to various communication cues. That is, intrapersonal communication may take place without communication in any of the other arenas, but communication in the other arenas cannot take place without intrapersonal communication.[6] Thus, intrapersonal communication provides the basis for all other communication arenas.[7]

Although the notion that "all communication ultimately becomes intrapersonal" is quite simple, it merits much attention. For example, we like to think of ourselves as empathic and others-oriented. We admire individuals who apparently can understand problems from another's viewpoint. As we endeavor to understand our associates, we try to see things "through their eyes." But, as we mentioned earlier, all communication is personal. We can never totally shed ourselves as we communicate with others—the intrapersonal phase in communication transactions can never be avoided. Intrapersonal communication, pro-

[6] Gordon Wiseman and Larry Barker, *Speech–Interpersonal Communication*, Chandler, San Francisco, 1967, p. 20.

[7] Dance, p. 298 (cited in footnote 4).

duced and reacted to by the self, occurs whenever there is communication in any arena.

INTERPERSONAL COMMUNICATION

Two people participating in a communication transaction provide the basic paradigm for interpersonal communication. The addition of a second individual has a marked impact on the complexity of the communication process. One way to realize that the addition of a second person increases the complexity of the communication process is to examine the notion of "awareness of presence."

Awareness of Presence

Two individuals, recognizing one another's presence, will change the character and content of their intrapersonal communication. This type of change will occur *even before* actual verbal interaction takes place.[8] For clarity, we like to look at the effects of "awareness of presence" from two perspectives—other and self.

Awareness of Others

When you become aware of the presence of another person, your communication is affected. For example, when you encounter a new acquaintance who you think is conceited, you may not wish to continue communicating with him. But if you are forced into an extended association with him, you may get to know him more personally, and perhaps will no longer interpret his behavior as an attempt to be superior. This may be because once you openly accept the conceited-appearing individual, he will change his behavior and no longer give cues that make him appear conceited. On the other hand, it may be because once you accept him, you will cease to be so critical or conscious of his mannerisms. Whichever is the case, awareness of another's presence affects the content and character of your communication transactions.

As you are consciously or unconsciously making adjustments that result from your awareness of another, he is also making similar adjustments as he becomes aware of you. He seeks to acquire information

[8] Dean C. Barnlund, "A Transactional Model of Communication," in Kenneth K. Sereno and C. David Mortensen (Eds.), *Foundations of Communication Theory*, Harper and Row, New York, 1970, pp. 98–99.

about you and he brings into play information he already possesses. He will make several evaluations of you, such as your socioeconomic status, your apparent attitude toward him, and your appearance. This information will help him define the situation and know what to expect of you.[9] Obviously, this initial impression is usually too incomplete for the communication situation to be defined adequately. As he acquires more information about you by getting to know you better, his perceptions of you will be altered just as your initial impression of his conceit changed.

Awareness of Self

Awareness of presence can also be looked at from a self-perspective. When you become aware of the other person, you will automatically realize that he has or may become aware of you, also. You know that your actions will influence the relationship. In fact, if he likes or respects you, the relationship that develops will be much different from the relationship that will develop if he dislikes you. Some individuals are so concerned about the initial impressions they make on other people that they consciously monitor the types of cues they give to others. The reasons for the impact of "awareness of presence" from a self-perspective are numerous. According to one author:

"Sometimes the individual will act in a thoroughly calculating manner, expressing himself in a given way solely in order to give the kind of impression to others that is likely to evoke . . . a specific response. . . . Sometimes the individual will be calculating in his activity but be relatively unaware that this is the case. Sometimes he will intentionally and consciously express himself in a particular way . . . because the tradition of his group or social status require this kind of expression. . . . Sometimes the traditions of an individual's role will lead him to give a well designed impression of a particular kind and yet he may be neither consciously nor unconsciously disposed to create such an impression."[10]

Whether you try to manage the situation or not, in the interpersonal communication arena you are certainly aware that your presence affects the other person and that his presence affects you. Most of us find it impossible to "be ourselves" in the absolute sense when we realize that another person is present.

[9] Erving Goffman, *The Presentation of Self in Everyday Life,* Doubleday, Garden City, 1959, p. 1.
[10] Ibid., p. 6.

Significance of the Interpersonal Arena

With the exception of the intrapersonal arena, which is inherent in all communication, the interpersonal arena is the most significant of all the arenas. It is within this arena that most meaningful relationships are formed and maintained.[11] In an interpersonal transaction, one individual can most easily communicate *directly* with another individual.

All of us have observed interpersonal communication that is interpersonal by definition only. We define it as interpersonal because two people are involved but mutual verbal exchange is almost nonexistent. This is the case when one of the individuals is a "dead pan." Try as you might, it is next to impossible to get a verbal response from the dead pan. He simply sits there, and perhaps smiles or frowns. In terms of the content of the transaction, he appears to be totally out to lunch. Communicators who find it very difficult to cope with this type of individual insert many verbal cues designed specifically to generate a response. This is especially true when the communicator is one who has a "high need for feedback." Such a person will constantly insert cues such as, "OK?" "Right?" "You know?" "Do you follow?" or "Hey, you still there?" A person with a high need for feedback will often be mentally exhausted and frustrated when he leaves a conversation with a dead pan.

At the other extreme, we have all experienced an interpersonal communication situation with a "gum flapper." You know the type, he constantly flaps his gums and gives little, if any, opportunity for the other person to participate at the verbal level. When exposed to a gum flapper, one often inserts verbal cues in an attempt to participate in the development of the substance of the conversation. A person may insert cues such as, "But . . ." "Yes, I . . . ," "No, I . . . ," "Did you . . . ," or "Uh-huh . . ." In such a situation, one often leaves the transaction in a state of confusion and exhaustion. As the person tears himself away from the gum flapper, he can be seen shaking his head and sighing, "Whew!" It seems reasonable to conclude that the gum flapper and the dead pan would get along quite nicely. Neither would experience any pressure from the other and both could leave the transaction in a fairly comfortable state. The "normal" communicator, however, will be tired and frustrated following a communication encounter with either a dead pan or a gum flapper.

Although the gum flapper and dead pan represent the extremes of over- and underparticipation in the interpersonal arena, when interpersonal contact is *perceived*, a transaction exists; that is, both parties

[11] Wiseman and Barker, pp. 8–9 (cited in footnote 6).

are concurrently observing and participating in the transaction. Potentially, the opportunity for participating and observing is *equally* divided between the two communicators.[12] As noted earlier, it is within this arena that people deal with each other as individuals, and this is where interpersonal needs are manifested.

Interpersonal Needs

In the interpersonal communication arena, each of us can realize fulfillment of our basic interpersonal needs. Scholars have classified these needs in different ways. According to William C. Schutz, the basic interpersonal needs within each person are *affection*, *inclusion*, and *control*.[13]

Affection

This is the need to feel that the self is loveable. A person who adequately fulfills this need is labeled "personal." One who fails to fulfill the affection need is called "underpersonal" or "overpersonal."

The underpersonal person tries to avoid close ties with others. Although he tries to remain emotionally distant from others, his main fear is that no one loves him. He has a marked interpersonal need for affection, but feels that people will not like him because he does not deserve it. Consequently, he tries to keep everyone at the same distance so that he does not have to treat anyone with personal warmth and affection. Such a person is superficially friendly to everyone, but genuinely friendly to no one. His basic relationships are formed and maintained within the interpersonal arena, but they are never allowed to develop to a personal level. To the underpersonal person, the interpersonal communication arena can be extremely threatening. An underpersonal individual is rather difficult to label "from a distance." He is friendly and responds to people when they speak to him. However, he avoids sustained communication transactions with the same people. Often, he is classified as a "nice guy." He is willing to lend you his car or his notes from a class you may have missed. Few people, if any, however, ever get to know him very well. He is the type of person whom you later remember as being pleasant, but you cannot remember his name.

In contrast, the overpersonal individual thrives on establishing close

[12] Ruesch and Bateson, pp. 279-280 (cited in footnote 2).

[13] This classification system and portions of the treatment that follow are taken from William C. Schutz, *The Interpersonal Underworld*, Science Behavior Books, Palo Alto, 1966, p. 25–33.

relationships with others. His overriding need is for affection. He may overtly seek approval by being extremely personal and confiding. Upon being accepted, he may attempt to control his friends by being overly possessive and blocking all their attempts to establish other friendships. To the overpersonal person, the interpersonal communication arena is overly essential.

An overpersonal individual appears quite normal until you have the opportunity to relate to him in the interpersonal arena. Immediately, he begins telling you his problems and secrets. He demands your understanding and sympathy. Once he generates understanding and sympathy from you, he clings to you. It is almost as if you "owe him something" since he has confided in you. He wants to make sure that you do not reveal to others what he has told you and does not like others to have the opportunity to confide in you. He is the type of person whom you may like at first, but later find yourself purposefully avoiding.

The personal individual is secure in his fulfillment of his affection need. He can deal with others within a close interpersonal relationship and he can handle more distant contacts as well. He wants to be liked, but if he is not, he does not conclude that he is an unlovable person. The communication behavior of the personal individual is admirable. He is at ease in the interpersonal arena and is pleasant to talk with. He can handle personal compliments when they are directed toward him and can make confidential statements to others without being embarrassed. He does not, however, get "up tight" if one does not confide in him, and he is not compelled to share his inner feelings with others.

Inclusion

The interpersonal need of *inclusion* is the need to feel that the self is significant and worthwhile. Those who have not successfully fulfilled this need are called "undersocial" or "oversocial." The undersocial person wants to be alone because, like the underpersonal, he finds the interpersonal arena threatening. His biggest fear is that people will ignore him, so he does not want to take the risk of giving them the opportunity to do so. Such an individual is extremely shy. He hardly ever initiates conversation with others and even appears nervous when someone tries to communicate with him. He is the "loner" who goes to the theatre by himself and would rather watch television alone than go to a party. He finds it very difficult to make an oral contribution in a classroom setting. He tries to avoid saying anything that might draw attention to himself. He would rather accept a low grade on an examination that was graded incorrectly than to point out the error to his instructor.

The oversocial individual also fears being ignored, but his approach is to make people pay attention to him. He always seeks interpersonal relationships and dislikes being alone. Like the overpersonal person, he thrives on the interpersonal communication arena. Such a person can be seen popping from room to room in the dormitory to "get a party going" or just to chat. He probably finds it difficult to study alone, but is quite willing to study with others. He is often so talkative in a class that other students resent him.

The "social" individual has no problems with inclusion. He can be comfortable alone or with people. He likes being with others, but often takes a walk by himself. He feels good about paying attention to others, and is comfortable when he is in the limelight.

Control

This interpersonal need refers to the need to feel that one is a responsible person successfully coming to grips with his environment. Those who have not satisfied this interpersonal need are labeled "abdicrats" or "autocrats." The abdicrat is extremely submissive in interpersonal relationships. He is a follower and avoids making any decisions or accepting responsibilities. He has no confidence in himself and perceives himself as stupid and irresponsible. The interpersonal communication arena, to the abdicrat, is quite threatening. Although he initially manifests what might be labeled as healthy interpersonal communication behavior, later when it appears that someone is going to depend on his guidance, he becomes nervous and shy. He can be seen sitting and looking at the floor at a first meeting of a committee that has the initial task of electing a chairman. Such a role would be extremely threatening to him. He is always willing to go along with others to a football game, but would not consider initiating or organizing the plans. He will order a beer if the others do, but not if the others order soft drinks. Like the undersocial person, he does not want to draw attention to himself.

The autocrat, on the other hand, is one who attempts to dominate others. He takes control in all interpersonal relationships. He is afraid he is not a responsible person, but attempts to prove otherwise. To him, the interpersonal communication arena is crucial. In organizational meetings, he makes obvious moves to take command. In an interpersonal transaction, he tries to dominate the conversation and affect the other's decisions. He sees his suggestions for action as just a little more reasonable than those presented by others. He gets excited about a party or meeting if he is the one who thought of it and is allowed to organize it. When asked for assistance in solving a problem, he not only assists—he takes over.

The "democrat" has successfully fulfilled his control need. He feels he is a capable person and he is not concerned about either shrugging or demanding responsible roles. He is able to take the lead when he feels he should, but is quite willing to follow and help others when they are in charge. He does not personalize the issue of leadership; he can see the merits of another's proposals or ideas as well as the merits of his own.

Some individuals, hopefully most, are quite satisfied in their fulfillment of their interpersonal needs of affection, inclusion, and control. It is within the interpersonal arena that we normally perceive fulfillment or lack of fulfillment of our personal needs. To some individuals, interpersonal communication is extremely threatening, to some, it is overly essential, and to others, it is quite attractive. Obviously, these "types" of communicators are extreme examples; but they do illustrate that people attempt to serve their needs for inclusion, affection, and control in widely divergent ways in the interpersonal communication arena.

Characteristics of the Interpersonal Arena

The interpersonal arena has many unique characteristics. Communication in this arena is subject to more than one person's perceptions. More sense modalities are operable than in the other arenas. You see, smell, hear, taste, and touch more. And, because a person is close to you, feedback to one another is immediate.[14] As a result, people discover more information about one another than in the other arenas. And, interestingly enough, communicators are perceived as less manipulative in interpersonal communication than in small group, public speaking, or mass situations.[15] Most scholars agree that if one has a choice in determining which communication arena to utilize when he wants to affect the attitudes and behaviors of others, he should definitely choose the interpersonal arena. In fact, communicators in the other arenas "have an effectiveness relative to the closeness with which they duplicate the dyadic-communication behavior" of the interpersonal arena.[16]

The interpersonal arena certainly merits concentrated, continued

[14] Bruce H. Westley and Malcolm S. MacLean, Jr. "A Conceptual Model for Communications Research," in Sereno and Mortensen (Eds.), p. 74 (cited in footnote 8).

[15] Howard H. Martin and Kenneth E. Andersen (Eds.), *Speech Communication: Analysis and Readings,* Allyn and Bacon, Boston, 1968, p. 69.

[16] Dance, p. 298 (cited in footnote 4).

analysis. It is through this type of communication that we realize our fulfillment or lack of fulfillment of our interpersonal needs and establish and maintain meaningful relationships with others.

SMALL GROUP COMMUNICATION

As the addition of a second person altered the conduct of intrapersonal communication, the inclusion of any additional person has a significant impact on interpersonal communication behavior. The transaction is then so complicated that it is useful to discuss the communication of three or more people as communication in the small group arena. The nature of small group communication is primarily interpersonal since (1) it resembles dialogue, (2) all members have an equal opportunity to observe and participate, (3) feedback is immediate because all sense modalities remain operable, (4) correction of messages is still possible (though not as probable as in the interpersonal arena), and (5) meaningful personal relationships can be maintained.

A small group contains three or more people, but an upper limit on size is difficult to establish. "When the size becomes so unwieldy that a group begins to change character, it is no longer small. . . . In groups of thirteen or more, from five to seven people often hold the discussion while the others watch and listen. In permanent work groups larger than thirteen, people tend to form smaller groups (cliques) within the larger."[17] Thus, we cannot set a definite number for the maximum size of a small group. We are simply referring to small groups of people (three-?) in which individuals may communicate with one another on a basis that approximates interpersonal communication. If a group gets too large for this type of communication, the group becomes characterized as several small clique groups and still belongs within the small group communication arena.

For an aggregate of people to be classified as a group, they must have some dependence on one another. Keeping in mind our statements about the size of a group, "A group is a collection of individuals who have relations to one another that make them interdependent to some significant degree . . . the term group refers to a class of social entities having in common the property of interdependence among their constituent members."[18]

[17] Ernest G. Bormann, *Discussion and Group Methods: Theory and Practice,* Harper and Row, New York, 1969, p. 3.
[18] Darwin Cartwright and Alvin Zander (Eds.), *Group Dynamics,* Harper and Row, New York, 1968, p. 46.

Assumptions About Small Groups

We can make four basic assumptions about small groups.[19] First, "groups are inevitable and ubiquitous." That is to say, groups will always form and continue to exist when humans reside closely to one another. You have each known or heard about certain individuals who deny this first assumption and assert, "I refuse to join any groups—I want to do my own thing!" But, have you ever noticed how these free souls have a tendency to collect together in groups and conform to "nonconformity?"

The second assumption is "groups mobilize powerful forces that produce effects of utmost importance to individuals." Put simply, group memberships have a tremendous impact on the shaping and maintenance of a person's personality. An individual's sense of self-identity is developed, to a large extent, by transactions that occur within groups. The family group, social clique groups, church groups, and professional groups all play a part in developing one's identity.

Third, "groups may produce both good and bad consequences." Groups can supply necessary motivation and reinforcement; but groups, using pressure or exclusion, can also impart severe, undesirable consequences on an individual. Take for example, the child who has a habit of telling "little white lies." The parents, in order to teach the child a lesson, may ignore his presence and refuse to communicate directly with him. The potential psychological tension within the child can be very damaging—especially if his membership in the family group is extremely important to him.

The fourth basic assumption is that through research, group behavior can be better understood, and as a result desirable consequences from groups can be enhanced. Put simply "groups can be made to serve better ends."

Types of Groups

Groups may be classified in a variety of ways. Until recently, the speech communication profession has primarily categorized small groups in terms of *format*, for example, panel, symposium, and forum. We, however, find more utility in classifying groups in terms of *function*. From this perspective, groups are primarily socioemotional or task oriented.

[19] These four assumptions and explanations are taken from Cartwright and Zander, pp. 23–24 (cited in footnote 18).

Socioemotional Groups

The primary function of these groups is the fulfillment of interpersonal needs. The feelings of individual members are of highest priority in the group. High school cliques, bridge clubs, fraternities and sororities, and bowling clubs are examples of socioemotional groups. Their function is to contribute to the social and emotional needs of the members. Such groups often provide the opportunity for the development and maintenance of lasting interpersonal relationships. They can also serve as task groups, but their primary function is socioemotional in nature.

Task Groups

The main function of these groups is solving or completing a given problem or project. Administrative councils within a university, executive councils within a fraternity or sorority, volunteer fire departments, chambers of commerce, and organizational committees are examples of task groups. These groups often fulfill socioemotional needs of members (in fact, they may be unsuccessful if they do not), but their primary function is to make decisions, solve problems, or complete projects.

Most groups serve both task and socioemotional functions, but we categorize them on the basis of their *primary* function. Ofter, a group will be formed for one function but will end up serving another. For example, a service club, when it comes into existence may not have a definite task function. In order to sustain itself to fulfill socioemotional needs, however, tasks must be selected that give the group a definite, concrete purpose.

Regardless of the type of small group, there are certain elements that emerge that have a significant impact on the group members. We will briefly explicate some of these concepts.

Concepts About Groups

Cohesion

Within a small group, cohesion influences member communication. Cohesion is defined as "the resultant of all the forces acting on the members to remain in the group."[20] It is directly related to the attractiveness of the group to a given member. An individual will be more attracted to a group if the results he expects to derive from that membership are desirable.[21] Perhaps the problem to be solved (how to raise

[20] Leon Festinger, "Informal Social Communication," in Cartwright and Zander (Eds.), p. 185 (cited in footnote 18).
[21] Cartwright and Zander, p. 96 (cited in footnote 18).

enough taxes to finance his child's school system) or task to be completed (the building of a community swimming pool) is crucial to him. If so, the potential outcome of membership within the group is desirable. If, however, membership is not desirable (the group takes a public stand opposite to the individual's stand), the forces drawing him to membership may be cancelled. He may as easily leave the group as stay in it.[22]

There are several ways of determining group cohesiveness. It is important to note, however, that cohesiveness or attractiveness of a group varies with individual group members. To some members, maintenance of a certain group will be much more important than it is to other members. To determine if you feel the groups you belong to are cohesive, ask yourself questions such as "How many good friends do I have who are members of this group?" "If I had to choose between this group and another specific group to which I belong, which would I choose?" "Do I really feel that I 'belong' to this group?" If each member of the group answered these and similar questions, you could determine the overall cohesiveness of the group. Picture for a moment two groups to which you belong that have varying levels of cohesiveness to you, personally. Do you notice any different types of communication behavior on the part of yourself or other members?

Individuals who are the most enthusiastic about the group and contribute frequently to the communication probably perceive the group as the most cohesive. You may find a certain group to be cohesive to you while one of your friends may not evaluate the cohesiveness as highly. On the other hand, that same friend might be much more attracted than you are to another group to which you both belong. Obviously, your communication behaviors will vary with your perceptions of group cohesiveness. For example, if you value your membership in a group, you will try to promote good socioemotional relationships, assist the group in accomplishing its goals, and in general, provide supportive communication. If you do not feel that you belong, your communication may be directed toward dissolving the group or your membership in it. On the other hand, you might remain as a member and become silent.

Norms

The more cohesive a group is, the more pressure there will be for the members to adhere to group norms. Norms are simply "the rules which govern the behavior of members of the group."[23] These rules may

[22] Festinger, p. 185 (cited in footnote 20).
[23] Clovis R. Shepherd, *Small Groups: Some Sociological Perspectives*. Chandler, San Francisco, 1964, p. 25.

be unwritten. Some of the standards of group membership behavior are often not talked about or perhaps even recognized by members in a group—but they are there and they have a significant impact on the communication patterns that develop in the small group arena.

Formal Norms

These norms are determined by the role structure of a group. Roles are those expectations that refer "to the relative status and prestige of members and to their rights and duties as members of the group."[24] Whether a person assumes or is assigned a certain role, expectations or norms will emerge according to the particular role.[25] If you are elected secretary, for example, you will be expected to behave differently than if you are just a regular member. We usually adopt these role expectations without being told to do so.

Informal Norms

These norms are developed exclusive of the group role structure. They are "shared behaviors." They are meant to apply to all group members (except, perhaps, when a particular individual must deviate from these shared behaviors because of his particular role). Examples of shared behavior expectations that influence communication are the degree of personableness of the communication, the style of language used by members (for example, formal language, informal language, and profanity), and the directness of the comments (for example, bluntness).[26]

Norms and Pressures

It is interesting to watch norms emerge within a group. They begin to develop during the early stages of group formation. During these early meetings, roles are assigned or assumed and normative behavior according to roles begins. Also, the "tone" of the group begins to develop and it affects the way members will communicate with each other.

Norms are extremely important in the maintenance of a small group. "One of the most definite conclusions of small group research is that groups exert great pressures on their members to conform to the group norms."[27] Experimental research evidence that supports this notion is readily available. For example, in one study, individuals were assigned

[24] Ibid.
[25] Bormann, p. 184 (cited in footnote 17).
[26] Bormann, pp. 260–276 (cited in footnote 17).
[27] Bormann, p. 268 (cited in footnote 17).

to participate with a group in "assessing the length of lines." The individuals who joined each group were not aware that the other group members had been instructed to make incorrect judgments of the lines. The experimenters wanted to determine if an individual would conform to the group's inaccurate assessment or if they would stand out as individuals against the majority opinion. Some individuals maintained their minority opinion without exception, but one third of the experimental subjects "displaced the estimates toward the majority in one half or more of the trials."[28] Pressure to conform did indeed exist. It is interesting to note that the preceding results were obtained in a group situation in which cohesion was almost nonexistent. The group was not one that the individual belonged to because of personal preference. Because pressure was found to exist in groups with low cohesion, you can speculate about the pressure that is applied to you and that you apply to yourself and to others in your highly cohesive personal groups.

All groups exert pressures on members to conform. Some groups, such as churches, fraternities and sororities, and families, establish formal pressures to conform. Other groups, such as bridge clubs and friendship clubs, develop more informal norms, ones that still exert pressure to conform.[29] Conformity is not necessarily an indication of weakness or lack of individualism. Membership in a group makes a person more aware of his relationships with others; this awareness causes him to respond positively to the thoughts and opinions of his respected peers. Even if conformity is not intentional, membership in a group determines many of the things an individual will see, hear, do, learn, and think about.[30]

The major question that remains concerning norms and conformity pressures is "How do groups deal with members who continually violate group standards?" The procedures for dealing with deviant, norm-violating members are quite predictable, and apply to all types of groups. As you read these procedures, try to visualize a personal experience in which you were a deviant group member or a situation where you were a group member dealing with a deviant.

The first step in applying conformity pressure is to delay action, hoping that if you ignore a deviant member he may automatically "come

---

[28] S. E. Asch, "Effects of Group Pressure Upon the Modification and Distortion of Judgments," in Eleanor E. Maccoby, Theodore M. Newcomb, and Eugene L. Hartley (Eds.), *Readings in Social Psychology,* Holt, Rinehart and Winston, New York, 1958, pp. 174–183.

[29] Cartwright and Zander, p. 141 (cited in footnote 18).

[30] Cartwright and Zander, p. 140 (cited in footnote 18).

around." Second, group members will talk among themselves about the deviance and begin directing some communication, often of a light, humorous nature, toward him. The hope is that "light" suggestions will be sufficient to correct the deviance. If the deviance persists, in the third phase of pressure application the humor becomes ridicule. Here, the strategy is simply that the group recognized the behavior as (1) different, and (2) something of which to be ashamed. The fourth step in the process is to make the directive communication "serious" persuasion, perhaps revealing threats and severe criticisms. Finally, if the deviance persists, the group will ignore, isolate, and reject the member (either by retracting his membership or by freezing him out in future meetings).[31] At any step in this pressure procedure, an individual may conform. If he does, the amount of communication directed toward him will decrease, and he will again be accepted and treated as a regular group member. If he fails to conform, however, he will ultimately be rejected.[32]

Alteration of Norms

One should not conclude from this brief discussion of norms and conformity that once norms are established they are not subject to change. Pressures from the external environment can cause the norms to be changed. For example, the president of an organization (external environment) can pass an edict that says all standing committees will meet during the noon hour twice a week. The committee norm may be to meet twice a month, but because of pressures from the external environment, they will probably change the norm.

Another way in which norms can be altered is for group members to change the norms when they become dissatisfied with them. This type of change rarely occurs, however, with what can be termed "substantive" norms. "Procedural" norms, such as time of meeting or place of meeting, are much more subject to change by existing group membership than norms that have their roots in existing philosophies of some group members. For example, a university academic department rarely adopts sweeping changes in a curriculum solely on the desires of the existing departmental members. Such changes do take place, but usually as a result of pressures from the external environment (students and administration) or as a result of several new group members. Proposed changes by new members are difficult to achieve, however, unless there is a significant number of new members. Visualize the changes you have observed taking place within a certain organization

[31] Bormann, p. 269 (cited in footnote 17).
[32] Stanley Schachter, "Deviation, Rejection, and Communication," *Journal of Abnormal and Social Psychology* (1951), *46*, 190–207.

such as a church, or a university academic department. What caused the changes—pressure from the external environment? Initiative on the part of exiting members? Infiltration of new members? Or a combination of these causes?

Norms may *need* to be changed. They can outlive their usefulness and inhibit the workings and efficiency of a group. They are like habits and can be identified, evaluated, and changed.[33] Such optimism, however, is often difficult to convey to a new member of a group who wants to change existing norms. Without sufficient support from the external environment, existing members, or other new members, he will probably fail in his proposed changes. If he fails, he will ultimately either conform to existing practices or withdraw and be rejected or ignored by the group.

Leadership

Of all the topics studied by those interested in the small group communication arena, the nature of leadership has been investigated most persistently over a long period of time.[34]

Leadership Traits

One approach to leadership has been termed the "trait" approach. From this perspective, one views group leadership as "a function of personality and designation."[35] "The belief that a high level of group effectiveness can be achieved simply by the provision of 'good' leaders, though still prevalent . . . , now appears naive in light of research findings." Advocates of the trait approach to leadership have made startling speculations such as "Leaders tend to be bigger (but not too much bigger) and brighter (but not too much brighter) than the rest of the members."[36]

It is apparent that the trait approach to the understanding of leadership has problems. For example, the characteristics that get a person into a position of leadership may be rather different from those that make a person an effective leader once he becomes a leader.[37] We see this discrepancy quite often in a democratic state. The person for whom

[33] A similar treatment of changing norms can be found in Bormann, p. 272 (cited in footnote 17).

[34] Cartwright and Zander, p. 301 (cited in footnote 18).

[35] Edward M. Bodaken, "An Attempt to Define Purposes of Group Discussion with Suggestions for Appropriate Leadership Style," a Ph.D. Prelim Paper, Michigan State University, 1969, p. 1.

[36] Cartwright and Zander, pp. 301–302 (cited in footnote 18).

[37] Cartwright and Zander, p. 303 (cited in footnote 18).

we vote is often different from the person whom we are to follow after he has been elected. It is apparent that the requirements for good leadership in one situation are vastly different from the requirements for good leadership in another situation. Thus, it appears to be impossible to specify inherent trait requirements for "good" leadership.

Leadership Functions

The other approach to the study of leadership is called the "functional" approach. Instead of concentrating on some static trait, the focus is on the *relationship* among participants. From this perspective, one realizes that many group members can (and usually do) serve vital leadership functions. Any action by a group member that helps in the achievement of some specific group task or aids in the maintenance or strengthening of the group task or aids in the maintenance of strengthening of the group itself (socioemotional dimension) is called a leadership function.[38] Thus, extended to its extreme conclusion, any member of a group exerts leadership to the extent that the workings of the group are modified by his presence in the group.[39]

From the standpoint of teaching communication skills, the functional approach to leadership is much more profitable than the trait approach. Rather than training individuals to be the stereo-type of an impressive, articulate leader, individuals are encouraged to become functioning members who are sensitive to group and interpersonal needs. This type of sensitivity to needs for task accomplishment and group maintenance helps individuals realize their worth in the small group communication arena. All individuals are important, for they have the capacity to supply needed leadership functions in this arena.

Small Group Obstacles

The communication process within the small group arena is, without question, extremely complex. The addition of individuals increases the number of all types of communication cues so that the existing communication network is more than the total of the individual communication networks. For each encoded or observed cue, there are many decoded perceptions. Each decoded perception is different from what it would be if an individual were to perceive the cue within the intrapersonal or interpersonal arenas. The addition of cues, interpersonal

[38] Cartwright and Zander, p. 306 (cited in footnote 18).
[39] R. Cattell, "New Concepts for Measuring Leadership in Terms of Group Syntality," *Human Relations* (1951), *4*, 161–184.

needs, and group needs (cohesion, norms, and conformity) necessitate careful analysis of the small group arena. Understanding of the needs allows us to visualize the necessary leadership functions that must be fulfilled if the needs are to be met.

The potential interpersonal obstacles that exist among members in small groups are many. "In general, group members usually have a much better understanding of the task obstacles than they do of the interpersonal obstacles which inhibit group effectiveness.[40] One must acquire a sense of group and interpersonal needs. If one is motivated only by his personal, self-centered needs, he will reduce the effectiveness of the group.[41]

How about your own communication behavior within the small group arena? Are you sensitive to the multiplicity of group and interpersonal needs which exist? Do you fulfill a leadership function at times to assist in dealing with the needs? How do you react to the normal pull of cohesion? Can you recognize the covert as well as the overt norms? If you acquire an understanding of these basic small group concepts, you can become a more capable observer and participant in this arena.

PUBLIC SPEAKING

The primary characteristic of the public speaking arena that distinguishes it from the intrapersonal, interpersonal, and small group arenas is that *one individual* has the major responsibility for communicating a verbal message to a group of receivers. That one individual, however, is not the *only* communicator in the communication transaction. We know that all individuals who are present (and sometimes those who are noticeably absent) communicate. In this arena, the *major* responsibility for the main message rests in the hands of one communicator. He (the speaker) is most actively engaged in encoding that message, while the audience is most concerned with decoding it. Thus, within this arena the opportunities for receiving and transmitting the main message are *unequally* divided among the participants.[42]

In this arena, unlike the interpersonal and small group arenas, people are not usually treated as unique individuals. Although the speaker may "know" each member of his audience, as in the case of delivering a message to his basic speech class, he cannot *focus* on the uniqueness of each individual throughout his entire formal message presentation. Because one person is given the major responsibility for

---

[40] Barry E. Collins and Harold Guetzkow, *A Social Psychology of Group Processes for Decision-Making*, John Wiley, New York, 1964, p. 88.

[41] Ibid., p. 89.

[42] Reusch and Bateson, p. 280–281 (cited in footnote 2).

message presentation and because he cannot deal with each audience member individually, the communication is essentially a monologue.[43] In contrast, in the interpersonal and small group arenas the communication is mostly in dialogue form. If there is dialogue in the public situation, it is much more restricted than the dialogue that exists at the interpersonal level.[44]

Feedback in this arena is also different from feedback in the other arenas. Feedback from the "audience" to the "speaker" and from the "speaker" to the "audience" does exist, but it occurs with only limited cues. The feedback from the receivers to the speaker is almost totally nonverbal. There is seldom any opportunity for a receiver to become a source of spontaneous, verbal feedback. The speaker's feedback to the audience, that is, his response to their feedback, can be both verbal and nonverbal; but the audience usually attends most closely to the verbal feedback. Verbal feedback from the audience to the source is often too threatening and disruptive; therefore, it is not normally permitted. When it does take place (for example, when a "heckler" stands and verbally confronts the source), the public speaking event begins to break down and confusion often results.

Another distinguishing characteristic of this arena is that the verbal communication message is highly organized and premeditated. This planned nature of discourse contrasts sharply with the spontaneous, impulsive, and fragmentary character of communication within the intrapersonal, interpersonal, and small group arenas.[45] Rarely does one go into a public communication encounter as the primary source without a measurable amount of preparation.

Even though it is true that in the public speaking arena (1) one person has the major responsibility for delivering a specific verbal message to an audience, (2) people are not treated as unique individuals, (3) the situation resembles a monologue rather than a dialogue, (4) feedback is restricted, and (5) the message is structured and premitted. When it does take place (for example, when a "heckler" stands meditated, *communication in this arena can still be described as transactional*. Messages other than the speaker's main verbal message exist during the speaking situation. Audience members, no matter how hard they try to avoid it, emit nonverbal cues while the speaker is speaking. Furthermore, the speaker usually decodes some of these audience cues while he is speaking. Because the speaker and the audience members are actually simultaneously encoding and decoding communication cues, the public speaking arena is transactional in nature.

[43] Brooks, p. 11 (cited in footnote 1).
[44] John W. Keltner, *Interpersonal Speech-Communication,* Wadsworth Publishing, Belmont, 1970, p. 322.
[45] Barnlund, p. 11 (cited in footnote 8).

There are aspects of interpersonal and small group transactions in the public speaking setting, also. For example, you are affected by the presence of others (perhaps those sitting close to you or others you know are in attendance). Furthermore, the public speaker attempts to make the aggregate audience a cohesive group. It is necessary for elements of interpersonal communication to be present because, in part, the overall effectiveness of a public communicator is determined by his ability to have audience members perceive his communication as interpersonal. If the speaker can break down the "interaction expectations" of his audience members and get them to feel the actual transactional nature of the public speaking arena, he will be quite successful. When audience members begin to perceive that they are engaging in a personal communication transaction with the speaker, they will enjoy it more and the speaker will be more successful. Some skilled college professors can generate the essence of transaction in large lecture classes. The students become involved and feel that they are actually engaging in a personal communication transaction. Others, who are not so skilled, are incapable of creating a feeling of transaction. At best, a student might perceive he is in an interaction. Again, this arena is transactional; but only skilled speakers can lead the audience to perceive this transactional nature.

It is difficult to estimate with precision the effects due to speeches. It does seem, however, that few significant policy changes or important decisions are made *solely as the result* of one public speech. It is a rare speech that excites a nation and becomes a focal point for social change, but those events have occured. For the most part, single speeches, just like single conversations, do not yield dramatic results. The public speaking arena is used more often for the dissemination of information rather than as a catalyst for change. Put into proper perspective, the public speaking arena is usually not the most effective arena for personal communication because it is so difficult for most speakers to personalize the communication transaction. However, there are some communicators who are more personable as speakers in the public speaking arena than they are as participants in interpersonal or small group situations. For them, the public speaking arena is the most effective.

MASS COMMUNICATION

This arena is similar to the public communication situation in that one source has the major responsibility for message transmission. As a result, opportunities for receiving and sending messages are *unequally* divided among the participants.

The main feature that distinguishes this arena from the public speaking situation is *the audience's relationship to the source.* We indicated earlier that the highly personalized character of interpersonal and small group encounters was diminished in the public speaking situation. In the mass communication arena, this personalized character is diminished even further. There is no direct contact between audience and source, and there is usually no direct contact among all audience members. In the public speaking arena, all audience members are assembled together; but a mass media audience consists of numerous separate small groups of people or single individuals. Because audience members are widely separated and direct feedback to the source is either delayed or totally omitted, simultaneous encoding and decoding among the participants does not occur. Thus, mass media communication is primarily an *interactive* rather than a *transactional* process.

Again, some characteristics of all the arenas are present in this type of communication. As with public speaking, most studies suggest that to be successful, mass communication must be perceived as interpersonal communication.[46] Many people insist that the major reason for the success of Franklin D. Roosevelt's fireside chats on national radio networks was his ability to sound as though he was speaking individually with each listener. Some of the more popular television shows succeed because the performers appear very personal in a mass medium presentation. We know a delightful child, Amy, who was quite upset when she visited with Bozo the Clown, her favorite television performer. She was upset because Bozo asked her what her name was. Later, it became apparent that Amy was no longer angry with Bozo. She said to her Mother, "He was just kidding, Mommy—he really knows my name—he sees me every afternoon when I watch his show."

Thus, even though mass communication is interactive rather than transactional, many of the successful communicators in this arena have the ability to lead their viewers to perceive that they are engaging in a transaction. Often, avid fans of a television performer actually feel (just like Amy), that they have a personal relationship with the performer even though they have never met him. It seems reasonable, therefore, that a communicator in the mass communication arena will be more successful as he improves his ability to appear that he is transacting in the interpersonal communication arena.

Obviously, the mass media play an important role in our society.

[46] Wiseman and Barker, p. 9 (cited in footnote 6).

They serve as important conveyors of information as well as entertainers. The media are relatively ineffective, however, in *changing* our attitudes about issues that are important to us. Their prime role is to reinforce decisons already made. The type of personal influence that normally occurs within the interpersonal and small group arenas is much more effective in changing our attitudes and behaviors than are the mass media.[47]

CONCLUSION

By now it should be apparent to you that the communication arenas are more alike than different. They do have primary distinguishing characteristics, however, which merit separate attention. In the rest of this book, you will notice that the distinctions among the arenas assist us in discussing and simplifying various topics. Also, awareness of the arena characteristics can assist each of us in our attempts to understand and analyze what happens in our various communication transactions. We must remember that even though each arena has distinguishing characteristics, with the exception of the mass communication arena, *the essence of all communication happenings is transaction*. And, even in the mass communication arena, perceived transaction is extremely important.

Exercises

1. Give a speech on a topic of your own choosing to the class so that the situation contains the elements of a mass media presentation. Place a barrier between yourself and the class so that no transaction can take place. Then, remove the barrier and give the identical speech to the class. As a class, discuss how interpersonal needs may or may not be met in each of the two situations.
2. In small groups, draw up a list of the most favored TV personalities. List the communication characteristics of those people.
3. To illustrate the pervasive nature of intrapersonal communication, think of *anything* but do not think of a white polar bear.
4. Get into small groups and discuss if and how this class manifests

---

[47] Walter Weiss, "Effects of the Mass Media of Communication," *Handbook of Social Psychology*, 2nd Ed., V, Gardner Lindzey and Elliot Aronson (Eds.), Addison-Wesley, Reading, 1969, pp. 77–195.

cohesion, what the norms are, and how leadership functions are distributed in the class.

5. Get into two-person groups (dyads). Sit facing each other and, maintaining eye contact, try not to encode or decode.
6. When sitting in small groups, see what the group members feel like when one member presents a prepared speech. Does such communication behavior violate your expectations?
7. As an individual project, observe a small group in action. See how the group members deal with deviants. Do they follow the steps we outlined in this chapter?

Suggested Readings

Robert C. Carson, *Interaction Concepts of Personality,* Aldine, Chicago, 1969.

Darwin Cartwright and Alvin Zander (Eds.), *Group Dynamics—Research and theory,* Harper and Row, New York, 1968.

Frank E. X. Dance (Ed.), *Human Communication Theory,* Holt, Rinehart and Winston, New York, 1967.

Howard H. Martin and Kenneth E. Andersen (Eds.), *Speech Communication—Analysis and Readings,* Allyn and Bacon, Boston, 1968.

Jurgen Reusch and Gregory Bateson, *Communication: The Social Matrix of Psychiatry,* W. W. Norton, New York, 1968.

William C. Schutz, *The Interpersonal Underworld,* Science Behavior Books, Palo Alto, 1966.

Chapter *3* ▶ *Communication Models*

Objectives

On completion of this chapter you should be able to:
1. Specify how concepts and models are interrelated.
2. Give examples that illustrate how models provide perspectives on such things as education, religion, and communication.
3. Orally describe the nature of a model.
4. Reproduce the basic elements of the models presented in the chapter.
5. Compare and contrast the models and list their strengths and weaknesses.
6. Describe the notion of process as it applies to communication.
7. Draw your own model of communication.

    Chapter 3 presents conceptualizations of human communication in diagram form. Similar to the proverbial elephant that the six blind men examine, the "communication beast" can be probed from many different directions. Visualization from one vantage point will highlight certain dimensions, while observation from another perspective will reveal other aspects. A graphic model is simply "a kind of classification system that enables one to categorize potential relevant parts of the process."[1]
    After reading this chapter, you should be able to discuss the diverse

Gerald Miller, *Speech Communication: A Behavioral Approach*, Bobbs-Merrill, New York, 1966, p. 53.

approaches toward communication taken by various scholars and diagram how you personally conceive of the communication process. Ultimately, you will become a capable "observer" of communication. Although this sounds simple, it is not. The capacity to observe communication will enable you to better understand why communication breakdowns and conflicts arise. This understanding will aid you in predicting potential communication problems and thus help you to avoid them. Also, it will assist you in being able to resolve communication conflicts once they occur.

One of us resisted learning about communication models for a long time. He often asserted, "These models turn me off! I don't see any purpose in learning about models and when I become a teacher I will not make my students study them." Knowledge of models and the resulting "observer perspective," however, has liberated him in his thinking about the communication process. This new insight has freed him of some of the shackles (narrow thinking) by which he was once bound. If you experience this type of growth, this chapter will have served its purpose.

THE PROCESS OF CONCEPTUALIZATION

It is impossible to think of an object, event, or a person without conceptualizing it. Our concepts or images reveal our orientations.[2] The concept of "the solar system" probably conjures up a mental picture of the earth and other planets revolving around the sun. Before the Copernican scientific revolution, however, people visualized the sun revolving around the earth. When the Copernican concepts emerged, there was great resistance to this new model of the solar system. Men who thought the earth was the center of the universe were faced with an opposing notion. Scientific and theological conflicts of great importance ensued simply because someone had a new model of the universe.[3]

Our personal concepts of elements in the world are continually undergoing change and affecting our behavior. Exposure to a religious prophet or educational critic, for example, may change your concepts of religion and education. If you become a convert to (or away from) a religion, events that you previously interpreted one way are seen in a

[2] For an excellent treatment of the importance of images, see Kenneth E. Boulding, *The Image,* University of Michigan Press, Ann Arbor, 1956.
[3] The nature of changing scientific notions are treated in Thomas S. Kuhn, *The Structure of Scientific Revolutions,* University of Chicago Press, Chicago, 1962.

new light: behavior previously viewed as normal now seems to be a "sin." Such a change in your concepts affects your own reactions to those behaviors.

If you have accepted the goals and methods of our educational system and then become exposed to books such as *Teaching as a Subversive Activity* and *Why Children Fail,* your whole notion of education may change. Suddenly the goal of the educational system seems to be the stimulation of students' thoughts instead of the transmission of facts and information. This kind of new model will obviously affect your classroom experience. A boring lecture that did not bother you in the past will disturb you now. Our concepts change, and those changes have consequences.

Although your own personal notions of communication may not have undergone any changes, other people's views of it have gone through important transitions. For example, the theatre (one communication medium) is changing. In traditional theatre, the audience participates vicariously in the play by identifying with the characters, even though they are physically separate entities. In some contemporary theatre, however, actors are no longer separated from the audience. Parts of the play are sometimes presented among the audience members and the audience actually participates in the action. This variation in theatrical practice signifies a change in how theatre is conceptualized. The relationship between the actor and the audience is seen from an entirely different perspective.

Also, views of "mass communication" have undergone changes. Originally people viewed mass communication as a totally effective device. Whatever message was transmitted was assumed to have been effective. This belief is labeled the "hypodermic-needle" view. It visualizes governments that control mass media systems as manipulators of people. From this perspective, the media and its masters are seen as omnipotent.

The views of the "all-powerful nature" of mass communication have been altered. Just because a communication source desires a certain effect does not mean that the effect will necessarily follow. The message transmitted is not necessarily "injected" wholesale into the populace. Instead, (1) the effects of mass communications differ from person to person because each person is different, and (2) a person's relationship with other people alters the effect of a message on him. One's attitudes, beliefs, personality traits, and communication linkages with others influence the effect of a mass message on him.[4] To under-

[4] For a more detailed account of different models of mass communication, see Melvin L. DeFleur, *Theories of Mass Communication,* 2nd Ed., David McKay, New York, 1970, Chapters VI and VII.

stand message effects, one must focus on the receivers because they are of prime importance.

The hypodermic-needle and recipient-centered approaches are simply diverse conceptualizations of the mass communication process. The way an event is conceptualized and diagrammed becomes a "model" of the event.

MODELS OF COMMUNICATION

As with mass communication, the other areas of human communication have been approached from various perspectives. These perspectives become apparent when historical writings on communication are compared with contemporary treatments.

Let us examine some of the various conceptual schemes of communication as they are presented in certain popular communication models. Just as a city or state "map" is a graphic representation of one conceptual scheme of a particular area, a communication model is a graphic representation of one conceptual scheme of communication. No single map is perfect (isomorphic) and no one model of communication is flawless.[5] Some maps have more social utility than others and some communication models provide more insight than others. As you read about models, view them with a critical eye. We will discuss the fundamental notions of the models. This should serve as a guide to your own critique of each model.

Historical Insights

The classical view of communication has a strong influence today. Although early rhetorical theorists did not present a specific diagram that represented their conception of communication, a diagram can be extracted from the seminal rhetorical concepts. The principal rhetorical thinker was Aristotle. The focus of *The Rhetoric* (Aristotle's treatise on communication) was that communication is persuasion. Figure 1[6] is an attempt to represent graphically how most scholars have interpreted Aristotle's description of communication in *The Rhetoric.*

Although there is some contemporary challenge to this interpretation of Aristotle's description of communication,[7] many scholars have

[5] If a map were isomorphic with an area, it would have to be the area. A model of communication is not communication, but an attempt to represent it.

[6] This diagram is from Howard H. Martin and Kenneth E. Andersen (Eds.), *Speech Communication: Analysis and Readings,* Allyn and Bacon, Boston, 1968, p. 9.

[7] Lawrence W. Rosenfield, "Rhetoric Criticism and an Aristotelian Notion of Process," *Speech Monographs,* (March 1966), *XXXIII,* 1–16.

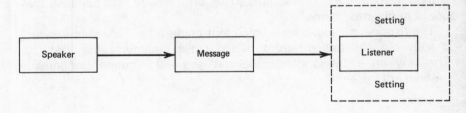

Figure 1

adopted this viewpoint. From this perspective, communication occurs when a speaker presents a speech to audience members in an attempt to alter their attitudes. As commonly interpreted, the important parts of communication were those related to the speaker, the speech, the audience, and the occasion. Aristotle said that persuasion could be achieved by who you are (ethos—your trustworthiness), by the manner of your arguments (logos—the logic in your position), and by playing on the emotions of the audience (pathos—the audience's emotions). This notion of communication was in harmony with public speaking, the primary means of influence and communication during Aristotle's time.

Throughout history, individuals have benefited by public speaking skills. Courses in public speaking have been designed to fill this need. The traditional public speaking courses in colleges and high schools are outgrowths of the common interpretation of Aristotle's conceptual model of communication, developed 25 centuries ago. The student in the course spends considerable time polishing his formal speech, because it is his only link with the audience.

The common Aristotelian model, as most models, can be used to generate relevant questions about speech communication. From this model, the speech itself becomes the central concern. For example, what elements of the speech produce persuasion in the audience? Are certain types of speech organization better than others? Does the style of language in a speech influence its persuasiveness? Does the speaker's prior reputation aid his persuasiveness? Note, also, that the model represents communication as a "static" phenomenon. The speaker speaks, the message travels to the audience, and the audience listens. The steps in the event follow one another instead of occurring simultaneously. Finally, the model concentrates on purposive communication, which occurs when one consciously tries to persuade another to accept his position.

Some aspects of communication are not highlighted in this Aristotelian model. For instance, the model does not illustrate the concept of feedback (where the speaker gets immediate cues from the audience about the success of what he is saying and alters his behavior accordingly). The nonverbal aspects of persuasion (all the elements of the situation other than the words in the message) are not explicitly treated by the model.

There are numerous other historical insights into communication, but they are either revisions of Aristotle's or have had little influence on concepts of communication.[8]

Contemporary Models

Berlo Model

The Berlo model (Figure 2), has had a definite impact on how scholars and students view communication.[9]

The model's advantages are apparent. The model is not limited to public speaking as the only form of communication. With the Berlo model, one can visualize interpersonal spoken communication and varieties of written communication. The model also has heuristic (research idea generating) values. It specifies elements that are vital to the communication process. For example, the model can lead you to investigate the effect of a receiver's communication skills on his acceptance of your message; or, you as a speaker might begin to realize that your social background affects the attitudes of your receivers.

The model also has limitations. Although Berlo wrote extensively about communication as a process,[10] the model, like Aristotle's, represents communication as a static rather than as a dynamic, everchanging phenomenon. Furthermore, the feedback the speaker receives from the audience is not graphically represented, and nonverbal communication is not considered important in influencing a message's impact on a person.

[8] Other contemporary insights are difficult to graphically represent. For example, Kenneth Burke's concept of communication based on "identification" is rather difficult to portray. See his numerous works, especially *A Rhetoric of Motives,* Prentice-Hall, New York, 1950.

[9] David K. Berlo, *The Process of Communication,* Holt, Rinehart and Winston, New York, 1960, p. 72.

[10] Berlo's discussion of process in communication was one of the first to appear and was a significant contribution. Ibid., pp 23–30.

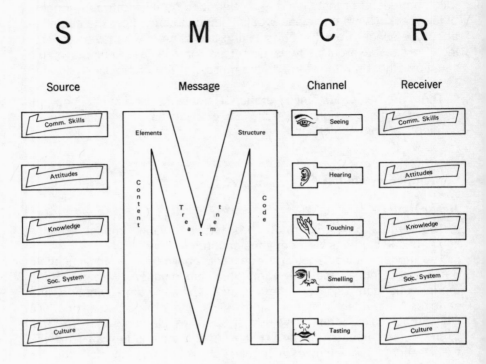

Figure 2

Information Theory Model

Shannon and Weaver were the prime movers in applying information theory to communication. Since Shannon worked with the Bell Telephone Laboratories, the focus of his concern was "accurate message transmission." Weaver extended Shannon's notions to all types of communication. In response to the question "What happens to information from the time it is transmitted until it is received?", they offered their model of communication (Figure 3).[11]

The model highlights several facets of communication. It focuses on information and leads to an examination of the **accuracy** of transmission. One of the barriers to fidelity of communication (fidelity is when the message is received and interpreted exactly as it was intended), is "noise." Noise is composed of unwanted signals that can disrupt mes-

[11] Claude E. Shannon and Warren Weaver, *The Mathematical Theory of Communication,* University of Illinois Press, Urbana, 1948, p. 9.

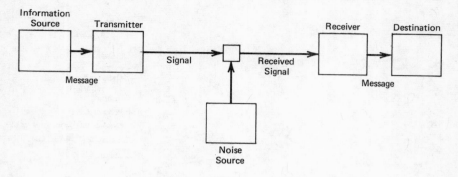

Figure 3

sage fidelity. In simplest terms, if a telephone connection is faulty, the message sent will be distorted before it reaches its destination. The noise can be from a faulty wire, bad receiver phone, or the presence of other messages in the same channel. In communication, we have extended the notion of noise to include "perceptual noise." You have probably experienced perceptual noise in your own communication experiences. Have you tried to talk to a friend about a concern of yours when he has an important exam the next morning? Describe his listening behavior. In such a situation, your friend's reception channel is probably overloaded with the perceptual noise resulting from his concern about the exam.

The Shannon and Weaver model can be applied to all communication arenas, that is, intrapersonal, interpersonal, public speaking, or mass. For example, the noise may be a receiver's accidental misinterpretation of a message. Noise causes the translated message to be different from the transmitted one.

Although the information theory model introduces new insights into communication, it gives only a partial picture of the process. Again, communication is treated as a static, one-way phenomenon. There is no graphic representation of feedback or the transaction that takes place within encoding and decoding.

Barnlund Model

We mentioned earlier that the Aristotelian model was specifically designed for the public speaking situation. Barnlund's model (Figure 4) is aimed at illuminating the interpersonal communication situation.[12]

[12] Dean C. Barnlund, "A Transactional Model of Communication," in Kenneth K. Sereno and C. David Mortensen (Eds.), *Foundations of Communication Theory*, Harper and Row, New York, 1970, p. 99.

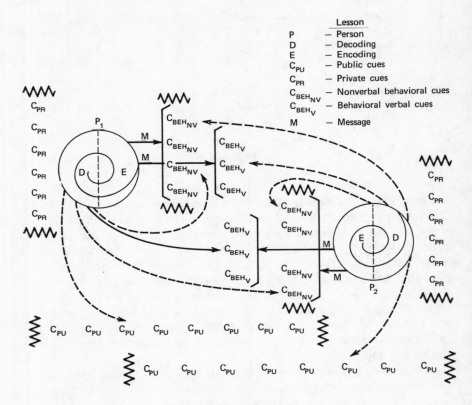

Figure 4

Figure 4 is not as difficult to interpret as it appears to be. The left circle represents person one (P_1), and the right circle represents a second person (P_2). The arrows emanating from the circles point to the kinds of cues (signals) a person processes from the environment (his immediate surroundings, his background and experiences, his physical state, and so on). Each person (1) sees the public cues (C_{PU}), those elements of the immediate environment (though the two persons perceive them differently); (2) is aware of private cues (C_{PR}), those aspects of himself such as fatigue, which alter his perception; (3) is producing and observing behavioral cues ($C_{BEH_{NV}}$) that are nonverbal, such as movements, posture, smells, spatial distance, and facial expressions;

and (4) is utilizing behavioral cues (C_{BEH_v}) that are verbal, the actual words of a message.

As you visualize two persons talking, it is clear that this model takes a unique perspective. It represents interpersonal communication as a dynamic, continuous, and complex process. Communication is no longer seen as a static event but as a transactional event. Each person is sharing in the encoding and decoding process, and each person is affecting the other. This model highlights the kinds of cues (public, private, and behavioral) that affect the meaning one attaches to a situation. From this perspective, the verbal message supplies only one part of the total meaning. Also, looking at one-half of the model, one-person (intrapersonal) communication can be examined.

Like all models, the Barnlund model is not complete. The cues are listed, but the elements that make up those cues are not fully specified. What parts of a verbal message are relevant to the establishment of communication meaning? What are the specific types of nonverbal cues? Are the cues of equal importance in determining one's meaning of a communication? The model obviously also needs to include more persons before it can be applied to small group, public speaking, and mass communication situations.

Westley and MacLean Model

This model applies to interpersonal and mass communication. Westley and MacLean recognized differences between interpersonal and mass communication; for example, interpersonal communication allows one to get more cues about the other person and feedback is more immediate; but they developed a model that stresses the similarities between the two.[13] The basic elements of the model are objects (X's), and people (A's and B's). In interpersonal communication (Figure 5, page 54), a communicator (A), in contact with objects in his environment (X's), selects and transmits a message (X') to B. Person B may or may not have the same objects as part of his environment, but in any event, he transmits feedback (f_{BA}) to A.

For mass communication, the model requires the addition of other persons (C's) (Figure 6, page 54).

Figure 6 graphically presents the "two-step flow" of information in mass communication. C's are "gatekeepers" or "opinion leaders" who select information from mass media sources (A's) and transmit to their own followers (B's). The mass media message then reaches B (Mr. Average Citizen) *after* it has been filtered through other people. There is not

[13] Bruce H. Westley and Malcolm S. MacLean, Jr., "A Conceptual Model for Communications Research," *Journalism Quarterly* (1957), 34, 31–38.

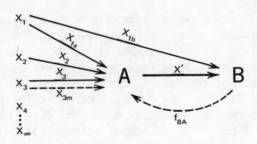

Figure 5

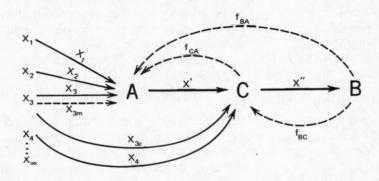

Figure 6

a direct, uninterrupted chain of events from a mass communication source to receivers. A message is filtered, digested, and analyzed.[14]

Westley and MacLean indicate that the messages (X″) that an opinion leader (gatekeeper) transmits to followers represent the opinion leader's selections from the messages he receives from the various mass media sources (X′) and his selections and abstractions from the objects in his own sensory field (X_3, X_4). Feedback moves from the followers to the mass media (f_{BA}), from the followers to the opinion leaders (f_{BC}), and from the opinion leaders to the mass media (f_{CA}). Westley and

[14] For a cogent summary of this process, see Paul F. Lazarsfeld and Herbert Menzel, "Mass Media and Personal Influence," in Wilbur Schramm (Ed.), *The Science of Human Communication*, Basic Books, New York, pp. 94–115.

MacLean develop their concept further by saying, "Clearly, in the mass communication situation, a large number of C's receive from a very large number of A's and transmit to a vastly larger number of B's who simultaneously receive from other C's."[15]

The prime value of the model is its generality. Using the same basic diagram, communication events ranging from interpersonal to mass media settings can be visualized. Another strength of the model is its perceptive representation of the two-step flow of communication. It also demonstrates the inherent nature of feedback in a communication system and accounts for environmental effects (public and private cues).

It is extremely difficult to describe the model verbally. Furthermore, the model does not represent communication as a process. The model leads one to conclude incorrectly that all communication has a definite beginning and end. For example, note that A, whether a person or a form of mass media, is not represented as giving feedback to anyone.

Wenburg and Wilmot Model

To conclude the discussion of the various communication models, we offer one of our own models, which stresses process. Seeing human communication as a process implies (1) that it is an ever-changing, on-going phenomenon; (2) that to select a source and a receiver is an artificial decision and must be recognized as such; (3) that it really has no beginning or end—each part is a beginning or end depending on where you are in the process; and (4) that its essence is transaction between or among persons and the "behavior of each person affects and is affected by the behavior of each other person."[16]

We feel that most authors have "frozen" the communication process beyond reasonable grounds with their models. Our model (Figure 7) is an attempt to fulfill, through visual representation, the four criteria of the process notion stated in the previous paragraph. At the same time, we have attempted to maintain the important elements of a communication event.

The basic diagram is the infinity symbol. As long as persons are in contact with one another, the transactions are endless. Actually, when realization of personal contact first exists (awareness of presence), *several loops of our infinity symbol model have already been completed*.

[15] Bruce H. Westley and Malcolm S. MacLean, Jr., "A Conceptual Model for Communications Research," in Sereno and C. Mortensen (Eds.), p. 77 (cited in footnote 12).
[16] Paul Watzlawick, Janet Helmick Beavin, and Don D. Jackson, *Pragmatics of Human Communication*, W. W. Norton, New York, 1967, p. 31.

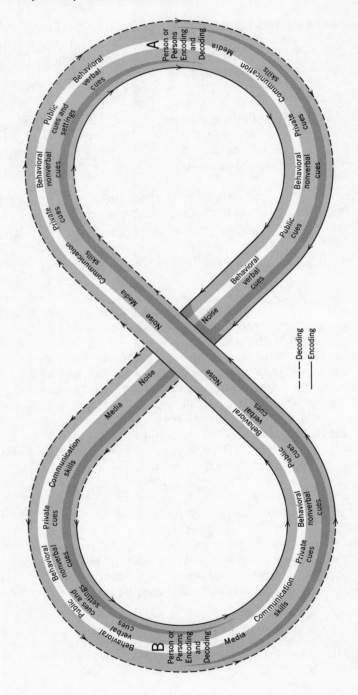

Figure 7

Interpersonal Communication

Now we will slow the process down, make some artificial distinctions (similar to designating units of time), and look at the essence of transaction. You are sitting in the student union and see a friend across the room. When you first see her, you are already decoding (receiving messages)—while still decoding, you react by a "Hi, Jill" (encoding, that is, creating messages)—she, already engaged in the process of decoding, in turn receives that information (more decoding) and responds (encoding)—you, still encoding and decoding, respond to her (more encoding)—she responds to that, and so on. Note that while you were encoding, you were simultaneously decoding, and when you were decoding, you were simultaneously encoding—and so was Jill. Both of you were sending and receiving cues simultaneously, more cues than we have represented in the example. To demonstrate this simultaneity, in Figure 7 the solid lines represent encoding and the broken lines represent decoding. Notice how they overlap.

While encoding a message, person A sends verbal and nonverbal behavioral cues. And, by now, person B has already emitted cues that reach person A. Person B perceives the public cues, certain behavioral cues (verbal and nonverbal), and private verbal and nonverbal cues. While B is going through this process, A is doing the same thing. Obviously, in a communication transaction, not all of the possible cues have an equal effect on meaning. In one transaction, the behavioral verbal cues may be the most important and in another, public or private cues may affect the participants more. In addition to the presence of cues, noise, or message and cue distortion, occurs in both the decoding and encoding processes.

Intrapersonal Communication

In this kind of communication—communication with oneself—the person is transacting with himself. He may be searching for a solution to a problem or thinking about what he is going to do the next day. He is encoding and decoding with himself. This type of intrapersonal communication is best represented by half of the infinity symbol of Figure 7. For example, if we look at the encoding and decoding of person B, and disregard person A and the right half of the symbol, "inner speech" or intrapersonal communication will be represented. The communication travels in a circle. B encodes and decodes without the presence of A or of A's encoding and decoding processes.

All of Figure 7 can be used to demonstrate intrapersonal communication that exists when one intends his message for a receiver who is not present; for example, writing a letter to someone. You impute message-receiving and message-sending qualities to the "imagined" receiver. Transaction, or imagined transaction, is still the key. In fact, some people enjoy letter writing because in the process of writing they imagine an actual conversation occurring. In these cases, a receiver is imagined, so the full infinity loop represents the process. B is a person and A is an imagined or intended receiver.

Even communication with God, animals, and inanimate objects can be shown by the complete model. For communication to occur, it is not even necessary to have real or imagined humans present. When a person is communicating with an object (for example, praying to the sun), he is making inferences about how that object will process the message and "respond." The more inanimate the object, the more one must "read into it" to communicate. The object is, essentially, personified and supplied with the human communication characteristics. For animate objects, the same process occurs, but to a lesser degree. When we communicate with a dog, he probably emits cues; but we, nevertheless, "read in" some qualities that are not there. When we want to communicate but transaction is in short supply, we supply it. Human communication, as demonstrated by our model, is, in all its forms, transactional.

Small Group and Public Speaking Communication

As noted in Chapter 2, although small group and public speaking situations differ in many respects, they are also very similar. Both contain more than two people who are in contact with each other. In the public speaking situation, the speaker may be the focus of attention, but the receivers are aware of one another's presence. In the small group, the receivers are even *more* aware of one another's presence. The adapted model in Figure 8 represents the real and potential interpersonal transactions of many people.[17]

Figure 8 demonstrates that the common notion that communication begins and ends with a formal speech is a limited perspective. A person is not a "source" or a "receiver" but a participant in a transaction. For clarity, some authors look only at the verbal messages. From that perspective, the initiator of the message—the group leader or the public speaker—is the "source." But, how can we ignore the other message cues (nonverbal, public, and private) that exist? Acknowledgment of the various cues makes it theoretically impossible to designate an original source. These cues, with the exception of verbal cues, occur

---

[17] Each of the loops in Figure 8 contains the specified cues that appear on Figure 7.

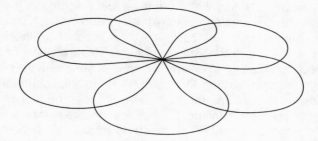

Figure 8

in every communication event. From this viewpoint, who is to say who the source and the receiver are? To understand small group and public speaking processes, we must focus not on a sender and receiver, but on the *continuing transaction* of persons simultaneously sending and receiving multiple communication cues.

Figure 8 is ideally suited to represent the intertwined participants in a small group. Its application to public speaking, however, may not be so obvious.

Let us take a specific example to illustrate the utility of the adapted model to public speaking. If a United States senator is going to present a speech, both he and the audience members have encoded and decoded messages prior to the speech. The senator has some idea of who will be present, to which political party they belong, their general attitudes on issues, and how they feel toward him. Also, the audience will have some reaction to the senator's previous messages and will have expectations of his feelings toward their party. When the senator enters the room (contact realization), the audience encodes by applauding. He encodes by responding. Since they are reacting to each other, both the senator and audience are encoding and decoding simultaneously. Many loops of the infinity model have already occurred *before* the speech begins because the encoding and decoding have been going on before. This prior transaction has an effect on the transmission and reception of the formal speech. When the speech begins, we are just continuing the transaction and entering another phase of the loop— *the infinity loops are constantly operable*. As you examine Figure 8, let any loop (petal) of the "daisy" model represent the senator and let the other loops represent audience members. Carefully study the nature of the communication. Notice that there is no initial source in the situation. Notice, also, the transactional nature of all the relationships existing in the public communication occurrence. The speaker is linked with the audience members and they all have some effect on one another and on the speaker. A public speaking event is a special type of interpersonal communication setting that involves more transactional patterns.

If one wishes to concentrate on the verbal message alone, and illustrate that the speaker has more influence on the event than do the audience members, a change in the daisy model will accomplish that goal. Simply make one loop of the daisy larger than the rest (Figure 9). The large loop represents the speaker and suggests that he has the task of creating the main verbal message. The small loops show the influence of the audience members on the verbal transaction.

The major strength of the Wenburg-Wilmot model is that it captures the essence of process by (1) representing personal communication as an ever-changing, on-going phenomenon, (2) highlighting the arbitrariness of identifying a source and a receiver, (3) showing there is no actual beginning or end in communication, and (4) stressing the impor-

Figure 9

tance of transaction in the personal communication process. Our model makes it clear that all participants in a transaction are important. In intrapersonal communication you are, of course, the only participant; but in the interpersonal, small group, and public speaking arenas, your presence is important regardless of your activities. At any point in the transaction, whether you are actively talking or passively listening, you are encoding and decoding; you are "attempting to get meaning."

The limitations of our model are similar to some of those of other models. For example, as with the Barnlund Model, the components of the public and private cues, and their relative importance are not fully specified. Also, as with the Westley-MacLean model, our model is difficult to describe verbally. Another limitation is that we have not diagrammed how persons get in and out of a transaction—we assume that people are always involved in communication.

FUNCTIONS OF MODELS

The values of models should now be apparent to you. Each model offers a fresh perspective into communication. The models we have presented are not a complete list, but they demonstrate the major approaches to communication.[18]

Organizing Function

Now that you have studied the chapter, you should be better able to "communicate about communication." We asserted that the models should serve an "organizing function;" if you have internalized this material, you should now be a more capable observer of communication. Now that you have been exposed to the "hypodermic-needle" and the "two-step flow of mass communication" postulates, mass communication per se should have new meaning for you. Your role as an observer of mass communication should be more sophisticated. The same is true for the public speaking situation. The Wenburg-Wilmot model represents a perspective very different from the Aristotelian model, but regardless of the approach, each model should help you organize your thoughts about a particular communication arena. Hopefully, you have gained similar insights into interpersonal and intrapersonal communication from the Barnlund and Wenburg-Wilmot models.

[18] Additional models can be found in sources such as F. Craig Johnson and George R. Klare, "General Models of Communication Research: A Survey of the Development of A Decade," *Journal of Communication* (March 1961), *11* 13–26.

Finally, you should be able to see similarities and differences among all forms of personal communication.

Heuristic Function

In addition to providing you with a better organization pattern from which to view communication, exposure to the models should have provided you with fresh, creative questions and insights about the communication process. The more research ideas and creative thoughts you can glean from a model, the better its heuristic value is.

SHORTCOMINGS OF MODELS

Models Provide a Partial View

Any view of communication is incomplete. When we organize and highlight certain parts of the communication process, we are ignoring other parts. The selective nature of any communication model necessitates overlooking some elements. Any single view of man's communication behavior is partial.

Confusing the Model for the Thing

Exposure to models often causes one to close his perspective prematurely. He fails to continue looking for fresh insights because he treats a model as the representative of a particular concept. Aristotle's writings on communication, as popularly interpreted, were accepted for thousands of years by many scholars as *the* representation of all communication. Such a myopic view, whether from the perspective of Aristotle's model or someone else's model, limits one's vision and chances for new insights. Kaplan argues that taking models too seriously can impede the truth. "When one doctrine, method, or technique comes to be regarded as the sole repository of truth, for my part I have no doubt that it is truth which suffers. The danger is all the greater with respect to model building. . . ."[19]

Hopefully, the models in this chapter have served an organizing and an heuristic function without restricting your views. Do not confuse them with reality—let them stimulate you both as an observer and as a student of communication.

[19] Abraham Kaplan, *The Conduct of Inquiry*, Chandler, San Francisco, 1964, p. 276.

Exercises

1. Carefully review each model and list the assets and liabilities of each.
2. Draw your own model of communication and analyze it. What assumptions do you make? What elements do you exclude?
3. Sit down with a friend or acquaintance not enrolled in this course. Ask him to describe one type of communication such as an interpersonal event or a mass media experience. Based on his description, construct a model of communication that highlights his assumptions.
4. Making models of communication is a process that entails assumptions. What aspects of communication that might be important cannot be graphically represented? Is it impossible to diagram some important elements of the communication process?
5. Diagram how you think mass communication works in Red China.
6. Sit where you can observe two people talking. Write down the specific public and behavioral cues that you observe. Make a listing of the kinds of private cues that you are aware of while you observe.
7. Draw a model of the "hypodermic-needle" view of mass communication.
8. See if you can diagram (a) your own view of the education process and, (b) the view held by (1) the teacher you enjoy the least and (2) the teacher you enjoy the most.
9. Assign various class members to "stage" the different models presented in this chapter or those constructed by some of the class members. Discuss the differences in the models that become apparent during this staging exercise. (Which model demonstrates the transactional preparation that existed in the classroom while you were preparing to stage the models?)
10. Create a situation in which class members can personally experience intrapersonal, dyadic, small group, speaker-audience, and, if possible, mass communication situations. Does any one of the models in this chapter adequately present the nature of all these communication paradigms?
11. Observe two people having a "friendly conversation" and then observe two people having a "friendly argument." Do you notice any differences in the types of noise (perceptual noise) that were present? Give your observations to the class in an oral report. (What kinds of noise were present during the time you were presenting the oral report?)

Suggested Readings

David K. Berlo, *The Process of Communication,* Holt, Rinehart and Winston, New York, 1960.

Kenneth Boulding, *The Image,* University of Michigan Press, Ann Arbor, 1956.

Melvin L. DeFleur, *Theories of Mass Communication,* 2nd Ed., David McKay, New York, 1970.

David Harrah, *Communication—A Logical Model,* M.I.T. Press, Cambridge, 1963.

Abraham Kaplan, *The Conduct of Inquiry,* Chandler, San Francisco, 1964.

Thomas S. Kuhn, *The Structure of Scientific Revolutions,* University of Chicago Press, Chicago, 1962.

Gerald Miller, *Speech Communication: A Behavioral Approach,* Bobbs-Merrill, New York, 1966.

Kenneth K. Sereno and C. David Mortensen (Eds.), *Foundations of Communication Theory,* Harper and Row, New York, 1970.

Norbert Wiener, *The Human Use of Human Beings: Cybernetics and Society,* Houghton Mifflin, Boston, 1950.

Chapter *4* ▶

Ethical Considerations in Communication

Objectives

On completion of this chapter you should be able to:
1. Discuss the classical views of communication ethics.
2. List some speech practices considered unethical by many speech communication scholars.
3. Compare and contrast universal, individual, and situational codes of ethics.
4. Specify your own code of ethics and relate it to other approaches.
5. Visualize how one's evaluation of another's ethics affects communication transactions.

We are all faced with decisions that have ethical overtones. We must make decisions that have consequences for us and others. Based on our own ethical code, we decide the rightness or wrongness of an act. As a student, you make decisions reflecting your value judgments. For example, you have to pass an examination and you know of a "sure-fire" method of cheating that will raise your grade. Do you cheat? Or, you have a friend sitting next to you who is not prepared for the exam. Do you make it easy for him to copy your answers? You are to give a persuasive speech in your introductory speech class and do not have sufficient time to find appropriate documentation. Should you create some fake evidence? Your fraternity or sorority has raised its annual dues and you need some additional funding from home. Knowing your parents already believe that the costs of the fraternity or sorority are unduly high, do you lie about the actual costs of your books for the semester or tell them your tuition fees have increased?

Others are also faced with ethical choices. During the first four to six years of your life, you parents led you to believe a fat man with a red suit and white beard lived at the North Pole and delivered gifts to good little boys and girls each Christmas. Is such deception desirable? The President of the United States, knowing that the CIA was actively engaged in a subversive movement in a foreign country, tells the United States public that the government was not involved in the action. The truth is later revealed and in answer to the falsification charges, he asserts that he was *not* aware of the involvement. Are his ethics questionable?

For centuries people have been concerned with how to make ethical choices such as these. To appreciate more fully the nature of ethics as it relates to *your* communication behavior, it is valuable to review briefly how others have tried to deal with it.

AN HISTORICAL PERSPECTIVE

To facilitate our discussion of the historical treatment of ethics in speech communication, let us view communication as an automobile. Inside that automobile are several passengers, such as sources, receivers, delivery techniques, word choice, ethics, and others. Where these various passengers have been seated in the car indicates their relative importance at a given time during the historical tradition of speech communication. At times, ethics has actually been the driver of the car; at others ethics has only been allowed a space in the trunk.

To the Sophists, teachers in Greece during the fifth century B.C., the goal of communication was the securement of belief. They established schools in which one could acquire the necessary skills for becoming an effective speaker. Although the ethical concerns of different Sophists varied, it is fair to say that ethics was generally placed in the back seat of the communication automobile. The Sophists were concerned with the enhancement of the speaker's image for the securement of belief, and ethics was not a central consideration. To them, truth was only a persuasive device that could aid in the securement of belief. Believability, not truth, was the goal. This exclusive concern with effectiveness left no guaranteed seat in the automobile for ethics.

Plato believed that ethics should be in the driver's seat. He argued that the establishment of truth should be the goal of communication. In

Gorgias,[1] he leveled harsh indictments against the common Sophistic treatment of communication. He criticized defining the end of communication as believability because, by that definition, truth, although permissable, was not inherently necessary. He also argued that the Sophists were concerned with the nonsubstantive techniques of communication and that they treated it as a knack rather than as a substantive concern related to philosophy and morality.

In *Rhetoric,* Aristotle stated what many believe is a more realistic position on ethical considerations in communication.[2] Although he advocated "ethical communication" in which truth is necessary for truth and justice to prevail, his position was very pragmatic. He implied that "communication is here to stay and not all communication is 'ethical communication'; let's look at it realistically so that we can better understand the ingredients." He provided a basic rationale for communication and defined it as the discovery of all available means of persuasion. He believed that if one loses while having the truth on his side, he has only his own ineptitude to blame. He contended that the Sophistic knacks such as techniques of generating attention that were criticized by Plato, were (1) amoral, and (2) often necessary because of the sorry nature of audiences. To Aristotle, ethics deserved a comfortable seat in the communication car, but did not have to serve as driver.

Many have extended Aristotle's "amoral" classification and contended that ethics is of no concern to communication, that is, communication, per se, is amoral. Thus, in many texts, ethics has been removed from the Communication Department car and forced to ride in an Ethics Department car. These scholars see speech as a *tool,* which, like fire, is used for both noble and base ends. It is maintained that speech is neither moral nor immoral—it is amoral. It takes on aspects of goodness or badness by how one uses it. Therefore, if a speaker elects to falsify evidence or use trickery, it is the fault of the speaker, not the speech process.

Quintilian's treatment of ethics also stands out in the historical tradition.[3] He was a successful teacher of communication in Rome in 100 A.D. He defined an orator as a "good man speaking well." Taken to the extreme, Quintilian's notion implies that unless a communicator is a "good man" he should not be studied by communication scholars. Thus, Mr. Ethics was again driving the car.

[1] Plato, *Gorgias*, trans. by W. C. Helmbold, The Liberal Arts Press, New York, 1952.
[2] Aristotle, *Rhetoric*, trans. by W. Rhys Roberts, Oxford Press, Oxford, 1924.
[3] Quintilian, *Institutio Oratoria,* trans. by H. E. Butler, Wm. Heinemann, Ltd., New York, 1921–1922.

In 1513, Machiavelli wrote a treatise on ethical philosophy.[4] The Machiavellian ethics holds that given an acceptable end (goal), any means (method) can be justified. If one adapts the "end justifies the means" philosophy to communication, he must look solely at the *intent* of the source. With this philosophy, one can argue, for example, that violence is permissable to achieve desirable civil liberties. Seen this way, ethics plays the role of a hitchhiker. It rides in the front seat of the communication auto for a few miles and is then dropped off to be picked up by someone else. And, like the hitchhiker, any car (goal) is acceptable for a ride.

The Sophistic, Platonic, Aristotelian, Quintilian, and Machiavellian positions are all espoused in today's society. Before we present our view of ethics, we will examine contemporary treatments of ethics. It is not our function to review all the approaches to ethics in speech communication, but we will try to demonstrate the general trends taken by most writers.[5]

VIEWS OF ETHICS

We noted earlier that most speech communication scholars have treated communication as a tool. This view was fostered because scholars, following Aristotle's lead, have only looked at the public speaking situation. The public speech has been treated as having a definite beginning and end, and speech critics have usually restricted their ethical judgments to the formal speech. Viewing communication as an event separate from man's everyday life is not an accurate portrayal of its true function. Communication is not just something one picks up from the shelf, uses it for a formal purpose, and then neatly replaces to its former spot. We use communication all the time; it is not like a faucet—turned on or off for a specific occasion—it is used constantly.

[4] Niccolo Machiavelli, *The Prince*, trans. by Luigi Ricci, The New American Library of World Literature, New York, 1952.

[5] There is a way of looking at ethics that is undeveloped in the field of speech communication. Ethics can be viewed as a communication variable—a variable that *explains* human behavior. Instead of just examining the concept of communication ethics from a value perspective, it can be viewed empirically as an individual personality characteristic that affects the way one receives messages. In Chapter II, we discuss personality variables such as predisposition and self-esteem. Perhaps a person's ethical code is a basic variable that affects other personality variables and governs a person's behavior.

Viewing speech as an integral part of man's everyday actions instead of as a ceremonial tool does not absolve us of ethical questions. In fact, if we view ethics as a set of standards for *all* our communication behavior, ethical considerations are more central to communication. Although we will be concerned with ethics in all situations, we need to concentrate briefly on public speaking to illustrate the central themes in previous approaches to ethics.

What should be the ethical concerns of the public speaker or advocate? Are there any choices he must make? Certainly, whether we are aware of it or not, the public speaker must make many value-oriented decisions. From the selection of speech material to the actual delivery, ethical decisions are made.

Many writers believe that the function of speech is to achieve specific ends in public situations, and that because men try to influence others, they need a guiding ethic or some set of principles to judge right from wrong. Guiding principles have been enumerated by various writers. They hold that the public speaker should, as a rule, heed the following admonitions:

1. Do not distort or falsify evidence.
2. Do not use specious reasoning.
3. Do not make unsupported attacks on your opponent.
4. Do not deceive the audience about your intent. If you represent an organization, do not conceal that fact.
5. Do not use irrelevant emotional appeals to divert attention from the basic argument.
6. Do not pose as an authority when you are not.[6]

Some speakers may break these rules consistently, while others slip only in a moment of weakness. What about yourself? When you support a position, do you load the case? Do you purposefully fail to bring information to the surface that, although it would make for a better decision, would ruin your particular case? If you do not behave according to the above principles, why? Are the rules unrealistic and dysfunctional or are you just a dishonest person?

It is easy to justify *not* following the principles. The end in sight was just too big to pass up ("the vote was crucial to the success of the

[6] This list represents the usual prescriptions for ethical speaking behavior. See H. L. Ewbank and J. J. Auer, *Discussion and Debate,* 2nd Ed., Appleton-Century-Crofts, New York, 1961; Austin J. Freeley, *Argumentation and Debate,* 2nd Ed., Wadsworth Publishing, Belmont, 1969; Winston Lamont Brembeck and William Smiley Howell, *Persuasion,* Prentice-Hall, Englewood Cliffs, 1952; and Kenneth E. Andersen, *Persuasion,* Allyn and Bacon, Boston, 1971.

program and that's why we covered up the flaws"). Or maybe we do not believe the receiver of our message deserves the truth. ("They are so unknowledgable about encyclopedias, they deserve to be cheated.") If we see the receiver, according to our standards, as an unethical person, we can certainly justify our falsifications. ("The federal government is corrupt anyway, so why should I not cheat on my tax return?")

If a communicator can so easily cast off the general rules for ethical speaking, perhaps the principles are not functional. One attempt to update the standard approach has been made that is (1) firmly grounded in our cultural norms, and (2) applicable to all communication situations.[7] The basic premise underlying this approach is that in the West, we believe men should be free to make their own decisions, and that the principles of argument and persuasion are available for free and public use. It follows that allowing men to make free choices is a desirable goal.

The ethical standard derived from this goal is that "The ethical touchstone is the degree of free, informed, rational, and critical choice —significant choice—that is fostered by our speaking."[8] In interpersonal relations, ethical communicating would be defined as the amount of freedom left to the receiver. Can he make his own decision? Does he feel forced to certain actions that he would not carry out under his own free will? Is he being manipulated? In a public speaking situation, if the receiver is to have a free rational choice, the speaker must be fair and adhere to high standards of conduct. The speaker will not, therefore, falsify evidence or use coercion on the listeners. He will let them make their own decisions. If the use of a particular appeal will short-circuit the reasoning process, it should not be used. The receiver, whether he is a personal friend or an audience member, should not feel as though he is being coerced, manipulated, or that advantage is being taken of him.

This position has the advantage of applicability to all communication situations, but it leads us to the same admonitions to the communicator that the more traditional prescribers have recommended for the public speaker. It stresses the general philosophic base underlying the traditional prescriptions.

We want to approach ethics from a different perspective. Instead of specifying a set of standards for a communicator, we offer a description of general ethical codes. We will primarily describe rather than prescribe (since prescription seems futile anyway).

[7] Thomas R. Nilsen, "Ethics and Argument," in Gerald R. Miller and Thomas R. Nilsen (Eds.), *Perspectives on Argumentation,* Scott, Foresman, Chicago, 1966.

[8] Thomas R. Nilsen, *Ethics of Speech Communication,* Bobbs-Merrill, New York, 1966, p. 38.

CHOICE OF ETHICAL APPROACHES

The ethical codes available to an individual can be classified in numerous ways. We suggest three primary options: (1) a universal code, (2) an individual code, and (3) a situational code.

Universal Code

A universal code must contain standards that can be applied by *all* people in *all* situations. The code specifies behaviors that are to be judged independent of a particular circumstance, time, or culture. For example, the Ten Commandments are often selected as an appropriate guide. "Thou shalt not kill" is an admonition not dependent on time, place, or circumstance.

The prime difficulty with a universal code is its nonuniversal acceptance. In many cultures, the Christian Bible is not acceptable to the people, just as the Koran is not fully accepted by most Americans. Furthermore, even Christian cultures violate the injunction against killing by executing a convicted murderer. Since situations should not mitigate the force of the injunction, the universal code is not universally applied. What set of standards can be universally applied? Certainly the existence of thousands of religious dogmas attests to the unlikely possibility of a universal ethical code.

Others suggest that the development of a universal code is possible, but that the source of the standards should be various academic disciplines. In the development of this type of code, each discipline would be asked to list unethical behaviors. A combination of these lists would constitute an acceptable universal code. Although the thought of developing such a set of standards is attractive, the task is difficult, if not impossible, to complete. The speech profession, for example, has not generated such a list for communication behavior that is acceptable to all people in the profession, let alone the entire society. Even those few guides for ethical speaking (such as not distorting evidence) have not had universal acceptance.

Individual Code

An individual code is similar to the universal code in that a person must consistently apply a set of absolute standards in *all* situations. It is different from the universal code because *each individual* is asked to develop his own list of ethical behaviors rather than rely on a single set of standards derived for all. The individual code option is quite popular because all of us like to think that we have made our own decisions on what is ethical and that we can live up to our own expectations. A sample question from the universal code is, "Is premarital sex ethical?" From an individual code perspective, one would ask "Is premarital sex ethical for me?" Given a decision on such questions, an individual code advocate can then govern his own behavior and be consistently ethical in his own conduct.

Inconsistency is not acceptable in either the universal or individual code options. The "thou shalt nots" or the "I shalt nots" are rigidly applied to all situations.

Situational Code

For those who feel that "too many people at heart long for an ethical *system* of prefabricated, pretailored morality"[9] the situational code is the answer. In this third option, circumstances of a situation determine what is ethical. Behavioral inconsistency is perfectly permissible because the behavioral demands change as the circumstances change. The situationalist takes an absolute code as a reference point and tailors it to specific situations. Society, for example, takes the "thou shalt not kill" and gives it situational meaning. Killing in war, self-defense, or as punishment for a convicted murderer all are situational exceptions to the "absolute" rule. From such a perspective, any absolute code can be adopted as a starting point, but it is not applied to all situations. Even if we agree that distortion of facts is unethical, it is easy to imagine a situation where we would do it (to save your brother, a draft dodger, from prosecution by the government by saying that you do not know where he is).

One might argue that a situational approach to ethical concerns "bruises the intellect." How could something be both ethical and unethical? With this code, the question is, "In this situation do I think premarital sex is unethical?" Situational ethics aims at a contextual appropriateness—not the "good" or the "right," but the fitting. The universal and individual code proponents are *what* askers (what does the code say?). The situationalist is a *circumstance* asker (given this situation, what should I do?).

Thus, the universal code is for *all* people in *all* situations; the individual code is for *one* person in *all* situations; and the situational code is for *one* person in *one* situation. Under the first two codes, inconsistency in application of the code is not tolerated—it is hypocrisy. Under

[9] Joseph Fletcher, *Situation Ethics: The New Morality,* Westminster Press, Philadelphia, 1966, p. 134.

the situational code, inconsistent application of the general code is permissible.

Advantages and disadvantages are apparent in each of the code options. Our concern is not to advocate the adoption of one of the codes, but to inquire about how your use of an ethical system interferes with your communication behavior.

APPLICATION OF ETHICS TO COMMUNICATION

Normally, when one considers the code options, he asks himself, "Which of the three codes have I adopted for my life?" After considerable introspection one will usually admit that he has adopted a situational code. The next important question is, "Which of the three codes do I expect others to live by?" Unfortunately, the answer to this second question is usually different from the answer to the first. We justify a situational system for our own daily behavior but we fail to allow others those same justifications. Even if we do allow others the right to be situationalists, often this is the case only if the other person evaluates the situation the same way we do. Ethics becomes a barrier in communication when we as receivers "put it on" others. Unrealistic value judgments interfere with understanding and meaning. How many times have you said, or heard someone say, "My father tells me not to smoke pot because it harms me. At the same time, he drinks a lot of alcohol." In this instance, is the father putting unrealistic standards on his son? How about you, do you make unfavorable value judgments of your parents because they cheat on their income tax returns and at the same time advocate total honesty to you? Do you, while criticizing them for being dishonest, find it justifiable to "fudge a bit" when they ask you how many hours you study each week? Or, to get more personal, how about the male undergraduate who attempts to sexually exploit all of his female acquaintances and then will not marry a girl who is not a virgin?

As indicated earlier, judging another unfavorably creates a lack of respect that interferes with communication. If we have the right to select our own code to govern our behavior, should not others have the same right? If we permit ourselves to be situationalists, should we expect others to be consistent universalists or individualists? Individuals should apply reasoned answers for *themselves* about *their own* ethical *code* and let others have those same prerogatives. With this philosophy, communication barriers created by unreasonable value judgments can be minimized. If one applies reasoned answers for himself on ethical questions and lets others have the same privilege, he will probably conclude that the best moral principle for guiding human communication is simply to "treat others in all communication transactions with dignity and respect—view them as people to be respected, not as people to be judged or objects to be manipulated."

To illustrate the difficulties one encounters when making ethical judgments, we offer the following story.

A Lie is Always a Lie

I remember a lively discussion one day in my catechism class between the boys who were being prepared for confirmation and the parish priest. The subject was a marionette show at which we boys had been present with the priest the day before. It was about the dramatic adventures of a child who was persecuted by the devil. At one point the child-marionette had appeared on the stage trembling with fear and, to escape the devil who was searching for him, had hidden under a bed in a corner of the stage; shortly afterwards the devil-marionette arrived and looked for him in vain. "But he *must* be here," said the devil-marionette, "I can smell him. Now I'll ask these good people in the audience." And he turned to us and asked: "My dear children, have you by any chance seen that naughty child I'm looking for hiding anywhere?" "No, no, no," we all chorused at once, as energetically as possible. "Where is he then? I can't see him," the devil insisted. "He's left, he's gone away," we all shouted. "He's gone to Lisbon." (In our part of Italy, Lisbon is still the furthermost point of the globe, even today.) I should add that none of us, when we went to the theater, had expected to be questioned by a devil-marionette; our behavior was therefore entirely instinctive and spontaneous. And I imagine that children in any other part of the world would have reacted in the same way. But our parish priest, a most worthy, cultured, and pious person, was not altogether pleased. We had told a lie, he warned us with a worried look. We had told it for good ends, of course, but still it remained a lie. One must never tell lies. "Not even to the devil?" we asked in surprise. "A lie is always a sin," the priest replied. "Even to the magistrate?" asked one of the boys. The priest rebuked him severely. "I'm here to teach you Christian doctrine and not to talk nonsense. What happens outside the Church is no concern of mine," and he began to explain the doctrine about truth and lies in general in the most eloquent language. But that day the question of lies *in general* was of no interest to us children; we wanted to know, "Ought we to have told the devil where the child was hiding, yes or no?" "That's not the point," the poor priest kept repeating to us rather uneasily. "A lie is always a lie. It might be a big sin, a medium sin, an average sort of sin, or a little tiny sin, but it's always a sin. Truth must be honored."

"The truth is," we said, "that there was the devil on one side and the child on the other. We wanted to help the child, that's the real truth." "But you've told a lie," the parish priest kept on repeating. "For good ends, I know, but still a lie."

To end it, I put forward an objection of unheard-of perfidy, and considering my age, considerable precocity: "if it'd been a priest instead of a child," I asked, "what ought we to have replied to the devil?" The parish priest blushed, avoided a reply; and as a punishment for my impertinence, made me spend the rest of the lesson on my knees beside him. "Are you sorry?" he asked me at the end of the lesson. "Of course," I replied. "If the devil asks me for your address, I'll give it to him at once."[10]

This story demonstrates the difficulty of trying to judge the actions of others by prescribed standards. A crucial concern has to be the other's "intent," which is difficult, if not impossible to determine. The only "intent" we can safely judge is our own. The result is that many people judge themselves by their *intent* but judge others by their *actions*. The unreasonableness of such judgments is obvious.

Lying, is it unethical? Yes . . . well, maybe . . . not always . . . it depends . . . I don't know! *Your* answer to the question, "Is lying unethical?" is the important consideration. Whatever your answer, it will affect your communication behavior—both when you are primarily responsible for encoding and for decoding. Is falsification of evidence justifiable? Does one have the right to remain silent when he is the only one who can expose certain information? Is it permissible to "trick" a person or group of people when you think that doing so will lead to a favorable decision for you? These are questions about communication behavior that you must answer for yourself. When you answer these questions for others by evaluating their behavior from your prescribed standards, you do not *really* know their intent. Ethical judgments influence one's perception and evaluation of communication cues from others. This, in turn, effects future communication transactions—an effect that is analogous to the killing of a butterfly in "The Sound of Thunder." As we stated earlier, if one applies reasoned answers for himself on ethical questions and lets others have the same privilege, he will probably conclude that the best moral principle for guiding human communication is simply to "treat others in all communication transactions with dignity and respect—view them as people to be respected, not as people to be judged or objects to be manipulated."

[10] From *The God That Failed*, Richard Crossman (Ed.), Harper & Bros., New York, 1949, p. 84. Reprinted in I. J. Lee, *Customs and Crises in Communication*, Harper, 1954.

Exercises

1. Based on your reading of "A Lie is Always a Lie," *is* a lie always a lie? Write a short paper on this question and then, as a class, discuss the various points of view.
2. As a class, develop a list of behaviors considered by the American society as unethical for a communicator in the following situations.

   (a) Two friends having an informal chat.
   (b) A public speaker addressing undecided voters and trying to get them to vote for his candidate.
   (c) A speaker addressing a mass audience through television.

3. As a class, adopt an absolute code for ethical communication behavior that is independent of our American culture.
4. Ask each member of the class to read, "The Spelucean Explorers."[11] Using this case as a reference, is "murder" justifiable? Discuss this in small groups and then see if the class, as a whole, can reach consensus on the issue.
5. Are silence and lying sometimes more "ethical" than the truth? More "desirable" than truth? More "humane" than truth?
6. Go out into the nearby community and poll diverse groups about behavior (including communication behavior) they consider unethical. Compare the basic assumptions inherent in each list of unethical behavior.
7. Ask those same people in the groups how they react to a speaker or acquaintance who violates their list of ethical behaviors. Based on that exploratory work, do you think that ethics is a variable that can be used to predict response to communication?
8. What are the mechanisms that individuals use to impose their ethical standards on others? Why do they do that?
9. Keep a diary for a week on all the important decisions that you make regarding your communication behaviors. What kind of ethical code do you follow in your everyday communication activities? Do you profess to follow a code that is discrepant from your actual use of it?

[11] Lon L. Fuller, "The Spelucean Explorers," *Harvard Law Review*, February 1949 62 (4), 616–645. Also appears in Harry P. Kerr, *Opinion and Evidence: Cases for Argument and Discussion*, Harcourt, Brace & World, New York, 1962, pp. 4–28.

Suggested Readings

Aristotle, *Rhetoric*, trans. by W. Rhys Roberts, Oxford Press, Oxford, 1924.

Joseph Fletcher, *Situation Ethics—The New Morality,* Westminster Press, Philadelphia, 1966.

Richard L. Johannesen (Ed.), *Ethics and Persuasion,* Random House, New York, 1967.

Niccolo Machiavelli, *The Prince*, trans. by Luigi Ricci, The American Library of World Literature, New York, 1952.

Thomas R. Nilsen, *Ethics of Speech Communication,* Bobbs-Merrill, New York, 1966.

Plato, *Gorgias*, trans. by W. C. Helmbold, Liberal Arts Press, New York, 1952.

Richard M. Weaver, *The Ethics of Rhetoric,* Regnery, Chicago, 1953.

Part II ▶

The Exchange of Ideas Through Oral Communication

Chapter 5 ▶ *Message Mainstays: Verbal Elements*

Objectives

On completion of this chapter you should be able to:
1. Distinguish between signs and symbols.
2. Specify some situations where humans fail to acquire language.
3. Discuss theories of language acquisition.
4. Know that language and thought are related.
5. Say why the word is not the thing.
6. Understand that meanings are in people.
7. Clearly distinguish between denotative and connotative meanings.
8. Describe language as a dynamic process.

THE NATURE OF LANGUAGE

If the proverbial man from Mars were to visit Earth and observe humans in their everyday activities, he would notice that they are almost constantly communicating. They make strange sounds that seem to have meanings for others. Humans spend much of their time sending and receiving sounds in order to influence one another.[1]

Marty Martian is so fascinated by the strange sounds he hears that he decides to examine them further. In one place, which the Earthlings

[1] Walter Logan, "What Language Reveals," in James B. Macdonald and Robert R. Leeper (Eds.), *Language and Meaning,* Association for Supervision and Curriculum Development, NEA, Washington, 1966, pp. 63–73; Dorwin Cartwright and Alvin Zander's Martian observed small groups in action, *Group Dynamics: Research and Theory,* 3rd Ed., Harper and Row, New York, 1968, p. 3.

call a "college campus," the sounds are rampant. Marty follows one person, called a student, around all day to discover what sounds the student makes and to which sounds he listens. The student goes to large rooms, sits closely packed with other students, and listens to older people stand up front and utter sounds for fifty minutes. The sounds appear to fall into units the humans called "words"; Marty, fascinated by all the "words" floating around, starts counting. The student he was following heard approximately 100,000 words that day, and read another 90,000 units of ink set on paper. Considering each ink grouping as a word, Marty calculated that the student would have been exposed to ¾ of a billion words in an Earthian year. On his way home, Marty remarked to his friends, "Ehotpziqackdm."[2]

Signs and Symbols

We humans use a lot of words. Each cultural group of humans has developed a language—many words used in specified ways. We "think" and "talk" to ourselves in our language, and our language also allows us to make contact with others. In fact, our language facility is what makes us uniquely human.

It is often said that animals have developed their own languages. It has been claimed that dogs, dolphins, bees, and other animals have language facilities. True, animals can communicate with one another. One beaver can signal danger to another, bees can indicate the direction of pollen to other bees, coyotes can "sing" to other coyotes across the canyon, and monkeys emit all kinds of sounds to other monkeys.[3] These and other animal *signs* are passed from generation to generation by animals. They are hereditary and remain unchanged and extremely simple.[4] Furthermore, a *sign*, such as the beaver slapping his tail on the water to indicate danger, *has a one-to-one relationship with its meaning*.[5] Each sign has a special purpose.

Humans, like animals, use signs. Stop signs, some hand gestures, and police whistles each have a special purpose. But these human signs have to be learned.[6] They are not passed on by heredity from

---

[2] Translation: "They sure use a lot of words."

[3] Some of these examples come from David McNeill, *The Acquisition of Language: The Study of Developmental Psycholinguistics,* Harper and Row, New York, 1970.

[4] John B. Carroll, *Language and Thought,* Prentice-Hall, Englewood Cliffs, 1964.

[5] Joseph R. Royce, "Psychology At The Crossroads Between The Sciences And The Humanities," in Royce (Ed.), *Psychology and the Symbol,* Random House, New York, 1965, p. 16.

[6] Ibid.

human to human. Through social contact, humans acquire meanings for the signs. Human signs may be (1) unintentional clues (a deer track, a clue left at a murder scene), (2) markers (road signs), or (3) labels or marks of identification (putting your name on an object).[7] Unlike other animals, however, humans employ *symbols*. Symbols (1) take on diverse meanings, (2) represent some object or event, and (3) are transmitted by tradition.[8] While *signs* have a *one-to-one* relationship to meaning, *symbols* have a *one-to-many* relationship.[9] One symbol can have different meanings. Symbols can be manipulated and can be used to stand for whatever we wish.

Every known human society has a language, but animals do not have any technology of communication called language.[10] It appears at times that animals can learn words. If they could not, the "no" shouted at your cocker spaniel puppy when she is relieving herself on your new carpet would have no effect. "Come here" would be a worthless command if the dog had not acquired a response for it. But learning a specific response to a command is far from effective symbolization.

In the early part of this century, it appeared that a horse had learned "language." The horse, Clever Hans, was first taught how to do simple counting. His owner would place a number of objects in front of Hans and, after some training, Hans would tap his foot once for each object. Hans then learned addition, multiplication, subtraction, and division. He could even give the correct answer to questions dealing with fractions. During public performances, Hans could give the correct number of people in the audience, count any number of selected objects, and give the date of any day that he was asked. It appeared to all that Clever Hans was a symbol-manipulating animal—the first one in history. An investigating committee even gave Hans a favorable report. A second investigating committee found, however, that Hans had not acquired language. He could give the correct answer to a question only as long as the person asking the question knew the answer. Although it was unintentional, all the questioners gave Hans subtle cues that indicated he should stop tapping. They would relax their posture and make slight head movements that were a sign to stop tapping.[11] Thus, Clever Hans had not acquired language.

[7] Hubert G. Alexander, *Meaning in Language,* Scott, Foresman, Glenview, 1969, p. 30.
[8] Ludwig Van Bertalanffy, "On Definition of the Symbol," in Royce (Ed.), p. 29 (cited in footnote 5).
[9] Royce, p. 16 (cited in footnote 5).
[10] Roger Brown, *Social Psychology,* The Free Press, New York, 1965, p. 246.
[11] A more complete report of Hans is in Roger Brown, *Words, and Things,* The Free Press, New York, 1958, pp. 172–175.

The story of Clever Hans and the other examples cited lead us to conclude the following:[12]

Language is human.
Language is a form of symbolization.
Language is systematic.
Language is verbal.
Language is a means of transmitting information.
Language is a form of social behavior.
Language is acquired.

Obviously, language is an important aspect of human existence. Since our use of symbols is so central, it would be helpful for us to (1) understand why language sometimes is not acquired, (2) be able to theorize about normal language acquisition, and (3) discuss the relationship of language and thought. Such information, as well as being interesting, can assist us in viewing the role of language in communication transactions.

LANGUAGE ACQUISITION

Failure to Acquire Language

Whenever humans are raised in human communities, language develops. But in no case have humans raised among animals developed language.[13] Humans raised by animals (such as the Hessian wolf-boy of 1349, the Lithuanian bear-boy of 1661, and Wild Peter of Hanover of 1724), did not acquire language when denied contact with humans. There have, however, been cases where children have been raised by animals, placed in human society, and then learned how to talk. In the 1920s, a wolf "adopted" two children as her cubs. One of the children, after returning to human society, learned to talk.[14]

If humans raised by other humans are isolated from communication transactions, they will not acquire language. In the 1940s the shocking case of six-year-old Isabella was reported. She was the illegitimate daughter of a deaf-mute. She was kept in a dark room separated from the rest of the family. When Isabella was discovered, she could not

[12] This is a partial listing of the characteristics given by John A Rycenga and Joseph Schwartz, "Language: By Way of Definition," in Rycenga and Schwartz (Eds.), *Perspectives on Language,* Ronald Press, New York, 1963, p. 4.
[13] Brown, p. 192 (cited in footnote 11).
[14] These and other cases are reported in Brown, pp. 186–193 (cited in footnote 11).

speak, but could only utter croaking noises. Isabella was given intensive care by doctors and clinical psychologists, and within two years had acquired a normal language facility.[15]

Isolation from human stimulation can prohibit language development; similarly, if a child has a mental problem, his language development may be impaired. Mentally retarded children have delayed language development.[16] Schizophrenics, who experience impairment of their abstracting ability, symbolizing ability, and ability to integrate into society, manifest serious language problems. They characteristically distort the relationship between words and what the words represent. The result is confused meaning.[17]

Learning a language seems to be a simple, straightforward process until we examine cases where it does not develop. Those unfortunate individuals who were deprived of necessary human contact demonstrate the requirements of speech.[18] Language acquisition requires (1) a functioning human with adequate cognitive development for recognition, identification, comprehension, and reproduction of speech, and (2) stimulation from communication transactions with other humans. If any of these ingredients are missing, normal language will not occur. The complexity of the acquisition process is evident when one examines the many theories of *why* it occurs when all the prerequisites are met.

Normal Language Acquisition

Verbal Behavior, by B. F. Skinner, advanced the best tested, and most hotly contested, theory on language acquisition.[19] The view maintains that our language is learned by operant conditioning. Basically, it means that when a child utters the correct syllables for a culture (like da-da), the child is rewarded. The reinforcement of certain sounds and combinations of sounds makes them more likely to appear in the future. For example, a one-year-old child, Jason, has learned how to bark like his dog. When Jason says "boof boof," his parents cannot restrain themselves; they always laugh. The pleasing laughter is rewarding to him so he keeps imitating the dog. For the most part, how-

[15] Brown, pp. 191–192 (cited in footnote 11).

[16] Harold J. Vetter, *Language Behavior and Psychopathology,* Rand McNally, Chicago, 1969, pp. 65–78.

[17] Harold J. Vetter, "Introduction," p. 8, and Joseph Richman, "Symbolic Distortion in the Vocabulary Definitions of Schizophrenics," p. 56; in Harold J. Vetter (Ed.), *Language Behavior in Schizophrenia,* Charles C Thomas, Springfield, 1968.

[18] This listing is, in part, from Carroll, p. 31 (cited in footnote 4).

[19] B. F. Skinner, *Verbal Behavior,* Appleton, New York, 1957.

ever, the reinforcement process assures that a child will acquire language appropriate to his community.

While the defilers and defenders of conditioning doctrine are many, the strongest defense has been made by a recent modification of the basic theory. Through experiments on the meaning of words, it has been shown that meaning can be altered by conditioning methods.[20] Once a child gets meanings for words, new combinations of the words are the "natural products" of the conditioning. Put simply, once a child acquires word meanings, new combinations of those words automatically follow.

Theoretically, the entire process works as follows. The parents' voices become reinforcing for the child because the voices are associated with dry diapers, food, and other bodily comforts. As the child begins babbling, those sounds closest to what he associates with his parents are most reinforcing. The child, therefore, makes those rewarding responses most frequently.[21]

Higher order conditioning explains how the child begins to manipulate words and symbols. Words get their original meaning by direct association with an object or experience. These words, in turn, become the base for conditioning the meaning of other words. Based on this principle, new combinations of words and meanings for the words are acquired.[22] Humans, therefore, have words for which there are no direct referents. Many objects to which words refer, such as witches, hobgoblins, dragons, and spirits, do not exist; yet these words elicit meanings for many people.[23]

One of the main critics of the operant conditioning theory is Noam Chomsky.[24] He maintains that conditioning theory does not account for the sentences a child can construct that he has never heard before. According to Chomsky, novel language usage cannot be explained by the conditioning approach. If Chomsky is correct, then language cannot be taught by using only "reinforcement schedules" of rewards.

Chomsky writes that grammar, the structure of languages, is part of our behavior—we are endowed with it. The acquisition of complex sentence structure is, therefore, derived from an innate ability, because it cannot have been imitated and rewarded. One example is often used

[20] Arthur W. Staats, *Learning, Language, and Cognition,* Holt, Rinehart and Winston, New York, 1968, pp. 16–22.

[21] Ibid., p. 68.

[22] Ibid., pp. 34–50.

[23] Ibid., p. 50.

[24] Chomsky's critical review of Skinner's *Verbal Behavior* can be found in *Language* (1959), XXXV, p. 26–58. See also J. P. Allen and Paul Van Buren (Eds.), *Chomsky: Selected Readings,* Oxford University Press, London, 1971.

to illustrate the point. The children of immigrants often learn their second language so well that their speech is no different from that of the native-born people. The parents of these children, however, are often unable to sound "native" no matter how hard they try. In short, there are "some fundamental processes at work quite independently of 'feedback' from our environment." These processes can be discovered, hopefully, by examining the similarities in the "generative grammars" of languages. In other words, there are certain language universals that can account for the structure of languages. Researchers, therefore, should try to find these universals so the process of language acquisition can be better understood.

Eric Lenneberg's work represents even another perspective on the acquisition of language.[25] Lenneberg argues that the capacity to learn language is not based on some "need" for symbolization, but is simply the outgrowth of maturation. Language is the result of maturation because (1) there are anatomic and physiologic correlates to verbal behavior, (2) the "onset" of speech is an extremely regular phenomenon, appearing at a certain time in the child's physical development," (3) language learning is difficult to suppress; even handicapped individuals often acquire it, (4) language cannot be taught to non-humans, and (5) there are language universals; all languages have semantics, syntactics, and phonology.

Lenneberg cautions us that his speculations are not a complete theory. The precise physical nature of language ability is "yet to be discovered." If Lenneberg is correct that language ability is rooted in biological processes, then cases of inadequate language development might be treated by some form of medical therapy rather than by a concentration on the reinforcement schedules.

The preceding positions on language acquisition are only a small portion of all the available approaches. They do, however, represent the major thrusts in theorizing. These and the other theories too, have *all* been criticized and found lacking in some respects. It is probably true that the learning process for language "may be of a type currently unknown."[26]

---

[25] See, for example, Eric H. Lenneberg, "A Biological Perspective of Language," in Eric H. Lenneberg (Ed.), *New Directions in the Study of Language,* M.I.T. Press, Cambridge, 1964, pp. 65–88; and "The Natural History of Language," in Frank Smith and George A. Miller (Eds.), *The Genesis of Language: A Psycholinguistic Approach,* M.I.T. Press, Cambridge, 1966, pp. 219–252.

[26] Jerry A. Fodor, James J. Jenkins, and Sol Saporta, "Psycholinguistics and Communication Theory," in Frank E. X. Dance (Ed.), *Human Communication Theory,* Holt, Rinehart and Winston, New York, 1967, p. 196.

Language and Thought

It is commonly believed that our language is just clothing over our thoughts. Expressions such as, "I know the answer, but I can't think of the words," and "I have the word right on the tip of my tongue" indicate a belief that we think and then express our thoughts in words. The relationship between thought and language is important; if we can specify it, we can probably improve (1) people's thinking abilities, and (2) their language facility.

One influential view of language development and its relation to thought maintains that a person's thought and language develop on a continuum. *Autistic* thought is on one end and *socialized* thought is at the other end. Autistic thought is removed from external reality. Its essence is created through imagination and dreams. Socialized thought is externally oriented. This type of thought is dependent on and directed to the immediate environment. A child's language development spans parts of this same continuum. Until the age of seven or eight, the child's language resembles autistic thought in that it is essentially egocentric. The child is "centered in himself and does not sense the information needs of others. He assumes that others have the exact same information he does."[27] Additionally, in egocentric speech, the child "takes no interest in his interlocutor, does not try to communicate, expects no answers, and often does not even care whether anyone listens to him."[28] As the child develops, his thought becomes more socialized. He begins to attune himself to the presence and needs of others. His thoughts and words become directed and adjusted to others around him. "One might say that an adult thinks socially even when he is alone, and a child under seven thinks and speaks egocentrically even in the society of others."[29]

One critic of this early language-thought formulation conceptualizes the development of speech and thought quite differently. He sees language as developing from social thought to egocentric thought and then to inner speech.[30] From this view, "thought is not merely expressed in words, it comes into existence through them." We have all experienced this process because our thoughts often undergo changes while we are speaking. Thought and speech grow and change together. Just as communication is a process, the relationship between thought and

[27] Brown, p. 342 (cited in footnote 10).
[28] Lev Semenovich Vygotsky, *Thought and Language,* M.I.T. Press, Cambridge, 1962, p. 15.
[29] Ibid.
[30] Ibid., p. 19.

language is a process. There is a "continual movement back and forth from thought to word and from word to thought."[31]

The relationship between language and thought is certainly an unsettled issue. The process of discovering the precise nature of the relation is still in full swing. There are, for example, many diverse guesses about "inner speech."[32] One investigator says in exasperation that it all "remains a mystery to me."[33] There are related issues of language and thought that are also unsettled. The fascinating hypothesis of Benjamin Whorf is one.

The Whorfian Hypothesis

Whorf has reversed the notion that language is determined by thought. He argues that language *shapes* thought, it does not just reflect it. According to this theory, man's very view of nature is molded by the language he uses.[34] The language spoken by a community orients it to a particular view of nature. For example, in English, the word "snow" is used for all forms of snow. On the other hand, Eskimos have a separate word for snow on the ground, falling snow, and snow in drifts.[35] They actually see and think about snow differently than we do. Americans think about colors differently than people in some other cultures. In the Bassa language, blue-green is one end of the color spectrum and red-orange is the other. The Zuni people see all oranges and yellows as belonging to one group. But English-speaking people have names for hues ranging from red to purple. One last example is our word "aunt." It applies to all possible aunts. For example, both your father's sister and your mother's brother's wife are called "aunt." Other cultures have aunts categorized in all possible ways. Some have separate names for each one and some have them grouped.[36]

The Whorfian hypothesis does have some merit. It demonstrates that in some cases, language can shape thought and that the two are interdependent. However, the instances where these effects have been observed are "limited and localized."[37] Language only seems to exert a "moderately powerful"[38] effect on thought.

[31] Ibid., p. 125.

[32] For example, Carroll, on p. 77, disagrees with Vygotsky's account of inner speech (cited in footnote 4).

[33] Brown, p. 347 (cited in footnote 10).

[34] See Benjamin L. Whorf, "Science and Linguistics," in Sol Saporta (Ed.), *Psycholinguistics,* Holt, Rinehart and Winston, New York, 1961, pp. 460–468.

[35] Alexander, p. 90 (cited in footnote 7).

[36] Brown, pp. 315–316 (cited in footnote 10).

[37] Carroll, p. 110 (cited in footnote 4).

[38] Joshua A. Fishman, "A Systemation of the Whorfian Hypothesis," in Alfred G. Smith (ed.), *Communication and Culture,* Holt, Rinehart and Winston, 1966, p. 516.

GENERAL SEMANTICS

Word meaning and usage interests are chief products of research and speculation about language and thought. The field of general semantics focuses on (1) the relationship between words and their referents (what they refer to), and (2) on the behavior that results from language.[39]

Symbols and Referents

Words mean nothing by themselves. Marty Martian's word "Ehotpziqackdm" does not mean anything unless you know what it stands for. Through our thought processes, words gain meaning or "stand for" certain things. A symbol and what it refers to are connected by our thoughts.[40] There is, however, no *natural* relation between words and referents. If there were, different languages would not exist. The student studying his first foreign language is well aware of how arbitrary the meanings for words seem in the other language. And, of course, English words seem arbitrary to someone learning it as a foreign language.[41] Upon close examination, it becomes clear that there is "no necessary connection between the symbol and that which it symbolizes."[42] This important distinction has led to the following cardinal principle of general semantics.

The Word Is Not the Thing

We have two worlds, extensional and verbal. The extensional world is the "real" world that we come to know through our senses. We see events, observe objects, and have other direct experiences. On the other hand, we cannot experience everything. We learn things through our "verbal" world. The things that come to us through words (such as when others relate their experiences), make up our verbal world.[43] Thus, words *represent* aspects of the extensional world. Words are *not* the things they represent, just as a map of an area is *not* the area (did you ever try to hike or drive on the map itself?).

[39] John C. Condon, Jr., *Semantics and Communication,* Macmillan, New York, 1966, p. 3.
[40] C. K. Ogden and I. A. Richards, *The Meaning of Meaning,* Harcourt, Brace, and World, New York, 1923, p. 9–11.
[41] The diverse languages are not arbitrary in the sense that they may be derived from the same root languages. For example, Latin roots appear in many languages. But the original languages arbitrarily assigned words to objects and concepts.
[42] S. I. Hayakawa, *Language in Thought and Action,* 2nd ed., Harcourt, Brace, and World, New York, 1964, p. 27.
[43] Ibid., p. 30.

Often, people confuse the word or symbol for the thing. General semanticists want us to understand how this confusion can lead to undesirable consequences. The student who cheats on his exams to get his Phi Beta Kappa key is confusing the symbol "key" for the thing it represents (intelligence and scholastic accomplishment).[44] Students who argue that grades should not be emphasized so much can be interpreted as saying, "Society confuses the symbol (grades) for the thing (ability)."

Further examples of symbol-referent confusion are abundant. Chapter 3 notes that a model of communication is *not* communication, but a symbolic representation of it. An acquaintance of the authors enjoys pointing out that the symbol is not the thing. When people entering his office ask, "Oh, is that your wife?", he says, "No, that's a picture of her." And devoted fans of the monthly *Playboy* centerfold are aware that the playmate is more than what is actually on that page.

Some people carry the notion "the word is not the thing" so far that they think we should not react to words. After all words only represent things. Granted, if someone burns the United States flag he is not burning the United States. The act, however, is not inconsequential. The child who chants "sticks and stones may break my bones but names will never hurt me," is actually saying, "please don't call me names, they hurt my feelings." Words *do* have impact and we *do* react to them. Just because words are symbolic "does not diminish either the power or importance . . . of that which is symbolized or the symbol itself."[45] In communication, we must be realistic and see how the symbol actually affects behavior instead of spending our time trying to defuse the power of words. After all, if words did not carry meaning for us and if we did not respond to them, they would be of no use. Symbols have emotive impact because they are paired with referents.[46]

Meanings Are In People

Words have no *necessary* tie with referents. It is the association in our mind that gives the word meaning. Meanings are in people, not in words.[47] We do not transmit *meaning*, we transmit *words*. Words stimulate the meaning the other person has for them. Communication is a

---

[44] Ibid., p. 29.

[45] George N. Gordon, *The Languages of Communication*, Hastings House, New York, 1969, p. 64.

[46] Alexander, p. 42 (cited in footnote 7).

[47] David K. Berlo, *The Process of Communication*, Holt, Rinehart and Winston, New York, 1960, p. 175.

stirring-up process; the meanings we have for words determine the meanings we get from them. As long as the person has values that approximate our values for the words, the message will stimulate a meaning for him that is similar to what we want. Our "attempts to get meaning" will coincide. The arbitrary nature of words we choose is often not recognized. A child asks his parents, "Why is it called a table?" They reply, in all earnestness, "Because it *is* a table." To them, to call a chair a table and a table a chair is impossible. But, if back in the history of our language, people said "chair" for the thing they sat around for dinner, it would be called a chair now.

The meaning for a word is arbitrarily assigned by our culture, but specific meaning resides in our thought process. Therefore, people have different meanings for words—meanings based on their experiences. One of the chief difficulties in communication is that we take it for granted that others have the same meanings for words that we do.[48]

Denotation and Connotation

If words stimulate different meanings in people, then what are their "true" meanings? All you have to do is consult a dictionary to see if your connotative meaning for the word (the meaning specific to you) squares with the denotative meanings (the meaning accepted by society). Such an approach, however, makes us think that the connotative meanings we have are "incorrect."

Let us take a fresh perspective toward denotative and connotative meanings. Denotative meanings refer to the critical attributes of an object—attributes on which we all agree. Recognition of these aspects will bring reinforcement from those around us. If a child shows that by "dog" he means his pet, his response will be reinforced. If he points to a cow and says "dog," he is characterizing the wrong critical aspects for dog (four legs and horns) and will not be reinforced. The critical attributes of dogs are what others want him to recognize. Denotative meanings, therefore, refer to critical attributes on which we agree.[49]

Connotative meanings refer to noncritical attributes that occur with regularity in our experience. In the case of "dog," the additional attributes one may have for them (dogs are friendly) are not necessary for reinforcement by others around us.[50] You can use the word "dog" and have specific meanings for it that others do not. You may think of your

---

[48] Irving Lee, "They Talk Past Each Other," in Howard H. Martin and Kenneth E. Andersen (Eds.), *Speech Communication,* Allyn and Bacon, Boston, 1968, p. 164.

[49] Carroll, p. 40 (cited in footnote 4).

[50] Carroll, p. 41 (cited in footnote 4).

black labrador when you say the word, and your friend may visualize his toy poodle, but they are both dogs.

Denotative and connotative meanings differ with how critical the attributes are to which they refer. Denotative meanings place objects in a classification, while connotative meanings are noncritical additional elements in the meaning. Denotative meanings are more in agreement across persons than are connotative ones. They can probably best be discovered by perusing the dictionary. Connotative meanings, however, are "dynamic rather than static."[51] They are personal and as such are more likely to change than are denotative meanings, which are cultural.

THE DYNAMICS OF LANGUAGE

It is rather easy to ascertain that language is a dynamic process. The language element of "meaning," by itself, renders language a process. Meanings are in people, are unique for each person, and change over time. For example, when a young man named Keim was a small boy, he pointed at the letter "C" on the typewriter keyboard in his father's office and said, "Daddy, see the *moon*?" To Keim, the letter "C" was a crescent moon. Within a few months, however, when Keim became exposed to the alphabet, the letter "C" had a different meaning. Each of us experiences this type of meaning change. The word accident, for example, will have a different meaning for a person after he experiences a serious accident than it did before the accident occurred. Certainly personal experiences and experiences related to us by others constantly modify our meanings for words.

People in different cultures have different meanings for words. Imperialism is certainly a different concept for us than for people in underdeveloped countries. Private enterprise means something different for an affluent capitalist than it does for a starving Marxist.

Not only do words mean different things to people, each word may have a different meaning in different contexts or settings. "Go fly a kite" means something to a child standing on a deserted field with a high wind, and quite another when spoken to a man in a tavern. The word "crop" for example, can be used as follows.

The stone stuck in the bird's *crop*.
She carried a riding *crop* in her hand.
The shepherd watched his sheep *crop* the grass.
The farmer reaped a *crop* of barley.[52]

[51] Vygotsky, p. 124 (cited in footnote 28).
[52] Logan, p. 67 (cited in footnote 1).

Thus, in the personal human communication process, language is an important element. It renders the process "human," for it is the variable that distinguishes us from all other forms of animal life. It renders the process "personal" because language usage varies with each individual.

Language, like communication, must be looked at from a process perspective. Any discussion of language and meaning is somewhat static because all process notions are extremely difficult to describe in process terms. For example, the phrase "language acquisition" suggests that acquiring language is a lengthy event that has an identifiable completion point. This is hardly the case. One is engaging in the process of language acquisition throughout life. Language meaning is constantly changing within, between, and among people.

Exercises

1. Demonstrate to yourself that meanings are in people. Select a highly abstract word such as love, democracy, theory, God, morality, death, immortality, capitalism, or communism and have each member of the class write down his meaning of the word.
   Compare the meanings and discuss them. Then look the words up in the dictionary and determine which of the meaning attributes are critical (denotative) and which are personal (connotative). Why do the connotative attributes vary from person to person?
2. Have two or three students illustrate phrases to the class that can take on almost contradictory meanings based on how they are said. "Hello," "good-bye," and "get lost" are a few examples.
3. Present a short speech to the class, discussing a personal experience in which you and another person had difficulty communicating because you had different meanings for words or phrases you used.
4. The next time you have an argument with a person, make a rule that before either of you can state anything new, the person has to restate the other's last statement to the latter's satisfaction. Once meanings are understood, what happens to the argument?
5. List and discuss communication settings where there is opportunity to check accuracy of meaning (fidelity) between the encoder and decoders. What are the characteristics of those situations?
6. Specify words in the English language that sound alike and can be misunderstood in oral communication (for example, to, too, and two).

7. Did you and the person sitting next to you in the class get the same "meaning" from this chapter on language? Compare what each of you "got out" of the chapter. Do you see any difficulty authors might have using words to write about words and word meaning?

Suggested Readings

Herbert G. Alexander, *Meaning in Language,* Scott, Foresman, Glenview, 1969.
Roger Brown, *Social Psychology,* The Free Press, New York, 1965.
Roger Brown, *Words and Things,* The Free Press, New York, 1958.
John C. Condon, *Semantics and Communication,* Macmillan, New York, 1966.
Etc. (Journal of the International Society for General Semantics).
George C. Gordon, *The Languages of Communication,* Hastings House, New York, 1969.
John A. Rycenga and Joseph Schwartz (Eds.), *Perspectives on Language,* Ronald Press, New York, 1963.
Sol Saporta (Ed.), *Psycholinguistics,* Holt, Rinehart and Winston, New York, 1961.
Harold J. Vetter (Ed.), *Language Behavior and Psychopathology,* Rand McNally, Chicago, 1969.

Chapter **6** ▶

The Language
of Nonverbal
Communication

Objectives

On completion of this chapter you should be able to:
1. Give examples of nonverbal communication cues.
2. Explain the four axioms of communication and give examples of their application to nonverbal communication.
3. Explain the importance of tone of voice, distance, eye contact, posture, and body orientation as nonverbal cues.
4. Generate some ideas for research in the area of nonverbal communication.

Only a small portion of the meaning one gets from face-to-face communication comes from the actual verbal cues used in the interchange. It has been estimated, for example, that only 35 percent of the meaning in a communication situation comes from the verbal symbols.[1] All the other elements, the nonverbal aspects, contribute the rest of the meaning that one attaches to the encounter. The phrase, "It isn't **what** he said, it's **how** he said it," illustrates that nonverbal elements of a communication transaction are very important.

What are some of the nonverbal aspects present when two or more people are talking? Below is a partial listing.

[1] Randall Harrison, "Nonverbal Communication: Explorations into Time, Space, Action, and Object," in James H. Campbell and Hal W. Hepler (Eds.), *Dimensions in Communication: Readings,* Wadsworth Publishing, Belmont, 1970, p. 258.

Personal apparel.
Physique and posture.
Facial expression.
Vocal expression (tone of voice).
Setting for the communication.
Gestures.
Voice quality (for example, raspy voice).
Distance between persons.
Eye contact.

There are innumerable possible variations in each of the nonverbal elements in the preceding list. We have, for example, the capacity for thousands of vocal sounds, and our faces can make 250,000 different expressions.[2] A gruff tone of voice signals us when a person is mad, busy, does not want to be bothered, has a sore throat, is playacting, or is experiencing any number of other possible feelings. Our forms of nonverbal behavior seem to operate "in accordance with an elaborate and secret code that is written nowhere, known by none, and understood by all."[3]

For our purposes, the nonverbal elements of a situation are *all the cues that are not words*. As noted in Chapter 3, in a communication transaction there are private and behavioral nonverbal and verbal cues, and public cues.[4] Of those, many public cues and all private and behavioral nonverbal cues fall under the general heading of nonverbal cues. *Public* cues such as room size and other situational factors are nonverbal. *Behavioral nonverbal* cues are the elements of vocal expression such as inflection, pitch, and tone. Certain private cues, such as being tired or having a hurt knee, are nonverbal in that they are readings of the physical state of the body.

Some scholars of nonverbal communication are primarily concerned with the nonverbal public cues. They want to examine the effects a

[2] Ray L. Birdwhistle, *Kinesics and Context: Essays on Body Motion Communication*, University of Pennsylvania Press, Philadelphia, 1970, pp. 7–8.

[3] Edward A. Sapir, "The Unconscious Patterning of Behavior in Society," in David G. Mandlebaum (Ed.), *Selected Writings of Edward Sapir in Language, Culture, and Personality*, University of California Press, Berkeley, 1949, p. 556.

[4] Nonverbal cues can be classified in numerous ways. For example, Jurgen Ruesch classifies nonverbal cues as (1) sign language—a hitchhiker thumbing; sign language of the deaf, (2) action language—all bodily movements that are not used exclusively for signals, for example, walking, and (3) object language—the intentional and unintentional display of material things, clothes, and so forth. See Jurgen Ruesch, "Nonverbal Language and Therapy," in Alfred G. Smith (Ed.), *Communication and Culture*, Holt, Rinehart and Winston, New York, 1966, pp 209–213.

Figure 1

situation has on a person. They focus, for example, on the "persuasive" nature of music, nazi marching, and other situational factors that may affect people. Such concerns would lead one to analyze the effects of symbols such as those in Figure 1.

No doubt, these symbols are a potent form of communication. Party or national identification seems to be solidified by the use of symbols that represent it. Ask any antiwar group that tried to display the Viet Cong flag in the United States whether nonverbal symbols communicate. The occasional punch in the nose to the carrier of the flag seems ample evidence of the effectiveness of nonverbal signs.

Other public cues extrinsic to the communication situation also have an effect on the persons involved. For example, the size of a room, its physical qualities, and even the placement of the desks "communicate" something to persons involved with that room. In fact, one of the authors of this text feels that desk placement affects relationships; consequently, his office is arranged so that students who come to visit sit beside him, rather than on the other side of the desk. He is obviously trying to communicate nonverbally.

Our focus in this chapter will be on behavioral nonverbal cues we emit in a communicative transaction[5] rather than public or private nonverbal cues. Even though most of the illustrations of nonverbal behavior that we will use are within the interpersonal communication situation, nonverbal cues are also present in small group, public speaking, and mass communication situations. For clarity, we will organize our treatment of nonverbal behavioral cues under different axioms of communication. These axioms could be introduced at several different points in this book, as they deal with all aspects of communication behavior. Since they cause us to focus on various elements of nonverbal communication behavior, we have included them here.

AXIOMS OF COMMUNICATION

Four tentative axioms, or rules, of communication can be set forth. While the axioms may seem obvious, it was not until recently that they were succinctly stated.[6]

Axiom I. One Cannot Not Communicate

When we are in interpersonal contact with another person, everything we do, or do not do, communicates. Sitting in a room with someone and not talking to him communicates something. Our posture, physique, physical dress, race, height, and other elements communicate something because we are giving off nonverbal cues by our very presence. Put bluntly, "From the moment of recognition until the moment of separation, people observe each other with all their senses."[7] Therefore, when we are in contact with another human, we are *always communicating*.

To illustrate that we are always communicating, although at times unintentionally, examine the concerns of people with physical attractiveness. The girl who regularly combs her hair and applies makeup is definitely communicating. Similarly, the girl who goes braless, wears no makeup, and wears overalls to class is communicating. People will probably perceive that both girls are revealing their values and con-

[5] Erving Goffman classifies cues, both verbal and nonverbal, as embodied or disembodied. Embodied cues are such things as a frown or a word—they are sent by current bodily action. Disembodied messages are received from letters or residues left after the organism behaves. To extend it a bit, all nonverbal cues extrinsic to the organism can be considered as disembodied cues. See Erving Goffman, *Behavior in Public Places,* Free Press, New York, 1963, p. 14.

[6] These axioms come from P. Wazlawick, J. H. Beavin, and D. D. Jackson, *The Pragmatics of Human Communication,* W. W. Norton, New York, 1967, pp. 48–71.

[7] Dean Barnlund (Ed.), *Interpersonal Communication: Survey and Studies,* Houghton Mifflin, New York, 1968, p. 536.

cerns by their nonverbal behavior. The first may be trying to convey to others that she is a tidy person in word and deed, or, she may not be consciously trying to communicate anything. Perhaps she just dresses that way. Whether she is trying to communicate a certain impression is not the most important consideration. How she is actually perceived is the crucial concern. She may be perceived as a neat, tidy person, or she may be perceived as "Miss Straight" with various personal hang-ups. In any case, *she is communicating*. The second girl may be trying to convey that she is a liberated woman without some of the conventional hang-ups. Again, she may not be trying to communicate anything. She may simply prefer to dress that way. She may, however, be perceived as "liberated" or possibly "loose." Whether she wants to or not, *she is communicating*.

People interpret our nonverbal behavior. Those interpretations differ from person to person, but they are there. When the American goes to a different culture, the way he dresses, his approach to other people, walking speed, facial expressions, and other nonverbal behaviors communicate themselves to the nonforeigners. The male college student with long hair who returns home is, whether he likes it or not, communicating to his parents and their friends. Although he may not smoke pot or espouse revolutionary ideas, others may read those qualities into him. The intensity of the reaction of parents and friends may be overwhelming to the person who is accustomed to long hair styles and beards. One of the authors visited his parents just after finishing his Ph.D. He wanted to leave his pet dog with them while he and his wife traveled all summer. His parents were so affected by his long hair, beard, and headband that they refused to keep the dog until the son stopped looking like one to them. He got a haircut and a shave—and grew them back later.

We "cannot stop communicating through body idiom"; and, nonverbally, we "cannot say nothing."[8] We are *constantly* communicating "in our silent language—the language of behavior."[9] We *can* stop our verbal communication by not using words, but we cannot stop nonverbal behavioral communication. Our very presence (and, sometimes our absence) communicates.

Axiom II. Every Communication Has Both Content and Relationship Aspects

When we communicate, we do not normally send only nonverbal or verbal cues. Usually, in human transactions, verbal and nonverbal cues

[8] Goffman, p. 35 (cited in footnote 5).
[9] Edward Hall, *The Silent Language,* Fawcett, Greenwich, 1966, p. 10.

supplement each other; by the use of both types of cues, the relationship between the participants is defined. Verbally, we emit cues of information; nonverbally, we give contextual meaning to the verbal cues. The result is a defined *relationship*. For example, the army private, when addressing the captain, conveys in his tone of voice, posture, eye contact, and facial expression the fact that he is subservient to the captain (and if he does not, he will soon hear about it). One of the important elements in defining a communication relationship is observable nonverbal behavior. For example, when you talk with a friend, your relaxed posture, eye contact, and other nonverbal cues tell him that you value his association and feel comfortable in his presence. A faculty member, being interviewed by the college president, was struck by the fact that the president came out from behind his desk, took his shoes off, propped his stocking feet on the desk, and began conversing. The president was emitting cues about his informal relationship to the prospective faculty member. Thus, the nonverbal cues helped define the context of the verbal cues.

Another nonverbal element that is important in defining a communication relationship is your voice. Your tone of voice is extremely powerful in projecting your definition of a relationship. The previous example of the army private demonstrates the importance of "tone of voice" in defining relationships. As we might expect, vocal variations such as changes in pitch, volume, quality, and articulation, affect the way we perceive others.[10] Most of us can readily tell when we are being "talked down to," and we understand how the other person is defining our communication relationship. To illustrate to yourself the importance of tone of voice in defining relationships, try these two exercises. First, tell your dog (or some other pet that is responsive to you), in the nicest way you can, "I hate you." Notice how the animal responds to the tone of voice and ignores the words—he stands with his tongue hanging out and his tail wagging. Second, try saying common phrases such as "Hello," "I love you," and "Talk to me," in many different ways. It is obvious that "tone of voice" creates meaning and these meanings are indicators of the relationship between communication participants. Again, it is not necessarily *what* you say (verbal cues), but *how* you say it (nonverbal cues).

The realization that our communication has a relationship as well as

[10] See, for example, David W. Addington, "The Effect of Vocal Variations on Ratings of Source Credibility," *Speech Monographs* (August 1971), *XXXVIII*, 242–247; W. Barnett Pearce and Forrest Conklin, "Nonverbal Vocalic Communication and Perceptions of a Speaker," *Speech Monographs* (August 1971), *XXXVIII*, 235–241; and the review by Ernest Kramer, "Judgment of Personal Characteristics and Emotions from Nonverbal Properties of Speech," *Psychological Bulletin* (1963), *60*, 408–420.

a content aspect has important applications. One of the current theories of mental illness is essentially a communication theory. If one assumes that the "mentally ill can be better described in terms of their behavior rather than state of mind,"[11] all sorts of avenues of insight are opened. Seeing communication disorders as both the *cause and consequence* of mental illness implies (1) certain illnesses can be prevented, and (2) if not prevented they can, hopefully, be cured by training in communication behavior.

The conditions that lead to the development of autistic, withdrawn, and outright schizophrenic children, in the opinion of a communication-oriented psychiatrist, exist because "the parents' unresponsiveness in nonverbal terms prevents the child in the early years of life from learning how to relate through *movement and action*."[12] As a result, the schizophrenic's actions are jerky and uncoordinated, and he is unable to relate nonverbally in a conventional manner. Put another way, the emotionally disturbed have a greater capacity for misinterpreting the behavior of others. They have a lessened ability to modify their non-verbal behavior when it is "offensive or misunderstood by others."[13] And, severe manic-depressives, because of a lack of coordination of verbal and nonverbal cues, create phony and fraudulent impressions of themselves.[14]

The "double-bind" theory of schizophrenia is a systematic treatment of the nonverbal behavior of mentally ill persons. Briefly, the theory holds that schizophrenia is caused because the patient, in his every-day encounters with his family, receives contradictory cues. For example, a mother may say to a child, "Come here and let me love you," and yet emit nonverbal cues that clearly let the child know he is not loved (like having a "mean" look on her face). If the child obeys the verbal command, he is hit by the mother as soon as he comes close. In this instance he has obeyed her verbal cues but has ignored her "true" feelings, which were manifested nonverbally. On the other hand, if he disobeys the verbal cues, she will punish him for not "coming to me to be loved when I ask." There are two injunctions, one verbal and one nonverbal, which are contradictory; the child loses no matter which set of cues he obeys. He is in the "double-bind."[15] The child's continual

[11] Goffman, p. 243 (cited in footnote 5).

[12] Jurgen Ruesch, *Disturbed Communication*, W. W. Norton, New York, 1957, p. 133.

[13] Birdwhistle, p. 24 (cited in footnote 2).

[14] Ruesch, p. 139 (cited in footnote 12).

[15] For a more detailed analysis see Gregory Bateson, et al., "Toward a Theory of Schizophrenia," pp. 35–36; and other articles in Don D. Jackson (Ed.), *Communication, Family, and Marriage,* Science and Behavior Books, Palo Alto, 1968.

exposure to double-bind situations creates, over a period of time, schizophrenic behavior. The resulting behavior of a schizophrenic reflects the types of behavior that caused the illness. The schizophrenic as we noted above, has difficulty in emitting nonverbal and verbal cues that are in harmony; as a result, nonschizophrenic persons cannot accurately interpret the schizophrenic's tone of voice, gestures, and other nonverbal and verbal behavior.[16]

It needs to be stressed that the creation of a double-bind does not necessarily lead to schizophrenia. In fact, we have probably all experienced receiving contradictory verbal and nonverbal cues in certain situations and for short periods of time. Students, for instance, experience a double-bind at various times in school. While attending a seminar, a student disagreed rather vehemently with the professor's point of view. The disagreement became heated; since he could not "cool it," the student said, "I guess you just don't want me to disagree with you." The professor, with a red face and in a very loud, disagreeable voice, said, "I **want** you to disagree with me." The verbal and nonverbal messages were clearly contradictory—verbally the professor wanted disagreement, nonverbally it was abundantly clear that the professor was terribly upset by the disagreement. Again, the power figure had placed the other person in a double-bind dilemma.

In every act of communication, we are defining the situation, or as we said previously, defining the relationship between the persons.[17] This process of defining a relationship is probably best illustrated by the efforts of some people to **deny** that they are defining one. Such comments as "I think you should do that, but it's not my place to tell you so," or, "But professor, I wasn't being disrespectful when I answered you," are attempts to deny defining, or to control the interpretation of one's definition.[18] It is apparent, then, that we can gain insight into human communication by examining both the content and relational properties of human communication transactions.

Axiom III. A Series of Communications Can Be Viewed As An Uninterrupted Sequence

In Chapter 3, we stressed that a communication event is a transaction and that the designation of a source and a receiver is an artificial deci-

---

[16] Ibid., pp. 38–40.

[17] For further illustration, see Erving Goffman, *Presentation of Self in Everyday Life,* Doubleday, Garden City, 1959, p. 6, and Jay Haley, "An Interactional Description of Schizophrenia," in Jackson, p. 155 (cited in footnote 15).

[18] For the first example above and classifications of other ways to deny defining a relationship, see Haley, pp. 157–158 (cited in footnote 17).

sion. The third axiom of communication makes a related point. Communication is an on-going, simultaneous process of encoding and decoding activities. The nonverbal cues present in a communication transaction are a principal contributor to the simultaneous encoding and decoding activities. Whenever you are with another person, you both are "attempting to get meaning" simultaneously. You do not encode and decode back and forth like the movement of a ping-pong ball, you both "attempt to get meaning" at any point in time.

In everyday behavior, people "punctuate" communication events (stop the process and define some part as causing some other part). In fact, the essence of many marital struggles is a disagreement over how communication interchanges are punctuated. Take the couple that has the following punctuation of events. The wife says, "I nag my husband because he withdraws and won't communicate with me," and the husband says, "I withdraw because my wife nags me." They are stopping the process at different points and, as a result, are assigning different causes and effects.[19]

Punctuation of events can be illustrated in numerous other human communication situations. The United States and Russia separately punctuate the series of events leading to the arms race. They both say, "We have to build bigger and better weapons because the (Amercans —Russians) are." Each sees the other as the cause of the arms buildup. Only when the nations begin to say, "It is irrelevant *who* starts and continues the arms race, let's agree not to race," will the rigid punctuation of the communication cycle be broken.

Axiom IV. All Communication Relationships are Either Symmetrical or Complementary, Depending on Whether They are Based on Equality or Difference

Axiom II told us that nonverbal cues can play an important part in helping define a communication relationship. Axiom IV says that the relationship may be either symmetrical or complementary. When communicators treat each other as equals, they "mirror each other's behavior." This is known as *symmetrical* transaction. For example, when writing this book we did not play a game of "I'm superior, you're inferior"—the transaction was symmetrical.

Complementary transaction stresses that one partner is superior to the other. In marriages, regardless of which partner is dominant, it is readily apparent when complementary communication occurs. Whether

[19] This example comes from Watzlawick, Beavin, and Jackson, p. 56 (cited in footnote 6).

it is the wife on the phone telling the bowling crew that "We have decided that Harold doesn't want to go tonight," or a husband saying, "I don't **want** my wife to know how to handle the finances," it is clear that the marriage partners relate in a complementary fashion.

In a particular transaction, such as the prior marriage example, the nature of the relationship may be explicitly defined by the nonverbal elements. In another transaction, it may be that the type of relationship is ordered or structured into the situation. For example, a judge may speak to a defendent in a sympathetic and friendly tone of voice, but the relationship is still complementary.

A student's satisfaction with a course can often be traced to the kind of instructor-student relationship he prefers. If a student prefers a complementary relationship, he will probably select professors who teach a highly structured course. The syllabus is complete, the assignments are specific, and it is clear that the professor is superior to the students. For the student who desires equal status or a symmetrical relationship, a class based on equality of all is more appreciated.

Usually, when asked which type of relationship they prefer, people will assert they prefer symmetrical relationships where all people are equal. It is interesting to note, however, that some of these same people when placed in a symmetrical relationship, try to create a complementary relationship. This type of behavior is common on a college campus. Many students say, "I like a professor who is inductive in the classroom. One who does not impose predetermined requirements and present us with prepackaged information. I like the professor who will treat us as equals and let us determine what we want to learn." Often, these same students, when placed in a truly inductive classroom setting in which the student-instructor relationships are symmetrical, will be among the first to demand a syllabus.

Which is preferable—symmetrical or complementary relationships? It depends on the situation and the people involved. Some institutions, such as our court system, could not survive with symmetrical relationships. Other institutions would be vastly improved if symmetrical relationships were permitted to develop.

NONVERBAL CODES

One of the most common assumptions about nonverbal communication is that it is "natural"; that is, it is inherent, not acquired. Because young babies "smile" it is assumed that facial expressions, gestures, body stance, and similar nonverbal cues are natural. It is becoming well established, however, that nonverbal communication is *learned* from our relationships with others. Acquired verbal language is composed of discrete units, and even though nonverbal expressions have no clearly defined boundaries, both verbal and nonverbal "languages" are learned systems of rules.[20]

If nonverbal communication is composed of cultural rules, then interpretations of cues vary across cultures. Put bluntly, just as our verbal language system is not understood by a different culture, our nonverbal "language system" is misunderstood.[21] While persons in our culture point with the index finger outstretched, certain African groups that point with an outstretched lower lip consider our gesture "crude and vulgar."[22] Similarly, we show surprise by a gaping mouth and raised eyebrows while Eskimos, Tlingits, and Brazilians show surprise by slapping their hips.[23] "Just as there are no universal words . . . there are no body motions, facial expressions, or gestures which provoke *identical* responses the world over."[24]

SELECTED RESEARCH FINDINGS

Scholars are now trying to specify exactly which nonverbal cues produce what interpretations within a given culture. To aid in this study, Birdwhistle recently developed a sophisticated notation technique for recording the components of a nonverbal language. Every nuance of behavior, from the raising of an eyebrow to the shifting of body position, can be recorded.

By the process of informal observation, you can personally notice some interesting nonverbal behavioral occurrences. For example, in some cultures, such as the Arabian ones, the distance between people who talk (spatial relationship) is much less than in American culture. If an Arab is speaking with an American, the Arab, in order to feel comfortable, comes close. The American, in order to feel comfortable, moves back. The two of them can be seen moving across the room while they talk. The American retreats and the Arab advances. Both of

[20] This distinction is quoted and discussed in Barnlund, pp. 525–526 (cited in footnote 7).

[21] Weston, LaBarne, "The Cultural Basis of Emotion and Gestures," *Journal of Personality* (September, 1947), XV, 55.

[22] Leonard W. Dobb, "Communication in Africa," in Haig A. Bosmajian (Ed.), *The Rhetoric of Nonverbal Communication,* Scott, Foresman, Glenview, 1971, p. 69.

[23] Maurice H. Krout, "Symbolism," in Bosmajian (Ed.), p. 22 (cited in footnote 22).

[24] Birdwhistle, p. 34 (cited in footnote 2).

them, having their spatial relationship norms violated, are probably uncomfortable.

We have seen acquaintances retreat behind desks and other objects to get some distance between themselves and a person who talks from a *very* close distance. The obstacles keep the "offender" from closing in, but he can be seen frantically leaning over the desk in an attempt to have his face about four inches from the person to whom he is speaking because he is comfortable at that close distance.

Informal observations such as these, while they give insights necessary for beginning an analysis, are not conclusive evidence. Many times, informal observations are not consistent with one another. "Absence makes the heart grow fonder" and "out of sight, out of mind," are not directly related to nonverbal communication, but best illustrate the point. Research, conducted under controlled conditions, permits us to observe if a certain effect occurs with regularity. Following are some findings about our nonverbal behaviors in communication transactions (these findings are restricted to the American culture).[25]

Distance

Within an interpersonal communication situation, as our degree of liking for a person increases, the distance between us is reduced. Persons who have a positive feeling about others like to converse with them at a closer range than when communicating with someone they dislike. There is a limit, however, to the closeness. If one comes *too* close (for what we normally expect in our culture) that indicates a negative feeling. To be nose to nose with someone is usually a sign of violent disagreement that borders on physical assault.

Eye Contact

Eye contact serves two primary functions in interpersonal communication. It serves a *regulatory* function when it lets the other person know you want to establish or to avoid making contact with him. When riding in an elevator, for example, by not looking at other people's eyes, you are signaling them that you prefer not to talk. And, if you want to "break the ice," you use your eyes to make contact either prior to, or simultaneously with, the verbal message. Our eyes serve an *expressive function* by letting others know how we feel about them. Although the

[25] All of the research summaries in this remaining section come from Albert Mehrabian, "Significance of Posture and Position in the Communication of Attitude and Status Relationships," *Psychological Bulletin* (1969), *71*, (5), 359–372.

research is somewhat inconsistent for females, males use more eye contact with someone they like than with someone they dislike.

Body Orientation

The degree to which one person is turned in the direction of another during communication reveals that generally, we use a more direct body orientation toward another if he is of a higher status than we, or, if we are male, our direction orientation reveals a liking for the other. Women, on the other hand, give a moderately direct orientation to those they like and a very indirect orientation to those they intensely dislike.

A related area of research, the "accessibility of body—openness of arms and legs" besides being difficult to summarize with propriety, has shown inconsistent results.

A CHALLENGE

The study of nonverbal communication is just beginning and the findings are mostly speculative at this point. Once nonverbal communication is better researched, we can begin training in nonverbal communication just as we now give training in the use of verbal communication. Training in nonverbal behavior will help each of us become better communicators. There is every possibility that knowledge in the area will be advantageous for other reasons, such as treating mentally ill patients. Even though conclusive research in nonverbal behavior is still in its infancy, you, as a student of human communication, should be able to supply insights into the use and misuse of nonverbal behavior.

Exercises

1. Can you think of specific situations where the research findings on nonverbal behavior seem incorrect or do not apply?
2. What nonverbal cues can the class members agree on (other than distance, eye contact, and body orientations) that give standard impressions in our culture?
3. What nonverbal differences are there within subcultures of American life? Do poor and rich use the same nonverbal signs? Blacks and whites?

4. Observe a conversation taking place (or, produce one in front of the class). Specify what nonverbal (and verbal) techniques are used to define the relationship between the two people communicating. Draw up a list of possible ways for those two people to redefine the relationship and continue the transaction, based on different assumptions.

5. Secure some pictures of persons sitting or standing that represent many different postures, facial expressions, and other nonverbal cues. Conduct a miniexperiment with members of the class and get their impressions of the people in the pictures (have the class members visualize, for example, that they are walking toward the person in the pictures). After you have collected the responses, have the class members attempt to specify what cues, or combination of cues, stimulated their particular impression.

6. Read Robert Ardrey's, *The Territorial Imperative*. What does he see as the origin of nonverbal spatial behavior? Are there any cogent arguments against his thesis?

7. As a project, try to describe what happens to the nonverbal cues in different communication settings.

8. Each class member, from his own experience, might draw up a list of communication situations that illustrate individuals punctuating differently. Are there any similarities between the situations chosen?

9. Make a list categorizing your two favorite and two least favorite classes. Then, analyze each class for the communication behavior expected from you as a student. Do you find a personal preference for either complementary or symmetrical communication relationships? What basic values that you hold are highlighted by your preferred style of communication?

10. If your community has an institution that houses individuals with emotional or mental problems, get permission for a field trip, and observe the nonverbal and verbal behavior of the patients. Do the verbal and nonverbal cues sent by schizophrenics conflict? Are emotionally disturbed persons deficient in certain areas of nonverbal expression?

11. Volunteer to go in front of the class. Have the instructor give you a list of words for you to portray nonverbally to the class. Ask the class members to try to guess each word.

12. This evening, meet with one or two members of your class and watch a specified televison program with the sound off. Each person should keep notes on the prominent features of the programs, what the plot was, and similar aspects. Relate your separate notes

to the class. Do you find that you are more sensitive to behavioral nonverbal cues when words are missing?

Suggested Readings

R. L. Birdwhistle, *Kinesics and Context: Essays on Body Motion Com-
   munication,* University of Pennsylvania Press, Philadelphia,
   1970.
Erving Goffman, *The Presentation of Self in Everyday Life,* Doubleday,
   New York, 1959.
Edward T. Hall, *The Hidden Dimension,* Doubleday, New York, 1969.
Edward T. Hall, *The Silent Language,* Doubleday, New York, 1959.
Randall Harrison, "Nonverbal Communication—A Research Update,"
   Paper presented to the 1971 Speech Communication Asso-
   ciation Convention, San Francisco, California.
Paul Watzlawick, Janet Helmick Beavin, and Don D. Jackson, *Prag-
   matics of Human Communication,* W. W. Norton, New York,
   1967.

Chapter 7

Selectivity
in Communication

Objectives

On completion of this chapter you should be able to:
1. Discuss how your own behavior demonstrates selective attention.
2. Understand why language is selectively perceived.
3. Describe how you selectively perceive objects and people.
4. Recognize your own set ways of thinking.
5. Critique the selective exposure postulate.
6. Understand why we selectively retain certain information.

SELECTIVE ATTENTION

Human communication, by its very nature, is selective. One simply cannot attend to, perceive, or recall all internal and external stimuli that have potential meaning. Hopefully, the stimuli one selects are the important ones. If one fails to pay attention to some environmental cues, tragic consequences may occur. A coed, for example, who attends the verbal cues being shouted to her by a friend across the street, will be run over if she does not also attend the loud horn signal being sent to her by an approaching automobile. Various stimuli compete for our attention; since we cannot decode all of them simultaneously, we must select only certain ones. The selection process is extremely complex, but very important. A major cause of failure in the air traffic control

---

[1] There is a significant difference between a "honky horn" and a "horny honk." Both compete for attention, but one of them comes through much more loudly and clearly.

communication systems in airports is that the human operator has too many incoming stimuli to handle simultaneously, or that he reacts to an unimportant signal when he should be dealing with an important one.[2]

To attend anything, our attention must be selective. We have to make decisions about what to attend. We are usually not aware of this decision process, but it is definitely taking place. Sometimes one must make a **conscious attempt** to attend certain stimuli; for example, when you are in a large lecture class and the people next to you are engaging in interpersonal communication. In order for you to receive the information being transmitted by the instructor, you must concentrate on the verbal communication cues in his message.

"Paying attention—and not paying attention—are surely two of the most important abilities of human beings."[3] Try for a moment to attend all of the stimuli that are competing for your attention. You will soon discover that simultaneous attention to all signals is impossible, as well as frustrating and confusing.

To attend all stimuli, one needs to have all of his basic senses of seeing, hearing, feeling, tasting, and smelling operable at the same time. This, of course, is not feasible. Often, when one is trying to attend important stimuli that he is receiving through a particular sense channel, he must consciously shut off other sense channels. One day, Ed, while traveling down the highway with his family, thought he smelled something burning. He shouted, to his wife, DeAnn, "Be quiet and turn down the radio—I think I smell something burning!" The absurdity of this statement is obvious, but the reason for such a command is understandable. Too many senses were competing for attention. The wife who gets upset with her husband for reading the paper while she talks to him is aware of his selection of stimuli. He is directing his attention to the signals important to him at the time and treating all other stimuli as background "noise."

Attention is a mental process by which a stimulus or stimuli becomes sharper, more distinct, and more vivid in consciousness while other stimuli tend to recede.[4] That it is selective is a truism. Try as we might, we will not be able to "cure" our attention process of its selectivity. We can, however, understand it better, and by so doing, we can better understand our successes and failures in communication. To receive

[2] Donald E. Broadbent, "Attention and the Perception of Speech," in Alfred G. Smith (Ed.), *Communication and Culture,* Holt, Rinehart and Winston, New York, 1966, p. 277.
[3] Ibid.
[4] Kenneth E. Andersen, *Persuasion Theory and Practice,* Allyn and Bacon, Boston, 1971, p. 98.

insight into the selective nature of communication, we must study the selective nature of perception, exposure, and retention. It is difficult to discuss any one of the selective features of this process without discussing the others at the same time. For clarity, however, we will deal with each of them as a separate process.

SELECTIVE PERCEPTION

Perception of Language

We noted in Chapter 5 that an animal sign has a one-to-one relationship with its meaning. Each animal sign has a special purpose and passes from generation to generaton. Human signs, however, are acquired by each individual. They are not passed on by heredity without a social context. Humans also use symbols that have a one-to-many relationship to meaning. There is no necessary connection between the symbol and its referent. This arbitrary nature of our language makes "perception" a crucial consideration.

Perception may be defined as the way an organism gives meaning.[5] Chapter 5 indicated that there are several different theoretical explanations for the way in which an organism acquires meaning. Although the *process* of meaning acquisition may be standard, the *specific meanings acquired* are not standard. Again, meanings are in people—not words. This presents several problems for the communication process. We must realize that as no two people have identical meanings for words, no two people perceive words, happenings, experiences, or messages exactly alike. Perception, like attention, is by its very nature selective.

A major difficulty in communication is that each of us believes his perception is the "correct" perception and that others perceive or should be able to perceive objects and events the same way we do. Nearly all of us go through life firmly convinced that we see, hear, and touch what is truly there to be seen, heard, or felt. We think of ourselves as inside observers of outside reality.[6] This is hardly the case. Perceptions vary from person to person. What is a "stimulating lecture" to one may be a "boring spew of prepackaged information" to another.

[5] Bernard C. Hennessy, *Public Opinion,* Wadsworth Publishing, Belmont, California, 1965, p. 176.
[6] "Perception and Communication," Pamphlet for use in AID Communication Seminars, Michigan State University, p. 1.

Perception of Objects

Our perception or interpretation of stimuli is partially controlled by our previous experiences.[7] Each of our perceptions is the beneficiary of all our previous perceptions. Each perception is a link between the past, which gives it its meaning and the future, which it helps to interpret.[8] Some extend this notion to the point of saying that *all* differences in opinion turn out to be a reflection of different experiences.[9]

Empirical support for the belief that experiences affect object perception is readily available. In one experiment, ten-year-old children were required to adjust the size of a disc of light to equal the sizes of some coins. It was found that they overestimated the sizes of the coins and the more valuable the coins, the greater the degree of overestimation. In addition, children from poor homes overestimated to a greater extent than did those from well-to-do homes.[10]

Past experience influences perception, and also sets limits on the possibilities of fresh approaches to problems. Most of us engage in "vertical thinking"; thinking within narrow limits.[11] Our *natural* patterning of a situation or a communication encounter is the basis on which we generate ideas, points of view, and approaches to a problem. With preconceived perceptions we parcel up information into nice neat, little packages. We then process the information accordingly. We cannot escape or avoid developing a perceptual approach. For example, imagine that you have eleven socks in your dresser drawer. Five of the socks are red and six of them are blue. You are getting up early in the morning to go on a weekend trip. It is dark in the room and you do not want to turn on the light and disturb your roommate. Instead, you decide to take enough socks so that you know you will have a pair that matches. How many socks will you take so that you are absolutely sure you will have a matching pair? Think about this before you read further. Most people decide to take six socks. Why? We would take only three. This number would assure you of a matching pair. Most people would

[7] Andersen, p. 103 (cited in footnote 4).

[8] Hans Toch and Malcolm S. MacLean, Jr., "Perception Communication, and Educational Research: A Transactional View," in James H. Campbell and Hal W. Hepler (Eds.), *Dimensions in Communication: Readings*, Wadsworth Publishing, Belmont, California, p. 41.

[9] Dean C. Barnlund (Ed.), *Interpersonal Communication: Survey and Studies*, Houghton Mifflin, Boston, 1968, p. 351.

[10] J. S. Bruner and C. C. Goodman, "Value and Need as Organizing Factors in Perception," *Journal of Abnormal and Social Psychology* (1947), *42*, 33–44.

[11] Edward de Bono, "Thinking Sideways," *Bell Telephone Magazine* (July/August 1969), pp. 26–32.

take six, not because they enjoy carrying extra clothes, but because they approached the problem from a set way.[12]

The gentleman who relates this "sock" problem also tells of an experience he had with a group of engineering students. He asked them to help him solve the problem of summer suits, "which are often made of such a smooth material that the trousers tend to slide off clothes hangers." They produced a number of possible solutions, but missed what is probably the simplest answer. How would you solve the problem? Would you design an elaborate new hanger, as did the engineering students? Or, would you ". . . hang the trousers so that instead of both legs going over the bar from the same side, each leg goes over from a different side." This would prevent the trousers from slipping off, "But no amount of attention to the hanger itself would lead to this answer."[13] Again, we approach problems, and unfortunately also people, from our perceptual sets.

Cover all the following numbers with a sheet of paper. Then, move the paper downward so that one number is revealed at a time. Total the numbers out loud as they are revealed. For example, "One thousand, two thousand, two thousand twenty," and so on.

1000
1000
20
1000
40
1000
30
1000
10

What is the total? It was easy, the total is 6000, right? Wrong—the total is 5100. Perceptual set?[14]

Not only do past experiences influence our perceptions, the immediate environment surrounding an object can also affect them. For example, look at the objects in Figure 1.

Is the hat taller than the brim is wide? Is there a lopsided circle in the center picture? Are the columns in the right-hand picture different heights? Demonstrate to your own satisfaction that the answer to each question is no.

[12] Ibid., p. 29.
[13] Ibid., pp. 28–30.
[14] Adapted from "Counting Game" exercise for use in AID Communication Seminars, Michigan State University.

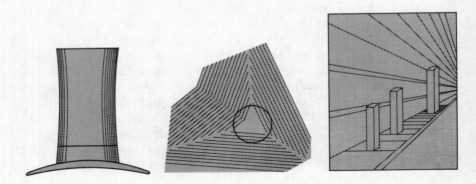

Figure 1

Interestingly enough, even when our past experiences and immediate environment do not measureably alter our perceptions, our perceptions may still not correspond to "reality." We often perceive some colors (for example, red and yellow) as "hot" and other colors (for example, blue and green) as "cool." But, certainly, they are the same temperature. People even paint rooms white to "expand" the perceived dimensions of a room. But, if anything, the room is smaller with one or two additional coats of paint on each wall. Obviously, we selectively perceive objects.

Even the *naming* of an object may affect the way in which it is perceived. In one experiment (Figure 2) two groups of people were shown a series of identical shapes. One group was given a name for each shape, and the other group was given a different name for each of the same shapes. After exposure to the shapes, people were asked to reproduce them. Figure 2 shows that the people produced shapes that were more like the names given the objects than like the original drawings.[15]

Not only can the names of objects influence our judgments, but the perceptions of words themselves can be altered. In one study, a group of subjects was told it would see words related to "boats." Another

[15] L. Carmichael, H. P. Hogan, and A. A. Walter, "An Experimental study of the Effect of Language on the Reproduction of Visually Perceived Form," *Journal of Experimental Psychology* (1932), *15*, 73–86. Also, for statement of a similar notion, see treatment of the Whorfian hypotheses in Chapter 5.

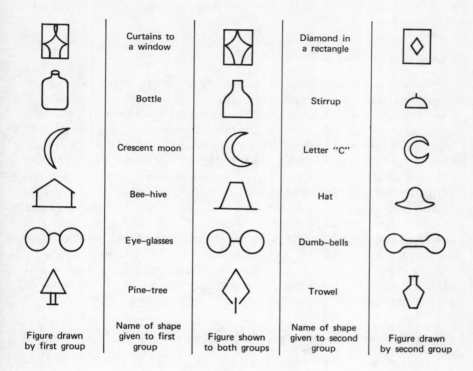

Figure drawn by first group	Name of shape given to first group	Figure shown to both groups	Name of shape given to second group	Figure drawn by second group
	Curtains to a window		Diamond in a rectangle	
	Bottle		Stirrup	
	Crescent moon		Letter "C"	
	Bee–hive		Hat	
	Eye–glasses		Dumb–bells	
	Pine–tree		Trowel	

Figure 2

group was told it would see words related to "animals." Both groups were exposed to "sael" and "wharl." The "boat" group perceived these as "sail" and "wharf," while the "animal" group perceived them as "seal" and "whale."[16]

Perceptual sets also operate in real life. For example, before you actually enrolled in the basic speech course, you may have asked a good friend of yours what he thought of the course when he took it last term. He may have replied, "It's a real bummer!" Although your friend was not purposefully trying to set your expectations, he probably did so. In such a case, you will initially perceive the course as a "real bummer." By now, if you were fortunate enough to receive an instructor you like, you may have modified that attitude set. Whenever a friend

[16] E. Siipola, "A Group Study of Some Effects of Preparatory Sets," *Psychological Monographs* (1935), *46* (210), 27–38.

relates a judgment to you, it influences your expectations and creates a perceptual set.

Perception of Persons

Since we selectively perceive objects, it should be expected that we selectively perceive people. For example, prejudice toward others affects perception of them. In one study, it was discovered that whites who had favorable attitudes toward blacks were more capable of distinguishing personal characteristics of blacks than were those whites who had unfavorable attitudes toward blacks. The whites with favorable attitudes could distinguish individual blacks in pictures, whereas those whites with unfavorable attitudes could not.[17] In another study, "prejudiced" and "unprejudiced" observers were exposed to some pictures of blacks and some pictures of whites. It was discovered that the prejudiced observers exaggerated the stereotyped racial characteristics such as width of nose and fullness of lips.[18] Studies of this nature support the notion of selective perception. Prejudiced observers classified all blacks as a homogenious group by accenting the imagined physical differences and failing to perceive the individual differences.

Perceptions and Expectations

Because perception is selective in nature, it not only makes us perceive things in a certain way, it also makes us *expect* to perceive things in a certain way. Prejudiced individuals perceive stereotype features because they expect to. ". . . one sees what one expects to see; one perceives what one expects to perceive."[19] The tendency to create expectations causes several communication problems. For example, we often interpret a message differently when it is attributed to different people. A group of experimenters developed three separate messages on the issue of busing children for the integration of schools. They termed one of the messages "probusing," one "antibusing," and one "ambivalent" or neutral. Six groups of college students were exposed to one of the three messages attributed to either Martin Luther King, Jr., or to George Wallace of Alabama. The students who heard the ambivalent message when it was attributed to King perceived it as

[17] V. Seeleman, "The Influence of Attitude Upon the Remembering of Pictorial Material," *Archives of Psychology* (1940), *258*, 1–69.

[18] P. F. Secord, W. Bevan, and B. Katz, "The Negro Stereotype and Perceptual Accentuation," *Journal of Abnormal and Social Psychology* (1956), pp. 78–83.

[19] Andersen, p. 103 (cited in footnote 4).

supportive of busing. The students who heard the message when it was attributed to Wallace perceived it as against busing. The "anti-busing" message when attributed to Wallace was perceived as significantly more "anti" than the same message when it was attributed to King. Similarly, the "probusing" message when attributed to King was perceived as significantly more "pro" than the same message when attributed to Wallace.[20] This is another example of selective perception (or distortion) based on perceptual sets.

We often misread the intent of a person because of perceptual sets. Two college coeds were having a conversation. One of the girls was visibly upset. They were discussing an encounter that the upset girl had with a certain male college student. The girl who was trying to calm down her upset friend said, "But, Charney, all Bill said was, 'When I gaze into your eyes time stops.'" Charney, with tears in her eyes replied, "Yea, Carolyn—but you don't know him like I do. What he meant was, 'Your face would stop a clock!'"[21]

How did Charney "know" what Bill "meant?" Maybe he did "mean" what Charney thought; but then, maybe he did not. To Carolyn, the observer, the implied message was not apparent. Who was "correct?" Actually, both girls were correct. To each individual, perception is reality. No matter how distorted one's perception may be to another person, it is accurate *to the perceiver*.

Perceptions of people in other cultures illustrate how we attach intent to others. One experimenter found that American school children, when asked why the Russians planted trees along the roadside said that the trees "interfered with vision" and "made work for the prisoners." These same children indicated that Americans plant roadside trees "for shade."[22]

The fact that perception is selective should now be very clear to you. It is regrettable that we selectively perceive language, objects, and people and behave from set perceptual platforms. Such regret, however, does not help us to improve the situation. We must recognize that perception *is* selective and we must cope with it. We must admit that we selectively perceive others and they, in turn, selectively perceive us. When we admit that we interpret our environment from a personal,

[20] J. W. Koehler, J. C. McCroskey, and W. E. Arnold, "The Effects of Receivers' Constancy-Expectation in Communication," Research monograph, Department of Speech, Pennsylvania State University, 1966, cited in James C. McCroskey, *An Introduction to Rhetorical Communication*, Prentice-Hall, Englewood Cliffs, 1968, pp. 174–175.

[21] The basic idea for this hypothetical example comes from John T. Kirk and George D. Talbot, "The Distortion of Information," in Smith (Ed.), p. 312 (cited in footnote 2).

[22] U. Bronfenbrenner, "The Mirror Image in Soviet-American Relations: A Social Psychologist's Report," *Journal of Social Issues, 17*, 45–56.

selective set, we may be able to stop and check our assumptions. By so doing, we may be able to "saw through some of our perception prison bars" and relate to others in a more empathic, understanding manner.

The basic perception problem that faces all of us as communicators is that we know ourselves and our environment only through our own senses. We cannot "get outside of ourselves" and check the "total" accuracy of all our perceptions, but we can do a better job than most of us do in our daily encounters.[23]

Advantages of Perception

Perceptual sets and expectations do not always hinder us. Sometimes they serve us well. As a matter of fact, the "better" our perception platforms are constructed, the more efficiently we can operate. The ability to recall previous experiences, sometimes involuntarily, is one feature that makes humans the highest form of animal life. We need this ability to survive in our environment. Set expectations enable us to make more rapid perceptions. For example, an individual who knows a sign is in a certain place along a highway can see that sign at night from almost twice as great a distance as a person who does not know the sign is there.[24] Without perceptual expectations, we would not be able to make any sense out of the world.

SELECTIVE EXPOSURE

Many scholars argue that we selectively *expose* ourselves to communication. Some scholars believe that the *most important* factor in the persistence of a person's attitudes is his selective exposure to communication stimuli.[25]

The term "selective exposure" has come to mean seeking and avoiding information so that one's present attitudes are maintained. The selective exposure idea has both a positive and a negative aspect. One prediction is that a person "seeks out information that confirms his preconceptions." The other prediction is that a person "actively avoids information that disconfirms his preconceptions." The way one seeks

[23] "Perception and Communication," p. 1 (cited in footnote 6).
[24] Andersen, p. 103 (cited in footnote 4).
[25] McCroskey, p. 43 (cited in footnote 20); See also Behavioral Sciences Subpanel, President's Science Advisory Committee, Report to the President, *Behavioral Sciences* (1962), 7, 277.

or avoids neutral or unimportant information is thought to be "between that for supportive and that for disconfirming information."[26]

The basic assumption underlying the selective exposure principle is related to the idea that man strives for consistency. He is comfortable when he is exposed to and interprets incoming stimuli that are consistent with his present beliefs. However, man becomes uncomfortable when he is exposed to stimuli that are inconsistent with his present beliefs. Inconsistency causes disruption in a person's mind; as a result, he purposefully avoids coming into contact with information that will threaten his existing beliefs.[27]

Early support for the selective exposure principle was generated by research in mass communication. Lazarsfeld discovered in 1940 that a radio series, designed to inform our society of minority group contributions to the country, was predominately listened to by members of the minority group being featured in the series. Cartwright found that most people who accepted free tickets to a documentary movie were the people who already behaved in the manner the movie was designed to encourage. Researchers also found that exposure to the media and the perceptions of the political bias of the messages surrounding the assassination and funeral of John Kennedy were related to people's previous political affiliations. Studies on voting behavior have found that a political candidate is usually listened to by voters who are already in favor of him. These studies are only a few that could be cited to support the first half of the selective exposure principle; that is, "a person seeks information that confirms his preconceptions."[28] We listen to people with whom we agree. We attend messages that advocate those things we already believe.

We can observe how such exposure is reinforcing to us. We seek people and information that confirm our preconceptions in our daily communication behavior. We surround ourselves with people we like. Students do this by joining certain groups, going to certain parties, searching for a familiar face in the union or cafeteria, and trying to arrange class schedules identical with friends' schedules.

Also, we pay special attention to information that supports our views. In our communication transactions with our friends, we accent those

[26] William J. McGuire, "The Nature of Attitudes and Attitude Change," in Gardner Lindzey and Elliot Aronson (Eds.), *The Handbook of Social Psychology*, 2nd Ed., Vol. III, Addison-Wesley, Reading, 1969, p. 218.
[27] For development of this and similar postulates, see Chapter 11.
[28] For an excellent review of the studies cited here, as well as others, see Walter Weiss, "Effects of the Mass Media of Communication," in Lindzey and Aronson (Eds.), V, pp. 77–195.

things on which we agree. One researcher found that college students select as their post-college friends and faculty advisers those people whose values are similar to their own. The researcher also found that the greatest similarity of values occurred when two students identified each other as a friend.[29] By thinking about our own communication exposure, we soon realize that we are, indeed, exposed to disproportionate amounts of supportive information in all the communication arenas.[30]

It is easy to see that we are exposed to a disproportionate amount of supportive information and people, but the reason "why" this is true is not so clear. We may "actively seek" supportive encounters; or, on the other hand, we may unintentionally adopt certain beliefs and associates because we are predominately exposed to them.

The second half of the selective exposure principle (a person *actively avoids* information that disconfirms his preconceptions) is, however, subject to serious challenge. Do we avoid information that does not support our views? Empirical support for this half of the selective exposure principle is very weak. "On the contrary . . . stimuli associated with pain and stimuli associated with pleasure both tend to enhance receptivity as compared with neutral stimuli." There may be less active seeking-out in some nonsupportive situations than in others, but overall there is "more seeking-out than avoidance of discrepant information."[31]

There are several reasons why one would purposefully expose himself to nonsupportive information—information that challenges his attitudes. The uniqueness or novelty of a person or message may be quite enticing even though we know we are in disagreement. Or, it is often desirable to know that the "other camp" or opposition is thinking about. Also, people find it desirable to appear to be "open-minded," and demonstrate it by attending to both sides of an issue.[32]

Thus, there is reason to question the generality of "one of the most widely accepted principles of mass communication and social psychology," that all voluntary exposure to information is highly selective.[33] Although we are predominately exposed to information and people we

[29] Joseph A. Precker, "Similarity of Valuings as a Factor in Selection of Peers and Near-Authority Figures," *Journal of Abnormal and Social Psychology* (1952), *47*, 406–414; Also cited in Elihu Katz and Paul F. Lazarsfeld, *Personal Influence*. The Free Press of Glencoe, 1964, pp. 60–61.

[30] Jonathan L. Freedman and David O. Sears, "Selective Exposure," in Leonard Berkowitz (Ed.), *Advances in Experimental Psychology II*, Academic Press, New York, 1965, p. 57.

[31] McGuire, p. 219 (cited in footnote 26).

[32] McGuire, pp. 219–220 (cited in footnote 26).

[33] Freedman and Sears, p. 59 (cited in footnote 30).

agree with, this may not be due to *purposeful planning* on our part. Also, it is fairly reasonable to conclude that we do not purposefully behave like ostriches with our heads in the sand to avoid information with which we disagree. To live in such a state of "blissful ignorance" would not be very efficient or effective.[34]

The important question that remains is, "Regardless of 'if' or 'why' we selectively seek-out or avoid certain information, what do we do with information once we are exposed to it?" Do we treat information that is inconsistent with our beliefs in the same manner as information with which we agree? Do we try to distort those things with which we disagree? Do we remember, objectively, as many of the things that upset us as we do those things that reinforce or comfort us?

SELECTIVE RETENTION

Research has shown that people remember material which supports their own view much more completely and accurately than they retain information which attacks their point of view.[35] Thus, retention, too, is selective.

There has not been much research on the process of retention. There is, however, support for the notion that we selectively forget those things which are unpleasant.[36] It seems reasonable to assume that one will "push unpleasant information into the shadow" of his mind. It is much easier and more comfortable to remember things the way we want them to be rather than the way they are.[37]

Is it any wonder we have so many communication problems? Initially, we selectively attend stimuli because we must sort out some specific stimuli from all those competing for our attention. Next, we selectively perceive those stimuli we have attended because we have only our past experiences on which to base our interpretation of "reality." Then, we even have a tendency to selectively retain the information that we selectively attended and perceived.

As communicators, we can be aware of our selective tendencies and become more "objective in our selectivity." Each of us can examine

[34] The term "blissful ignorance" comes from the ". . . blissful and cognitively consistent ignorance" statement by Leonard Berkowitz, "Social Motivation," Gardner Lindzey and Elliot Aronson (Eds.), p. 98 (cited in footnote 26).

[35] Joseph T. Klapper, "The Social Effects of Mass Communication," in Wilbur Schramm (Ed.), *The Science of Human Communication*, Basic Books, New York, 1963, p. 63.

[36] Weiss, p. 89 (cited in footnote 28).

[37] Martin and Andersen, p. 223.

his own communication behavior. By doing so, we become "more" objective by checking our assumptions about others and the things they say. If we can improve ourselves by not distorting other messages "quite so much," we will become much better communicators. Check your perceptions of events and people with others' views and you will find that they are not the same. By checking your own perceptions with the perceptions of others, you will find that no one is "correct." The resulting view, however, may be less distorted. Checking our perceptions and assumptions with others can lead to modified perceptions that will cause fewer communication problems.

Exercises

1. When your instructor gives you the signal, *stop, look,* and *listen.* Make a list of all the stimuli that are competing for your attention. Compare your list with those constructed by your classmates.
2. Give a speech in class in which you discuss how certain expectations you had for some aspect of college life have been fulfilled and how some of your other expectations have been proven inaccurate. If those initial expectations had been different, how would your present college situation be different?
3. Make a list of the things that you remember most from this chapter. Compare your list with those compiled by other members of the class. Why are the lists different? Be specific; analyze the differences.
4. Divide the class into small groups. Discuss instances where your perceptions of other people have hindered or assisted effective communication.
5. As a class, choose a well-known campus or national personality. Have each class member list what he believes are the five major characteristics of that person. Compare the lists. Discuss how the varied perceptions would affect communication transactions with the person.

Suggested Readings

Warren G. Bennis, et al., (Eds.), *Interpersonal Dynamics: Essays and Readings on Human Interaction,* Dorsey Press, Homewood, 1968.

Edward DeBono, *The Use of Lateral Thinking,* Jonathon Cape, London, 1967.

Albert H. Hastorf, David J. Schneider, and Judith Polefka, *Person Perception,* Addison-Wesley, Reading, Mass., 1970.

Renato Tagiuri and Luigi Petrullo, *Person Perception and Interpersonal Behavior,* Stanford University Press, Stanford, 1958.

M. D. Vernon, *The Psychology of Perception,* Penguin Books, Baltimore, 1963.

Chapter **8** ▶

Feedback: The Essence of Transaction

Objectives

On completion of this chapter you should be able to:
1. Specify what function feedback serves for a person encoding a message.
2. Discuss why feedback is just as important for "receivers" as it is for "sources."
3. Explain why one needs to receive feedback to his messages.
4. Describe why one needs to give feedback.
5. List some uses of feedback.
6. Discuss the effects positive and negative feedback have on a person giving a public speech.
7. Know the costs of allowing feedback.

THE NATURE OF FEEDBACK

Why is one frightened and frustrated when he presents a television or radio message for the first time? The large audience may be a factor, but the frustration one experiences in a mass communication arena is entirely different from the tension one experiences in a public speaking arena with a large audience. The *impossibility of observing the audience* is a major contributor to the differences in tension. In the public speaking arena, you at least have the opportunity to look at your receivers and interpret their reactions. In the mass communication arena, you cannot observe the receiver responses. It is quite common to hear the "first-time" radio or television performer say, "I couldn't believe it. You can't imagine what it's like to talk with a camera lens or a microphone staring at you." The main feature of communication which is temporarily omitted from this arena is immediate "feedback," that is, responses from the receivers. "Feedback provides the source with information concerning his success in accomplishing his objective."[1]

The notion of feedback in communication originated from the study of machines.[2] Machines, in order to function properly, must compare their *actual* performance to their *intended* performance. Without feedback about actual performance, the elevator would run amuck, the heating system would overheat, and our missiles would never get into space. The feedback to the machine is a form of control over future performance and the machine, in response to feedback, alters its performance. Likewise, a communication source can adjust his performance in response to feedback. The responses from receivers act as a monitoring device for a source. Like the elevator, if a communicator ignores the feedback being sent to him, he, too, can run amuck. You have probably had a professor who apparently ignores student feedback. Undoubtedly, his failure to adjust to the feedback harms his effectiveness. Feedback obviously serves a very important function as a corrective device for communicators.

Viewing feedback as a "corrective device," however, has its limitations. The notion structures our view of communication into the following format. The speaker speaks, the receivers respond, the response affects the speaker, and he gives an adjusted message, the audience responds again, and so on. As we indicated in Chapter 1, however, communication is not an interactive process—it is a *transactional* process. While the speaker is encoding, so is the receiver, and while the speaker adjusts to the receiver, the receiver is also adjusting to the speaker. In essence, *all* the persons present are sending messages and receiving feedback simultaneously. They are interdependent— each is a cause and an effect of the other.[3]

Receivers and sources are interdependent because they *both* get

[1] David K. Berlo, *The Process of Communication,* Holt, Rinehart and Winston, New York, 1960, pp. 111–112.

[2] See Norbert Wiener, *The Human Use of Human Beings: Cybernetics and Society,* Houghton Mifflin, Boston, 1950.

[3] Arnold Tustin, "Feedback," in Alfred G. Smith (Ed.), *Communication and Culture,* Holt, Rinehart and Winston, New York, 1966, p. 325.

feedback to the cues they emit. Feedback occurs when any encoder sending nonverbal or verbal cues perceives another's encoding as a response to his cues. In human communication, feedback consists of **cues an encoder perceives as being emitted in response to him**. It is the **perception** of the other's response that makes feedback. One can emit many dramatic, nonverbal cues to the oblivious professor; unless the professor perceives the cues, they are not feedback.

Some communicators are extra sensitive to feedback. They perceive all nonverbal cues as feedback to their messages. This can create problems since, as indicated earlier, we are always communicating nonverbally. One popular college lecturer was greatly disturbed in a new class because a girl in the back row "scowled" during his lectures. Throughout the semester, whenever he lectured, the frowning, disapproving face was always there. He got more and more nervous during the semester. He was on the verge of confronting the student when he discovered in the hall one day that the girl had a sight problem. Her "scowling" was mere "squinting." The negative scowl cues did exist, however, because the professor perceived them as negative cues. His perception, not her intention, made the negative feedback exist. Feedback exists "in the eyes of the beholder," and it is at the heart of personal communication transactions.

THE HUMAN NEED FOR FEEDBACK

Feedback is more than a "corrective device" in communication. In our daily lives, it serves to link persons involved in communication transactions. We all have a need to receive and give feedback in our communication encounters.

The Need to Receive Feedback

According to the words in a well-known song, "People who need people are the luckiest people in the world." Although both the tune and the words of this song are appealing, if you think about the phrase for a moment, you will discover that it is misleading. We would modify it to say, "People who need people are people." In other words, everyone needs people. Those who have fulfilled their personal need for others are "the luckiest people in the world." The way one becomes "lucky" is to perceive he is receiving feedback from others. "Through self-exposure and feedback persons can test assumptions about their acceptability or lovability."[4]

Two interpersonal needs that we all have are "inclusion" and "affection." You will recall that "inclusion" is the need to feel that the self is significant and worthwhile, and "affection" is the need to feel that the self is lovable.[5] To determine if you are significant, worthwhile, and lovable, you must (1) perceive feedback is being directed toward you by others (inclusion) and (2) perceive that some of the feedback directed toward you is supportive (affection). A child, for example, may be slow in language acquisition if (1) he receives no feedback from his parents in his attempt to speak, or (2) if he perceives only negative feedback from his parents. In the first case, he will not feel like a unique individual. In the second case, he will feel unique—but not worthwhile.

Each of us, like the child acquiring language, needs to receive feedback. "Our beliefs about ourself and our self image are a reflection of others' perceptions of us."[6] We are formed by our perception of the images others have of us. We receive these images through feedback. A student, for example, needs feedback in his student role. Through perceived feedback from his peers, parents, and teachers, he must feel like a unique, worthwhile, individual student. If he does not perceive that supportive feedback is being directed toward him, he will be unhappy. The same can be said of professors. They must fulfill their interpersonal needs of inclusion and affection or they will be unhappy with their careers. Students can help fulfill the professors' needs because students are important sources of feedback for them. If professors do not receive the necessary feedback, they will be unhappy in their professional roles and probably will not define that role as very important to them. The following statements often indicate a lack of receiving the necessary feedback to fulfill inclusion and affection needs: (1) the student who says, "I know I'm not a very good student; but I don't care—the only reason I'm here is because my parents made me come," and (2) the professor who says, "I don't care if the students think I'm a good teacher or not. To me, it's just a job." It seems reasonable that if a person does not perceive supportive feedback that enables him to fulfill his interpersonal needs in a particular role, he will

[4] Warren G. Bennis et al. (Eds.), *Interpersonal Dynamics: Essays and Readings on Human Interaction,* Dorsey Press, Homewood, 1968, p. 214.

[5] William C. Schutz, *The Interpersonal Underworld,* Science and Behavior Books, Palo Alto, 1966, p. 13.

[6] Bennis et al., p. 218 (cited in footnote 4).

diminish the importance of that role. This notion is applicable to such roles to mothers in their motherhood roles, ministers in their ministerial roles, friends in their friendship roles, and daughters in their daughter roles.

To illustrate our dependence on one another's responses, try to "not respond" to a friend in a communication situation. Avoid eye contact, do not give any verbal response, and act uninterested. You can expect the friend to get visibly upset. He may say such things as "Aren't you interested?" "Are you listening?", or "If you don't want to talk with me, just say so." Negative feelings are portrayed by refusing to respond to others. One who is badly treated, for whatever reason, can indicate his negative feelings by withdrawing from the relationship. The girl who learns of her fiance's infidelity may withdraw from all communication with him as a sign of her rejection. The commonly mouthed phrase of spurned lovers, "I'll never speak to him as long as I live" attests to this method of rejection. Likewise, persons who are seriously depressed often reduce their participation in group and interpersonal networks.[7]

The importance of feedback for interpersonal needs is also illustrated by the beneficial experiences people have when they are in isolation from others for a short period of time and in select circumstances. Moses, Paul, Mohammed, and Henry Thoreau all removed themselves for a period of time from communication transactions with others.[8] As a result, their religious and philosophic insights were considerably enhanced. They saw and discovered things that they would not have if they had remained in the continuing presence of others. The unfilled need for feedback made them temporarily more receptive to other experiences.

But if one is removed from human feedback for an extended period of time, the results are often harmful. Admiral Byrd, who was alone for six months in a small Antarctic hut, went there voluntarily to find some peace and quiet. After only three months, however, he became depressed and "felt a tremendous need for stimuli from the outside world, and yearned for sounds, smells, voices, and touch." Because he was deprived of transactions, he was losing his identity.[9] Once back in the company of persons, his identity was quickly reestablished.

The "mother-in-law syndrome" also illustrates the "need to receive feedback" point. The son-in-law, deeply concerned over a financial loss from a storm, says, "That was quite a storm. It ripped off half of my

[7] Jurgen Ruesch, *Disturbed Communication,* W. W. Norton, New York, p. 138.

[8] These examples are from Charles A. Brownfield, *Isolation: Clinical and Experimental Approaches,* Random House, New York, 1965, pp. 24–26.

[9] Ibid., pp. 13–14.

roof." She replies, "Yes, it was bad in our state, too. It was almost as violent as the monsoon of 1957. That was the year we took that nice vacation out West. We certainly had a good time. Have you traveled out West recently?" The mother-in-law has avoided giving direct responses to his major concern, the financial loss. Her tangential reply completely misses the point. The son-in-law expects a response to his message, but her "feedback" is only slightly related to it. After many similar experiences with her, he gets the impression that she really is not concerned about him because she always shifts the conversation to her own interests. Because we cannot not communicate, lack of response, or a tangential response, produces low confidence or hostility in the recipient.[10] All of us, student, teacher, fiancee, mother, or or son-in-law, need feedback.

Our need to receive feedback is pervasive, and our perception of feedback cues affects our communication behavior. For example, you undoubtedly prefer to communicate with some people and avoid others. Your perception of their feedback to you affects how often you communicate with them, how you express yourself when you are talking with them, and why you treat them as you do. In your attempts to fulfill your need for feedback, you may find that some feedback cues cause you to stutter and stammer. Other cues encourage you to keep talking, or perhaps restate in a different manner what you have said. You may find that some cues cause you to become silent or aggressive. Whatever the case, realization that you need feedback can give you insight into your own communication and aid you in understanding the communication behavior of others.

The Need To Give Feedback

The familiar cliche, "people need to be needed" highlights another important feedback principle. Not only does one person need other people, he needs to know that others need him. This resembles the third category of interpersonal needs, that is "control." Control refers to a need to feel that one is a responsible person successfully coping with his environment.[11] One way to realize fulfillment of this interpersonal need is to perceive that people care how you feel about them. The child who needed supportive feedback from his parents, for exam-

[10] Harold J. Leavitt and Ronald A. H. Mueller, "Some Effects of Feedback on Communication," in Dean Barnlund (Ed.), *Interpersonal Communication: Survey and Studies,* Houghton Mifflin, Boston, 1968, p. 258.

[11] Schutz, p. 13 (cited in footnote 5).

ple, also needs to know that his perceptions of his parents are important to them.

Most of us in our various roles need to give feedback. The student who can feel unique and worthwhile by perceiving feedback directed toward him must also feel that *others need his feedback* in their attempts to be unique and worthwhile. Examples of isolation from others illustrate the need to give, as well as receive, feedback. Dr. Alain Bombard spent 65 days alone in a small boat in the ocean. He was starved for communication and "wanted terribly to have someone who could confirm any impressions, or better still, argue about them."[12]

To prove that you, personally, have a need to give feedback and that this need affects your communication behavior, think about a time when you expressed your opinion about something to someone and it was apparent that they did not want your feedback. Or, think about communication transactions when someone was talking "at" you and not "with" you. You could tell that you were being talked "at" because all of your responses went unheeded. Most of us find these experiences very frustrating. We have a need to give feedback, and when another will not allow us that privilege, we find the communication transaction to be less than satisfying.

If you reflect about these experiences and understand your own need to give feedback, you may also begin to realize that other's have a need to give feedback, too. Do you give them the opportunity? The need to give feedback is an important need. It affects our communication behavior and that of others.

Thus, humans have a need for feedback—a need to *receive* feedback and a need to *give* feedback. By having the opportunity to receive and to give feedback, we can realize fulfillment of our interpersonal needs for inclusion, affection, and control. Understanding the feedback needs from our own perspective and from the perspective of others can assist us in facilitating and improving our communication relationships.

SOURCES OF FEEDBACK

Feedback, whether positive or negative, affects us differently depending on our relationship to the person giving it. Negative feedback from someone perceived as important causes anxiety. And the anticipation of unfavorable appraisals can measurably affect our state of mind.[13] That same feedback, from someone unimportant, can be easily

[12] Brownfield, p. 16 (cited in footnote 8).
[13] Harry Stack Sullivan, *The Interpersonal Theory of Psychiatry*, W. W. Norton, New York, 1953, p. 113.

dismissed or perhaps be perceived as positive. Similarly, positive feedback has differential effects. A husband complimenting his wife of 10 years, says, "Gee, honey you look great!" and he gets a yawn from her. If a stranger at a party that same night says he finds her attractive, she appreciates the compliment and she increases her liking for the stranger. She has come to expect positive feeback from her husband; therefore, although criticism from him might have a big effect, his positive feedback will not. Positive feedback from a stranger, though desired, is not expected; therefore, it has a noticeable effect.[14] You can easily visualize many other situations to demonstrate that your relationship to a feedback source has an impact on how you react to his comments.

EFFECTS OF FEEDBACK

Numerous studies have examined the effects that feedback has on a source. The research has focused on how feedback (1) improves the accuracy of message transmission, and (2) affects a source's speaking behavior.

One of the land mark studies investigated the effects of differing amounts of feedback on message transmission.[15] Students tried to construct geometric patterns described to them by instructors. The conditions were (1) zero feedback (instructors and students could not see each other or ask questions or make noise), (2) visible audience (instructor and students could see each other but no questions were allowed), (3) yes–no condition (audience could answer yes or no to instructor questions), and (4) free feedback (students had the freedom to ask questions and get information). The main results were that with greater degrees of free feedback, (1) task completion took more time, (2) the figures were drawn more accurately, and (3) the students felt more confident about their performance in completing the task. Feedback, therefore, makes for more accurate message transmission and more confidence in the task completion. It does, however, increase the amount of time necessary for task completion.

A series of experiments has also investigated the effects of feedback on the encoding process. Whether one is a speaker in a public speaking situation or a participant in an interpersonal communication encounter, his speaking is affected by the feedback he receives. Speakers make changes in the content of their speeches as a result of

[14] This example and analysis is from Elliott Aronson, "Who Likes Whom and Why," *Psychology Today* (August 1970), pp. 48–50, 74.
[15] Leavitt and Mueller, pp. 251–259 (cited in footnote 10).

perceived positive and negative feedback. They will alter the words used, and when the feedback is perceived as positive, make more opinion statements. Furthermore, the delivery is affected.

Speakers find negative feedback very disruptive. In a typical experiment, the audience has been trained to emit certain cues, but the speaker does not know they have been trained. When the speaker receives verbal "No's," head shakes, and other unfavorable cues from the audience, he becomes less fluent. He will stutter, repeat words and phrases, stumble and often say "Uh," and use incomplete sentences. And, he will say less at a slower rate. Positive feedback, on the other hand, encourages one to continue speaking and in a smoother manner.[16]

COSTS OF FEEDBACK

There are times when feedback is so "expensive" that all feedback channels must be blocked. As opportunity for feedback increases, the amount of time necessary for task completion increases.[17] Time can be an expensive commodity, especially in an organization where rapid decision making is necessary.

Another "expense" of feedback is that your decisions stand the risk of being altered when others are consulted. Hopefully, the altered decision is the best decision, but it will probably be different from the one you favored. The father, for example, who wants to take his family to Canada on a fishing trip for their annual vacation runs the risk of going to a coastal beach for a swimming trip if he consults his family and allows them to give him their feedback about the vacation plans. The same is true with the instructor who allows student feedback when planning course procedures. Whenever feedback is allowed, one runs the risk of decision alteration.

One needs to decide if (1) there is sufficient time to elicit feedback and (2) if the risks of decision alteration are sufficiently compensated for by the "good will" that is generated when those affected by a decision have a voice in the decision making. One large United States corporation had difficulty forcing its employees to follow company

[16] Reviews of numerous studies on feedback can be found in Mary Lou McCauliff, "A Descriptive Study of a Speaker's Response to Perceived Informative Feedback," unpublished M.A. Thesis, Central Michigan University, 1971; H. J. Ayers, "An Overview of Theory and Research in Feedback," paper presented to the International Communication Association Convention, Phoenix, Arizona, 1971; and James Carl Gardiner, "The Effects of Perceived Audience Response on Speaker Attitudes," unpublished Ph.D. Dissertation, Michigan State University, 1969.

[17] Leavitt and Mueller, p. 259 (cited in footnote 10).

safety regulations. After they gave the employees a voice in determining new safety policies, the employees followed the rules and personally policed all new employees to insure they followed the policies, too. People feel better about and are more committed to decisions they help formulate. But the father, employer, teacher, or whoever, has to be aware of the potential costs in time and ultimate decision alteration.

At the personal level, feedback can be quite expensive, too. In Chapter 2, we discussed individuals classified as underpersonal, undersocial, and abdicrat. In each case, we noted that the interpersonal communication arena is extremely threatening to them. The underpersonal individual, for example, has a strong need for affection. He is so afraid, however, that he will be rejected (receive negative feedback) that he avoids contact with others. To him the cost of receiving positive feedback is too high. He simply cannot afford the risk of receiving negative feedback in an attempt to get the positive feedback he so desperately needs. The same is true for the undersocial individual and the abdicrat. They would rather be alone than pay the costs for feedback. Each of us can probably recall instances when we felt that feedback was too threatening or expensive to warrant its existence. At times, it is much easier to prevent it or ignore it than to run the risk of receiving negative cues.

The personal communication process is permeated with feedback. The responses to our encoding behavior allow us to correct our messages and to know that others are involved in the transaction. As decoders, our feedback to others' encoding gives us a chance to influence their later encoding and can make *us* feel part of the transaction. Feedback, therefore, serves to link the participants in a communication transaction, because the heart of the process is people adjusting to others.

Exercises

1. Experiment with the "mother-in-law" syndrome. When you are talking with a friend, keep switching topics on him rather than continuing the discussion centered about his interests. What kind of reactions do you receive?
2. Make a listing of behaviors by others that are interpreted as positive or negative feedback in certain situations. Are some always interpreted the same way? Are some behaviors interpreted in opposite ways depending on the situation?
3. What exceptions to our thesis of the need for feedback can you

offer? Are there people who do not need feedback? Can you specify situations where giving feedback seems to hinder the fulfillment of the interpersonal needs?

4. Discuss the "gum flapper" and "dead pan" of Chapter 2 from the perspective of the need for feedback. Do they need or want feedback?

5. Observe a small group at work. Keep a record of all the cues that seem to be emitted in response to encoding behavior. Estimate the amount of total responses that could be classified as feedback. Who responds to whom, and why?

6. As an experiment, consciously ignore people who are trying to communicate with you. Do they go to extraordinary lengths to get your attention? Do they become angry? (After you get a reaction, explain to them what you were doing.)

7. Try, for one afternoon, not to talk to anyone. How does it affect you?

8. Give noticeable feedback where it is not expected, such as in certain classrooms or churches. What kind of response do you get? Do others' perceptions of you change when you give responses where they are not expected?

9. Your instructor will select a fellow student to describe some geometric designs to you under varying conditions. In the first condition (no feedback) he will face away from you. You are not allowed to ask any questions or make any responses as you try to reproduce the designs. In the second condition (limited feedback) he will face you and will observe your behavior as you reproduce the designs (but you still cannot ask him questions). In the third condition (free feedback), you are free to ask him questions as he describes the figures and he, of course, can answer the questions. At the conclusion of the experiment, see which condition (1) produced the most correct reproductions, (2) took the most time, and (3) was most satisfying to both the student describing the designs and the audience.

Suggested Readings

Charles A. Brownfield, *Isolation: Clinical and Experimental Approaches,* Random House, New York, 1965.

David C. Murray, "Talk, Silence, and Anxiety," *Psychological Bulletin,* April 1971, *75,* 244-260.

Alfred G. Smith (Ed.), *Communication and Culture,* Holt, Rinehart and Winston, New York, 1966.

Norbert Wiener, *The Human Use of Human Beings: Cybernetics and Society,* Houghton Mifflin, Boston, 1950.

Part III ▶   Constituent
Elements
of Oral
Communication

Chapter **9** ▶

The Sender's Influence: Source Credibility

Objectives

On completion of this chapter you should be able to:
1. Define source credibility.
2. Recognize that credibility is not an inherent trait of sources but is conferred on them by receivers.
3. Specify the dimensions of credibility.
4. See how credibility operates in the various communication arenas.
5. List some factors that affect credibility.
6. Distinguish between charisma and high credibility.

The source credibility variable has received more attention than any other single communication concept from the time of Aristotle to the present.[1] It is an important element in personal communication transactions, and it has a strong influence on opinion change.[2] In this chapter we will explicate the concept and discuss some of the research; it is remarkable that one notion has received so much attention and is still relatively difficult to understand.

[1] Many authors use the term *ethos* instead of source credibility.
[2] George A. Borden, *An Introduction to Human Communication Theory*, Wm. C. Brown, Dubuque, 1971, pp. 68–69.

SOURCE CREDIBILITY DEFINED

The first term to be clarified is "source." A source is an encoder who sends the message cues that we focus on for the purpose of description.[3] Source credibility is the degree of believability or acceptability a receiver gives to a source. The degree of believability or acceptability may range from high to low. Thus, source credibility is not a concept that is restricted to just "high" credibility sources.

Whether we are primarily sources or receivers, we are all concerned with source credibility. In the role of a source, each of us is concerned with his own image.[4] Also, as sources, what we perceive to be the credibility of our receivers (the "sources" who give us feedback) affects our communication behavior. In the receiver role, each of us is concerned with credibility because the amount of credibility we give to a source has an impact on our own responses to him. The information we receive is almost always colored by the feelings we have about the source of the information. He may be telling us the "truth," but if we do not trust him, we will not accept it. On the other hand, if we do trust him, we are much more reluctant to question the validity of the information.[5] Also, as receivers, the credibility that a source confers on us as "sources of feedback" will affect the way the source communicates with us.

DYNAMICS OF CREDIBILITY

It should be apparent from the above discussion that source credibility is a receiver phenomenon. According to Brooks, "the fact that thousands of years of study and more than thirty-five years of empirical research have brought little improvement to our understanding of the basis of source influence was due in part to a false assumption that source credibility is an inherent property of the speaker."[6]

The assumption that credibility is an inherent property of the speaker is incorrect. It denies the whole notion of process and individual differences in perception, attitudes, needs, and desires. Source credibility

[3] See, for example, Wallace C. Fotheringham, *Perspectives on Persuasion,* Allyn and Bacon, Boston, 1966, p. 261.

[4] Kenneth E. Andersen, *Persuasion: Theory and Practice,* Allyn and Bacon, Boston, 1971, p. 245.

[5] Borden, p. 58 (cited in footnote 2).

[6] William D. Brooks, *Speech Communication,* Wm. C. Brown, Dubuque, 1971, p. 163.

is a dynamic, not a static, notion. It is subject to constant reevaluation and change. In fact, it changes from receiver to receiver, from time to time, from topic to topic, and from setting to setting.

Receiver to Receiver

A source does not "possess" credibility; it is conferred upon him by his receiver(s).[7] Often we hear the statement, "He really has high credibility." Such a statement says more about the person making the statement than the person toward whom the comment is directed. A source simply does not *have* high credibility. Some people may evaluate him as a highly credible source; in fact, a large majority of people may evaluate him as such, but this does not mean that he *has* high credibility. In another's eyes, he may be a lowly credible source. For example, a college or university president may be perceived as highly credible by the board of trustees, the administration of his institution, the majority of his faculty members, most of the student population, and the general public. Whether he "has" high or low credibility cannot be measured, however, until he is confronted with a specific receiver(s). If the receiver is any of preceding, he will probably have high credibility. If the receiver is a leading campus radical or a faculty member who has recently been dismissed from his position, it is quite likely that he will have low credibility.

Time to Time

Source credibility changes from time to time in the same manner that it changes from receiver to receiver. Time changes can be seen both *during* a given communicative transaction (internal changes) and *between* various communicative acts (external changes).

Internal Changes

In any given communicative act, a communicator's credibility will constantly undergo changes that may be moderate, but are definitely changes. This changing status of source credibility demonstrates the transactional nature of communication. All cues during a communication transaction, that is, public, private, and behavioral (verbal and nonverbal) cues, affect our continual assessment of another's credi-

[7] Gerald R. Miller, *Speech Communication: A Behavioral Approach*, Bobbs Merrill, Indianapolis, 1966, p. 39.

bility. Empirical support for the varying nature of credibility is reported by Brooks in a summary of a series of studies. In these investigations, people were asked to evaluate a source with whom they were familiar, such as Malcolm X, James Hoffa, Richard Nixon, or Martin Luther King, Jr. They were then exposed to a brief recorded passage from one of the sources. After exposure to the brief passage, the people were asked to evaluate the sources again. Brooks summarized the results by stating, ". . . the results of these studies produce this limited conclusion: Audiences whose initial evaluations of speakers are clearly favorable or clearly unfavorable tend to shift in the opposite direction after a brief exposure to the source's recorded speech."[8]

This finding leads us to speculate that one's evaluation of a source changes throughout the communication situation. For description, the labels "pretransaction," "transactional," and "posttransaction" can be used to discuss the internal credibility changes.

Pretransaction credibility is a receiver's assessment of another person *before* a communication transaction begins. Determinants of pretransaction credibility may be our previous experiences, direct or vicarious, with the source; facts we know about the source, particularly those which provide us with information about his group memberships; knowledge of how others perceive the source; and the immediate stimuli leading to the actual communication transaction.[9] The college president we referred to earlier would automatically have some level of credibility conferred on him by some receivers before a given communication situation merely by virtue of his office and reputation. Status and reputation are two examples of many possible pretransaction determinants. Remember, however, although some of us may evaluate certain status and reputation elements in a positive way, others may evaluate them negatively.

Transactional credibility is a receiver's assessment of another person, produced *during* a communication transaction. Factors, such as language usage and tone serve to alter our perception of a person's pretransaction credibility.

Posttransaction credibility is a receiver's assessment of another person existing at the *completion* of a communication transaction. The changes from pretransaction to transactional credibility produce posttransaction credibility. Some refer to this concept as "source-message" interaction. That is, before a communication encounter, we have expectations about the potential source (pretransaction credibility). During a

[8] Robert D. Brooks, "The Generality of Early Reversals of Attitudes Toward Communication Sources," *Speech Monographs* (June 1970), *VII*, 154.

[9] Andersen, pp. 225–226 (cited in footnote 4).

communication encounter, our previous expectations serve as a basis of evaluation. Where our expectations are not fulfilled or are exceeded by the source, our assessment of the source's credibility changes (transactional credibility). All of these alterations become a basis on which we give our concluding assessment of the source (posttransaction credibility). Portions of this final image are activated in the receiver's mind and serve as *one* basis for the source's pretransaction credibility in the next communication encounter.[10] And, in that next encounter, the credibility will change again.

External Changes

As credibility changes *during* a communicative act, it also changes *between* communicative acts. A source's posttransaction credibility in one situation is only one determinant of his pretransaction credibility in the next encounter. As our own goals, desires, values, and knowledge change, our evaluations of other people change. What is admirable to us today may not be as admirable tomorrow. As we change, our attitudes, positions on issues, and methods of dealing with people change. We all undergo personal changes that affect our evaluations. The college president referred to earlier will be perceived differently by us two years from now than today—even if we are communicating with him in the same place and on the same topic.

Topic to Topic

Topical changes also alter perception and credibility. These changes, however, are less significant than the other changes we have discussed. For example, according to most people, especially nonsmokers, the United States Surgeon General is an extremely credible source on the topic of smoking and lung cancer. He probably is not perceived as quite so credible, however, on the topic of United States foreign policy. It is virtually impossible to be highly knowledgeable on all topics. Thus, when one is perceived as being less knowledgeable on one topic than on another, perception of his credibility should change. Some of us do, however, assess others as being highly credible on many divergent topics. If we are impressed by the status of "United States Surgeon General," per se, our perception of his credibility will be affected in all situations. This tendency to generalize credibility across many unrelated topics is called the "halo-effect." For example, if you have an extremely good biology teacher, you may perceive him as highly

---

[10] George A. Borden, Richard B. Gregg, and Theodore G. Grove, *Speech Behavior and Human Interaction*, Prentice-Hall, Englewood Cliffs, 1969, p. 200.

credible on many topics, such as civil rights, until he proves otherwise. Although credibility is influenced by topical changes, these changes may be quite minor.

Setting to Setting

Changes in setting alter our perception of another's credibility. Some of the reverence of a minister's words are lost, for example, in a fishing boat. Changes from one communication arena to another serve to alter credibility perceptions. We normally perceive a person's credibility differently on a one-to-one basis than in a public speaking situation. For example, think how a personal conference with a professor alters your perception of his credibility. After such a conference, your perception of him in the classroom will be different from before. You have all heard statements such as, "He's a pretty good guy once you get a chance to talk with him personally."

Thus, credibility is an unstable phenomenon. It changes like the wind. It is different after a communication act than it was before, it is different between communication acts, it is different from one topic to another, from one place to another, and most importantly it is different from one person to another. We do not "have it," it is "given to us" by others in a multiplicity of ways for many different reasons.

DIMENSIONS OF CREDIBILITY

Credibility in Public Speaking Settings

Aristotle suggested that source credibility is composed of three separate dimensions, character, sagacity (intelligence), and goodwill. Although the Aristotelian dimensions have been challenged, no one has denied the assumption that credibility has more than one dimension. Before we examine some of the specific ideas about the various components of source credibility, make a list of words that you would use in describing a person whom you perceive as highly credible in a given situation. What words do you come up with? Probably words such as knowledgeable, sincere, understanding, concerned, impressive, articulate, expert, and friendly. If you analyze your list, you may discover that most of the words can be placed under the three dimensions set forth by Aristotle.

Hovland, Janis, and Kelley speculate that a source's credibility consists of expertness, trustworthiness, and intention toward the receiver

Credibility Dimensions

Aristotle	Intelligence	Character	Goodwill
Hovland, Janis, and Kelley	Expertness	Trust-worthiness	Intention

Figure 1

as perceived by the receiver.[11] Notice how closely their speculations mirror Aristotle's ideas. "Expertness" is another word for intelligence, "trustworthiness" is related to character, and "intention toward the receiver" is another way of labeling perceived goodwill. Figure 1 shows the close relationship between the dimensions of Aristotle and Hovland, Janis, and Kelley.

Recently, with the use of computerized factor analysis, researchers have examined the dimensions more carefully, though perhaps not more accurately. Andersen found that two major dimensions were employed in making credibility judgments about sources. He identified these dimensions as evaluation and dynamism. It should be noted, however, that the respondents in the Andersen research were assessing "potential" sources. They were not actually exposed to messages delivered by the sources.[12] Figure 2 illustrates Andersen's research, as compared to previous theorizing.

Berlo and Lemert discovered three dimensions of source credibility. They labeled them "safety," "qualification," and "dynamism."[13] Notice how closely safety resembles the character dimension of Aristotle, the

[11] Carl I. Hovland, Irving L. Janis, and Harold H. Kelly, *Communication and Persuasion,* Yale University Press, New Haven, 1953, pp. 19–55.

[12] Andersen, pp. 221–222 (cited in footnote 4). The bipolar adjective scales that Andersen discovered that were descriptive of the evaluative dimensions were honest-dishonest, moral-immoral, fair-unfair, sympathetic-unsympathetic, good-bad, reasonable-unreasonable. Scales that were descriptive of the dynamism dimension were interesting-uninteresting, strong-weak, fast-slow, aggressive-nonaggressive, and active-passive. From this list, one can see that scales relevant to both character and intelligence went together to constitute Andersen's evaluative dimension. For example, honest-dishonest, moral-immoral, sympathetic-unsympathetic, and good-bad constitute a description closely related to character, whereas fair-unfair, and reasonable-unreasonable more closely resemble an intelligence or expertness dimension.

[13] James B. Lemert, "Dimensions of Source Credibility." Paper presented to the Association for Education in Journalism, August 26, 1963.

Credibility Dimensions

	Intelligence	Character	Goodwill	
Aristotle	Intelligence	Character	Goodwill	
Hovland. Janis, and Kelley	Expertness	Trust–worthiness	Intention	
Andersen	Evaluation			Dynamism

Figure 2

Credibility Dimensions

	Intelligence	Character	Goodwill	
Aristotle	Intelligence	Character	Goodwill	
Hovland, Janis, and Kelley	Expertness	Trust–worthiness	Intention	
Andersen	Evaluation			Dynamism
Berlo and Lemert	Qualification	Safety		Dynamism

Figure 3

trustworthiness dimension of Hovland, Janis, and Kelley, and a large portion of the evaluative dimension found by Andersen (Figure 3). Also, the qualification dimension is similar to the sagacity dimension forwarded by Aristotle, the expertness factor stated by Hovland, Janis, and Kelley, and the other portion of the evaluative dimension found by Andersen. The dynamism dimension duplicates the dynamism dimension set forth by Andersen. In a later study Berlo, Lemert, and

Credibility Dimensions

Aristotle	Intelligence	Character	Goodwill	
Hovland, Janis, and Kelley	Expertness	Trust–worthiness	Intention	
Andersen	Evaluation			Dynamism
Berlo and Lemert	Qualification	Safety		Dynamism
McCroskey	Authorita–tiveness	Character		

Figure 4

Mertz discovered that the dynamism factor was quite unstable and did not account for much of the overall source assessment.[14]

McCroskey, in an impressive series of studies designed to develop better credibility scales, found two dimensions. He labeled them as character and authoritativeness (Figure 4).[15]

Comparison of Credibility Dimensions

The two pieces of research, by Andersen and Berlo and Lemert, found dynamism as a "new" dimension of credibility. In McCroskey's research, however, dynamism did not emerge as a third dimension (Figure 4), because when the dynamism of a source was changed, it affected the other two dimensions. McCroskey found that a dynamic source was consistently perceived to be more competent, and usually more trustworthy, than a nondynamic source. He concluded that the dynamism of a source is important, but that it affects the other dimen-

[14] David K. Berlo, James B. Lemert, and Robert J. Mertz, "Dimensions for Evaluating the Acceptability of Message Sources," *Public Opinion Quarterly* (Winter, 1969–1970), *XXXIII*, 562–576. The scales that delineated the safety dimension were just-unjust, kind-cruel, honest-dishonest, and so forth. Some of the scales indicative of the qualification dimension were trained-untrained, qualified-unqualified, and informed-uninformed. The dynamism dimension was exemplified by such scales as aggressive-meek, emphatic-hesitant, and energetic-tired.

[15] James C. McCroskey, "Scales for the Measurement of Ethos," *Speech Monographs* (1966), *XXX*, 65–72.

sions of credibility, and, therefore, may not be a separate credibility dimension.[16] Figure 4 also demonstrates that the goodwill or intention toward the receiver dimension no longer appears, although it was set forth by Aristotle, and Hovland, Janis, and Kelley.

The lack of consistency between the goodwill and dynamism dimensions is, on the surface, very confusing. We attribute these inconsistencies to the ways in which the studies were conducted. The scales used to measure the dimensions of credibility in the research were constructed on an a priori basis. They were developed by having people describe qualities they liked or disliked in sources. The people were rating sources outside of any particular communication event. People were not exposed to a source in an actual communication transaction and then asked to describe the qualities they perceived in the source.

We have reason to believe that scales need to be developed specifically for the measurement of posttransaction credibility. Given the phenomenon of source-message interaction, there is a need to develop scales that assess a person's credibility *after* a communication transaction occurs. Such scales might (1) show a goodwill dimension emerging, and (2) demonstrate that dynamism is much more important than previously thought. Both goodwill and dynamism depend upon a transaction actually taking place. They might emerge if scales are designed to measure posttransaction credibility. In short, goodwill and dynamism are probably constituents of credibility in an oral interchange.

At any rate, there are at least two dimensions of source credibility that we as receivers in a public speaking situation, use to evaluate a source; those dimensions are character and authoritativeness. Only further research will illustrate whether we are correct about the importance of goodwill and dynamism.

Credibility from an Interpersonal Perspective

The preceding discussion of credibility dimensions was based on research done in the public speaking setting. When we look at credibility in other types of communication transactions, we can view the dimensions of credibility somewhat differently.

You will recall that every individual has three *interpersonal needs*: inclusion, control, and affection.[17] While the inclusion need does not

---

[16] James C. McCroskey, *An Introduction to Rhetorical Communication*, Prentice-Hall, Englewood Cliffs, 1968, pp. 60–61.

[17] William C. Schutz, *The Interpersonal Underworld*, Science and Behavior Books, Palo Alto, 1966, p. 13.

have a direct relationship to the credibility dimensions, control and affection do.

"Control" (the need to feel that one is a responsible person successfully coming to grips with his environment) is closely parallel to the authoritativeness dimension of credibility. The way to manifest control in a public speaking situation is to be perceived as knowledgeable. One's authoritativeness in a public speaking situation is comparable to his degree of control in an interpersonal event. In fact, it might even be hypothesized that the interpersonal need of control is what receivers see fulfilled by a speaker they perceive as knowledgeable.

"Affection" (the need to feel that the self is lovable) is related to the dimensions of goodwill or intention toward the receiver. Goodwill on the part of a speaker is probably a special type of interpersonal affection. The speaker has empathy for the audience members and has their best interests at heart—which is one way to show affection for them. While, in an interpersonal situation, it might be appropriate to say, "I love you," the public speaking setting will produce statements such as, "I want to do all I can for you."

It may be that each of us has dominant personal needs that become the basis of our evaluation of others in various communication situations. Perhaps our perception of a source's credibility in a public speaking situation is dependent on how we perceive the source with respect to **our own** needs of control and affection. Earlier in this chapter we asserted that to say "He really has high credibility," says more about the person making the comment than it does about the person toward whom it is directed. Perhaps the only way we will ever learn about how we evaluate others in communication will be first to understand our own dominant personal needs. For example, if you have a strong need for "control," then it is reasonable that you will hold another's "authoritativeness" as being extremely important. You may perceive an authoritative source as one who can help you achieve your own need for control.

The research on source credibility is seen in a new light when approached from an interpersonal communication vantage point. Interpersonal needs are closely parallel to the dimensions of credibility that exist in a public speaking situation. Since the public speaking situation is a special extension of interpersonal communication, it may be that interpersonal needs create the dimensions of credibility evaluation.

Credibility From a Mass Perspective

In the mass communication arena, a source who is popularly perceived as highly credible is often labeled "charismatic." Charisma is usually associated with a person who is perceived as highly credible by large numbers of people. Traditionally, authors in speech communication have made the following types of statements: "The best guess as to the nature of charisma is that it is the possession of many of the dimensions of credibility by a single individual and possession of those factors to a greater extent than is usual for the persuasive communicator."[18] "All through history there have been speakers whose words have swayed millions—Churchill, Hitler, Castro, Kennedy, King. The personal magnetism of such speakers is a quality called charisma."[19]

Some students attribute charisma to popular entertainers. Also, after John F. Kennedy's tragic assassination, it was common to hear students say, "No one can ever replace President Kennedy. None of the other national leaders has charisma like he had." Thus, many people believe that anyone who can collect a large circle of admirers has charisma.[20]

This is not an accurate understanding of charisma. The term charisma is not meant to be applied to a communicator in the mass communication arena, or, for that matter, to a communicator in any other arena. It is a concept that deals with a type of *leadership*, not necessarily the attributes of a communication source.

There are differences between charisma and high source credibility that need to be understood. Unless these differences are specified, charisma merely becomes a substitute label for high credibility conferred on a source with mass appeal. High source credibility does not explain the type of *total obedience* that followers give to a charismatic leader. The fact that sources with high credibility and leaders with charisma differ is quite easy to ascertain. Question: "Do all charismatic leaders have high source credibility?" Answer: "If a receiver believes that a leader has charisma, he will also think the leader is a highly credible source." Question: "Do all highly credible sources have charisma?" Answer: "Just because a receiver thinks a source is highly credible does not mean he will believe the source is a charismatic leader."

We noted earlier that source credibility fluctuates from receiver to receiver, topic to topic, time to time, and setting to setting. That is not necessarily the case with charisma. Charismatic sources completely control the attitudes of their followers. Followers give complete obedi-

---

[18] Erwin P. Bettinghaus, *Persuasive Communication,* Holt, Rinehart and Winston, New York, 1968, p. 117.

[19] John Hasling, *The Message, The Speaker, The Audience,* McGraw-Hill, New York, 1971, p. 53.

[20] A. Craig Baird, Franklin H. Knower, and Samuel L. Becker, *General Speech Communication,* McGraw-Hill, New York, 1971, p. 38.

ence to the charismatic leader.[21] To understand charisma, one must study a leader and his followers in a particular type of *social setting*.[22] Charisma, unlike high source credibility, is always a sociological happening. It can be said that the followers of a charismatic leader have "faith" in the leader, compared to the "respect" that a receiver confers on a source whom he perceives as highly credible.[23]

At the individual level, many of us have experienced the type of "faith" that followers have in a charismatic leader. This is especially true of children. Often a child will identify a person as an idol and give him blind obedience. The child may dismiss his own belief and value structure in an attempt to adopt his idol's behavior and beliefs. This type of happening at the individual level is quite common. You can probably identify such experiences in your own life.

Again, charisma is not just high credibility conferred on a source in the mass communication arena or on a source who has mass appeal. It is a unique product of a social system. We believe that high source credibility is the term that best describes sources who have appeal to receivers, regardless of the number of people appealed to or the arena in which the appeal is generated.

ENHANCING CREDIBILITY

We know that a source we perceive as highly credible will be more persuasive to us than a source we think of as lowly credible.[24] Since

[21] Max Weber, *The Theory of Social and Economic Organization,* trans. by A. M. Henderson and Talcott Parsons, Oxford University Press, 1947, New York, p. 359.

[22] James L. Winckler, "Charisma: An Empirical Explication," unpublished M. A. Thesis, Central Michigan University, 1971, p. 3.

[23] In the academic sense, charisma is meant to symbolize a type of authority rather than the attributes of a communicator. Charisma is a type of authority that centers solely upon an individual leader. It can be contrasted to "legalism," when a leader gets his authority from formal rules or laws, and "traditionalism," when a leader gets his power from precedent. True charismatic authority only emerges during a period of social upheaval. In such a situation, the charismatic leader becomes the source of stability and is the recipient of the "faith" of his followers who give him total, blind obedience. Only leaders such as Christ, Ghandi, Lenin, Hitler, and a few select others have been charismatic. For further development of these ideas, see Max Weber, "The Three Types of Legitimate Rule," trans. by Hans Gerth, in Amitai Etzoni (Ed.), *A Sociological Reader in Complex Organizations,* Holt, Rinehart and Winston, New York, 1969, p. 6; and Peter Blau, "Critical Remarks on Weber's Theory of Authority," *American Political Science Review* (1963), *LVII,* 308.

[24] A summary of research findings that support this belief is found in Kenneth Andersen and Theodore Clevenger, Jr., "A Summary of Experimental Research in Ethos," *Speech Monographs* (1963), *XXX,* 59–78. Another summary is found in Kim Giffin, "The Contribution of Studies of Source Credibility To A Theory of Interpersonal Trust in the Communication Process," *Psychological Bulletin* (1967), *68* (2), 104–120.

high credibility is more desirable than low credibility in all communication arenas, a critical question is, "How can I improve the way others initially perceive me?"

Pretransaction Credibility

Earlier in this chapter we discussed the determinants that controlled a receiver's initial evaluation of another's credibility. We stated that pretransaction credibility is determined by factors such as previous experiences with the source, facts we know about the source, knowledge of how others perceive the source, and the immediate stimuli that lead to an actual communication transaction. Your ideas on improving these various factors are as good as ours, but we will try to name a few anyway.

We noted that the previous experiences with the source can be direct or vicarious. Exposing potential receivers through mass communication, rumor mill, or any other possible way, to the experiences and accomplishments of a person should enhance their image of him. This approach is often used in the political arena. A political candidate going to Cozad, Nebraska or Upton, Wyoming to discuss the issue of beef imports with the local public wants high pretransaction credibility. Therefore, a definite attempt is made to expose the people to the candidate's previous "ranching" experiences or exposures to farm problems. This is one way the voters can be led to believe the candidate is well aware of their plight. Thus, they can identify with the candidate's past experiences.

A source's group memberships also give us information about him. Group memberships do more to influence a person's attitudes than any other single determinant; therefore, knowledge of a source's group affiliations can tell us a great deal about him. A source is wise when he tells his judges (receivers) about his memberships in groups that uphold the values cherished by his receivers.

Research has demonstrated that the credibility of the sponsor or person who introduces the source influences the pretransaction credibility of the source.[25] In other words, if you are going to be exposed to

[25] See, for example, James C. McCroskey and Robert E. Dunham, "Ethos: A Confounding Element in Communication Research," *Speech Monographs* (1966), *XXXII*, 456–463; Paul D. Holtzman, "Confirmation of Ethos as A Confounding Element in Communication Research," *Speech Monographs* (1966), *XXXII*, 464–466; Ivan G. Harvey, "An Experimental Study of The Influence of the Ethos of the Introducer as it Affects The Ethos and The Persuasiveness of The Speaker," unpublished Dissertation (Michigan, 1968), in Andersen, p. 225 (cited in footnote 4).

a certain receiver(s) it will be helpful for you to be sponsored or introduced by a person (or institution) respected by the receivers.

The immediate stimuli leading to an actual communication transaction can be manipulated to a certain degree by a source. As discussed in Chapter 6, things such as lighting and spatial arrangement have some effect on a person's perceptions. This knowledge can assist a source in making some relatively important decisions when preparing for a communication event. Also relevant is the research on communicator attractiveness.[26] Research indicates that attractiveness does influence perception of credibility. Although a communicator has no immediate control over his physical stature, he can change his appearance and thereby increase his attractiveness.

All the research and examples presented in the preceding discussion were geared primarily toward the public speaking situation, but the same speculations should hold true for other communication arenas. In the interpersonal situation, one does not normally premeditate massive communication strategies, but similarities do exist. The similarities are especially noticeable in a "planned" interpersonal situation. For example, you may want to attend a state university but your father wants you to attend the private liberal arts college from which he graduated. In this case, you will probably plan a communication strategy to use as you think about convincing your father of the appropriateness of your preference. All of the notions concerning previous experiences, facts about you, sponsorship effects, and immediate stimuli can aid you in enhancing your pretransaction credibility in that situation. These factors do not appear as crucial in spontaneous interpersonal transactions; but, more likely than not, you can observe these same techniques in use by yourself and your associates.

Transactional and Posttransaction Credibility

Transactional and posttransaction credibility judgments are ultimately the most important. Recently, researchers have moved away from studying the effects of pretransaction credibility and are examining how credibility interacts with the factors present in actual communication transactions. Message variables such as fear appeals, adaptation cues,

[26] See, for example, Judson Mills and Elliot Aronson, "Opinion Change as a Function of The Communicator's Attractiveness and Desire to Influence," *Journal of Personality and Social Psychology* (1965), *I*, 173–177; Franklin S. Haiman, "An Experimental Study of the Effects of Ethos in Public Speaking," *Speech Monographs* (1949), *XVI*, 190–202; Robin N. Widgery and Bruce Webster, "The Effects of Physical Attractiveness Upon Perceived Initial Credibility," *Michigan Speech Association Journal* (1969), *4*, 9–19.

and evidence usage have been examined. These topics are treated extensively in Chapter 10.

CONCLUSION

Source credibility is important for both the source and the receiver. The research indicates how important it is from a source's standpoint. Only you, however, know how important it is to you as a receiver. Since you spend more time being a receiver than a verbal source, it is your responsibility to understand how and why your perception of a person affects the way you relate to him. It would be nice if all of us either failed to evaluate other people and accepted messages on their face value, or evaluated others solely on the basis of objective merits—but, we do not. Assessments of another's character and authoritativeness (and perhaps goodwill) are reasonable assessments. But are our "reasonable assessments" *reasonable*? Each person has to answer this question for himself. Both intuition and research indicate that most of us base our judgments on seemingly unimportant elements. For example, how important is another's appearance? What does appearance actually have to do with the merit of an idea presented in a message? How important is race? In one study it was found that although a white engineer was not more effective than a black engineer when communicating about a mathematics topic, a white dishwasher was much more effective than a black dishwasher on the same mathematics topic.[27] How relevant are other factors such as word choice, group affiliations, delivery, and social status? While reading this book, you can probably sit there and say, "Those factors are not important at all!" That is merely wishful thinking. They are important. We as receivers make them important.

Exercises

1. Construct a hypothetical public speaking situation in which you are to be the speaker. Analyze the various potential determinants of pretransaction source credibility. What strategies would you use to enhance your pretransaction credibility in that situation? Present your ideas orally to the class.
2. On what bases do you evaluate people in communication situations? Which bases are relevant? Which are irrelevant? Do the

[27] Elliot Aronson and Burton W. Golden, "The Effect of Relevant and Irrelevant Aspects of Communicator Credibility on Opinion Change," *Journal of Personality* (1962), *30* (2), 135–146.

bases change from one type of communication situation to another? Why? Answer these questions, and then have the class divide into several small groups of five or six people and discuss the various evaluation bases mentioned.

3. To help you understand how people evaluate the credibility of others, place yourself in two divergent roles. First, make yourself as physically unattractive as possible. How do people react to you? The next day, make yourself as physically attractive as possible. Do people react differently? Report your experiences to the class. What insights have you gained about relevant and irrelevant considerations in evaluation?

4. Conduct a mini-experiment in which you introduce an acquaintance to two different groups of your associates, for example, to a group of friends who live with you, or to a group of friends from one of your classes. In one situation, introduce your acquaintance as a highly competent, respectable individual. In the other situation, attribute him with many undesirable characteristics. What types of differences in acceptance did you observe? How did pretransaction, transactional, and posttransaction credibility evaluations develop? How important was pretransaction credibility? (*Note:* In this exercise you will probably have to tell the two groups about your associate before they actually come into contact with him so that the introductions are not embarrassing.) Report your insights to the class.

5. Do some unstructured thinking. Do you evaluate friends on some bases that do not fall within the credibility dimensions mentioned in this chapter?

6. Draw up a list of situations where the dynamism of a speaker seems to be an important element in determining his effectiveness.

Suggested Readings

Kim Giffin, "The Contribution of Studies of Source Credibility To a Theory of Interpersonal Trust in the Communication Process," *Psychological Bulletin,* 1967, *68* (2), 104-120.

Carl I. Hovland, Irving L. Janis, and Harold H. Kelley, *Communication and Persuasion,* Yale University Press, New Haven, 1953.

James C. McCroskey, *An Introduction to Rhetorical Communication,* Prentice-Hall, Englewood Cliffs, 1968.

Gerald R. Miller, *Speech Communication: A Behavioral Approach,* Bobbs Merrill, Indianapolis, 1966.

James L. Winkler, "Charisma: An Empirical Explication," unpublished M. A. Thesis, Central Michigan University, 1971.

Chapter 10

Message Construction: Advice for Verbal Encoding

Objectives

On completion of this chapter you should be able to:
1. Understand that attempts to adapt a message to an audience are affected by source credibility.
2. Anticipate the effects that internal message organization patterns have on message acceptance.
3. Question the traditional distinction between logical proof and emotional proof.
4. Speculate about the limits of message discrepency that a decoder can tolerate.
5. Recognize the reasons for using evidence in a message.
6. Understand the interaction between levels of source credibility and levels of fear used in an appeal.
7. Distinguish between one-sided and two-sided messages.
8. Make informed decisions on potential message construction strategies.

As transactants in communication, we all need to create messages as well as receive them. We have already noted that both verbal and nonverbal messages play a part in communication, but we have not offered specific suggestions for you as an encoder of those messages. Because of limited research findings on nonverbal messages, not much advice can be given on how to encode those messages. Verbal messages, however, have been the subject of much thought and research. Both ancient scholars and contemporary behavioral scientists have focused their attention on verbal messages.

The traditional speech course emphasizes the verbal message. In fact, much of the emphasis in such a course is on the process of message construction.[1] The assumption behind traditional speech training is that different messages have different effects. Recently, several scholars have applied their scientific methodology to that assumption and are trying to determine what types of messages produce which effects in receivers. Some of the research findings are limited in usefulness and are inconclusive. Hopefully, however, a concentrated look at the research on messages will allow you to put the findings into perspective.

Messages can be examined in several ways: Presently four major message elements have received extensive experimentation: (1) adaptation (the things a source does in a message that makes the receivers believe the source is referring directly to them); (2) position (the side a source takes on a given issue); (3) types of appeals (the elements a source puts in a message to convince his receivers that they should do what he says); and (4) organization (the pattern of arrangement a source uses to make his message understandable and acceptable).

MESSAGE ADAPTATION

Most public speaking textbooks specify different kinds of speeches for different audiences and occasions. The ways one should prepare for speeches to inform, persuade, and entertain are supposedly quite diverse.[2] The choice of language, the type of appeal, and the general tone of the speech should be adapted to the specific audience.

An adapted speech should be more effective than one not tailored to the specific audience.[3] Some authors maintain that a speech can be partially adapted before a speaking situation and it can also be adapted during it. The speaker's prior audience analysis should provide a good

[1] The five "canons" or principles of rhetoric are the component parts of message creation and presentation. They are (1) invention, the gathering of ideas and arguments; (2) disposition, the arrangement of the materials and ideas you have brought together; (3) style, casting the verbal message in appropriate words; (4) memory, knowing your speech materials; and (5) delivery, the act of uttering your verbal message.

[2] It is our belief that the distinctions among types of speeches are unfruitful.

[3] See for example, Patrick O. Marsh, *Persuasive Speaking: Theory, Models, Practice,* Harper and Row, New York, 1967, pp. 90–96; and John F. Wilson and Carroll C. Arnold, *Public Speaking As a Liberal Art,* 2nd Ed., Allyn and Bacon, Boston, 1968, pp. 125–138.

"Where's that speech I use when I depart from my prepared text?"

Figure 1

starting point for understanding the audience; and, once the listeners begin reacting to his speech, he should make further necessary adaptations. A speaker should be able to adjust to audience responses and alter his messages accordingly.

The difficulty with all of the above generalizations is that they have received little systematic study. How *is* one to adapt his speech? What specific things should he do? What are the variables that produce an effect on an audience? If the situation is too formal and "stiff," should a communicator depart from his text and deliver his remarks extemporaneously? Whatever the tactic, he should concentrate on how the audience will perceive his attempts at adaptation. The gentleman in Figure 1 obviously thinks the audience will see his "unprepared speech" as superior to his "formal remarks."

A study by Wenburg directly dealt with some of the message adaptation questions.[4] Subjects in the study were given three types of messages about a persuasion course offered on campus. Some subjects were given an "unadapted" message (a factual description of the

[4] John R. Wenburg, "The Relationships Among Audience Adaptation, Source Credibility and Types of Message Cues," unpublished dissertation, Michigan State University, 1969.

persuasion course), others a "moderately adapted" message (that indicated why students *in general* should take persuasion), and the remaining students were presented an "adapted" message (that emphasized why students *in their present course* should take persuasion). The messages were adapted to the students by referring to group memberships. It was discovered during the study, however, that the students perceived the level of adaptation differently than what was expected. The students were then classified according to how *they* perceived the amount of message adaptation. One of the principle findings of the study was that perceptions of source credibility determined the perceptions of adaptation. This set the groundwork for a follow-up investigation.

Wenburg and Miller further demonstrated what the Wenburg research had indicated.[5] If a message is given by a highly credible source, the receivers perceive it as adapted, even if it makes no reference to their membership group. And, an "adapted" message given by a lowly credible source is perceived as *less* adapted than an "unadapted" message presented by a highly credible source. In both studies, the effects of credibility canceled the attempts at message adaptation. If you are lowly credible to your receivers, your attempts to adapt your message will probably go unnoticed. For example, if you are transacting with another person he will probably perceive your messages as more adapted to him if he believes you are highly credible instead of lowly credible. Messages that are perceived as "adapted," no matter in which arena one is transacting, will be more effective than messages perceived as "unadapted." Unfortunately, sufficient research has not been conducted so that a list of adaptation techniques can be constructed. We can say, however, if you are perceived as highly credible, your attempts to be concerned for the other person and to apply your statements to him will probably be appreciated and effective. If, on the other hand, you are perceived as lowly credible, you will have to work very hard to get your messages to be perceived as adapted.

MESSAGE DISCREPANCY

If you are going to present a persuasive message to an audience and you know the audience's position on the issue; what position should you take to get maximum effects? Should you represent your position as

[5] John R. Wenburg and G. R. Miller, "Effects of Source Credibility on Perceptions of Message Adaptation Level," unpublished study, Department of Communication, Michigan State University, 1969.

close to theirs as you can, as slightly discrepant (different), or as far from their position as possible? The more discrepant your message is, the more it is judged as less fair, less informed, less logical, less grammatical, and less interesting.[6] As your message falls farther and farther from the audience's position, its influence decreases.

As with message adaptation, the perceived credibility of the source delivering the message affects the impact of the message. If the source is highly credible, he can advocate a position farther removed from a receiver's position than can a lowly credible source. In both cases, however, there are limits to the degree of position difference the receivers can tolerate and still be persuaded. Past those limits, the receivers will reject the message, discredit the source, and not be persuaded.[7] Unfortunately, we cannot specify what the limits of effectiveness are for a specific speech in a given situation. But if a source is undecided about whether to "come on strong" and present an extreme position, or temper his views somewhat, the answer is easy. The less discrepant message will, in most cases, effect more attitude change in the recipients than an extreme message.

Most of us seem to understand that a slightly discrepant message is more appropriate and effective than is a greatly discrepant one, especially in interpersonal communication. Usually, when we are going to meet with someone and take a "hard line" on an issue, once we are in the presence of another person, we "soften" our position and take a less extreme stand. The presence of the other person or persons influences us and we realize that taking an extreme position is neither appropriate nor effective. In our personal transactions, therefore, we can affect the other person or persons more if our position on the issue is different, but not greatly different, from theirs.

TYPES OF APPEALS

Message position and levels of adaptation are not the only message elements that are important to a potential encoder. The specific types of appeals he uses may alter the impact of the message.

[6] William J. McGuire, "The Nature of Attitudes and Attitude Chance," in Gardner Lindsey and Elliot Aronson (Eds.), *The Handbook of Social Psychology*, 2nd Ed., *III,* Addison-Wesley, Reading, 1969, p. 221.

[7] There is a considerable body of literature dealing with the discrepancy issue. McGuire, pp. 223–224 (cited in footnote 6) provides a summary of the major issues. See also Chapter II.

Logical and Emotional Appeals

Aristotle observed in the *Rhetoric* that one can use three main types of appeals.[8] One can rely on ethos (credibility), logos (logical argument), and pathos (audience emotions). All of these appeals can be used to generate believability for the message. Aristotle's concepts have had an enduring impact. Most college and university catologs list logic as a separate course not related to the study of ethos or pathos. Speech Communication departments offer courses in persuasion that concentrate on winning an audience's favor by *emotional appeals,* and courses in argumentation that concentrate on the development of *logical argument* to win acceptance.

While the distinctions between ethos, pathos, and logos may be fruitful for teaching purposes, there is serious doubt that they are distinct kinds of appeals. Who can say that ethos or communicator credibility is independent of logical or emotional appeals? If you vote for a candidate because you believe he has high credibility, is that not a "logical" decision?[9]

The difficulty of separating emotional and logical appeals becomes apparent when one considers a receiver's perceptions. Presumably, receivers are able to distinguish between logical and emotional appeals. Lefford's research, however, shows that students could not tell if a pattern of argument was logical.[10] If the students agreed with the conclusion of the reasoning, they tended to perceive the reasoning as valid even though it was not. If, on the other hand, the students disagreed with the conclusion of the reasoning, they could detect the faulty reasoning.

Bettinghaus found that students who were trained in formal logic could detect faulty reasoning better than students who had not received training. Even the trained students, however, made more errors in detecting invalid reasoning when they agreed with the conclusion of the reasoning.[11]

The recognition of faulty reasoning is dependent on factors other than the type of appeal. Miller, in a review of research literature, notes that things such as attitudes, cognitive style, and prior training influence

[8] His general categories of appeals are artistic (those that come from within the speech), and inartistic (those that are external to the speech).

[9] McGuire, p. 202 (cited in footnote 6).

[10] A. Lefford, "The Influence of Emotional Subject Matter on Logical Reasoning," *Journal of General Psychology* (1946), *34*, 127–151.

[11] Erwin Bettinghaus, *Persuasive Communication,* Holt, Rinehart and Winston, New York, 1968, p. 158.

one's judgment of logical appeals.[12] Ruechelle found that neither experts nor students could consistently classify materials as logical or emotional.[13] And, finally, "logical" and "emotional" appeals do not, even when they have been classified by experts, seem to have different effects.[14]

Interestingly enough, even though audiences cannot distinguish between logical and emotional appeals, if they expect "logical" appeals in a formal speaking situation, the speaker would be wise to give the appearance of using logic. One study indicated that if the speaker uses such phrases as "Isn't it only logical . . ." the receivers will tend to see the message as logical rather than emotional.[15]

A precise distinction between logical and emotional appeals has not yet been made clear. For those who desire a distinction, McGuire has suggested the following difference. Logical appeals are those that argue for a belief by presenting evidence in favor of it, while emotional appeals consist of evidence that stresses the consequences to those who adopt or fail to adopt a given belief.[16] This approach gives a fresh perspective on emotional and logical appeals. It may enable us to distinguish clearly among the types of appeals in the future.

Evidence Usage

The use of evidence is the cornerstone of any persuasive appeal. Communicators are constantly advised to "get the facts" before trying to persuade an audience. The United States Congress traditionally allocates funds for "study and research" so that policy decisions can be based on evidence. And, we as recipients often reject a communicator's ideas because the evidence for his position is shallow.

Evidence can consist of (1) audience beliefs and knowledge, (2) opinions and assertions the speaker makes, and (3) opinions and facts stated by others.[17] Primarily, when a speaker "gathers evidence," he is pulling together facts and opinions that others have set forth. He hopes to increase the impact on his message by the citation of authorities.

[12] Gerald R. Miller, "Some Factors Influencing Judgments of the Logical Validity of Argument: A Critical Research Review," unpublished manuscript, Michigan State University, 1968.

[13] Randall C. Ruechelle, "An Experimental Study of Audience Recognition of Emotional and Intellectual Appeals in Persuasion," *Speech Monographs*, (1958), *XXV*, 58.

[14] For a review of the findings of numerous studies, see Stanley F. Paulson, "Social Values and Experimental Research in Speech," *Western Speech* (1962), *XXVI*, 133–139.

[15] Bettinghaus, p. 159 (cited in footnote 11).

[16] McGuire, p. 202 (cited in footnote 6).

[17] James C. McCroskey, *An Introduction to Rhetorical Communication*, Prentice-Hall, Englewood Cliffs, 1968, pp. 93–97.

Research indicates that if the speaker is perceived as highly credible, citing extensive evidence is not necessary. It does not increase his credibility or generate more receiver attitude change than if he does not use it. But, the use of evidence does make the attitude changes last longer. If a source is moderately or lowly credible to his receivers, the citation of evidence can enhance both his credibility and the effects of the message. If a lowly credible source's delivery is poor, however, evidence usage will not produce either effect.[18]

The student of oral communication would be well advised to use evidence. In a typical classroom assignment, for example, students do not normally perceive the student giving a speech as an authority on his selected topic, so evidence usage becomes necessary. The prestige of the sources you cite will help to dispose favorably your listeners to both you and your message. Even if your credibility is high, the use of evidence will help sustain the attitude changes your message produces.

Most of us have a tendency to use evidence in our communication transactions. Notice, for example, that in the interpersonal arena, it is common for you to quote an authority or cite statistics when you are trying to convince someone you are correct on a certain issue. Although you may not offer the evidence with the same degree of formality in the interpersonal or small group arenas that you would in the public speaking arena, the automatic tendency to rely on evidence usage is apparent in all communication arenas. In many cases, you may find that you admire or respect the person who always seems to "back-up" his position with examples and other types of evidence.

Fear Appeals

A speaker may use fear appeals in his message to produce anxiety in the receivers. Many believe that anxiety will make an audience more susceptible to a message. A fear appeal is an appeal that stresses the harmful consequences that will befall a receiver if he does not adopt the recommended course of action. Typical fear appeals that have been used in the fear appeals research are (1) the threat of tooth decay if one does not practice good dental hygiene, and (2) the possibility of bodily injury from failure to use seat belts.[19] A high fear appeal

[18] James C. McCroskey, "A Summary of Experimental Research on the Effects of Evidence in Persuasive Communication," *The Quarterly Journal of Speech* (1969), *55*, pp. 169–176.

[19] Irving I. Janis and Seymour Feshbach, "Effects of Fear-Arousing Communications," *Journal of Abnormal and Social Psychology* (1953), *XLVIII*, 78–92; and Leonard Berkowitz and Donald R. Cottingham, "The Interest Value and Relevance of Fear Arousing Communication," *Journal of Abnormal and Social Psychology* (1960), *LX*, 37–44.

forcefully stresses the dangers and consequences of tooth decay, but a milder appeal makes little mention of the harmful consequences.

High fear appeals can arouse anxiety that can produce two opposite effects in the receiver. The fear may motivate him to change his attitude because of the harmful consequences of not changing it, or it may cause so much anxiety that it interferes with his attitude change. The crucial issue is whether a communicator can achieve more attitude change using a high or a low amount of fear in his message. Overall, and without regard to other factors such as source credibility, most findings indicate that a high level of fear appeal is more effective than a low amount of fear.[20] When other factors are considered, however, the basic finding must be tempered. It has been noted, for example, that high fear appeals are more effective if the source is perceived as highly credible. Lowly credible sources are usually more effective using a low fear appeal.[21]

Factors other than source credibility also seem to influence the effects that levels of fear appeals produce. As the importance of the topic to the receiver increases, the level of fear that can successfully be employed can be increased.[22] Furthermore, the receiver's ability to successfully cope with anxiety-producing messages alter the effects of high and low fear appeals. Those able to cope with the anxiety are more persuaded by high fear appeals while "avoiders" (those who cannot cope with anxiety) are more moved by low fear appeals.[23]

These basic findings are far from conclusive. The search for appeals that are anxiety producing to all individuals and the search for techniques of differentiating more clearly between high and low amounts of anxiety are continuing. One suggested universal fear appeal is "social disapproval." Persons tend to be anxious when one person is criticizing another.[24] With the new research being conducted in this area,

[20] Howard Leventhal, "Findings and Theory In The Study of Fear Communications," in Leonard Berkowitz (Ed.), *Advances in Experimental Social Psychology, 5,* Academic Press, New York, 1970, pp. 119–186.

[21] Murray A. Hewgill and Gerald R. Miller, "Source Credibility and Response to Fear-Arousing Communication," *Speech Monographs* (June 1965), *XXXII,* 95–101; Gerald R. Miller and Murray A. Hewgill, "Some Recent Research on Fear-Arousing Message Appeals," *Speech Monographs* (November 1966), *XXXII,* 377–391; and Frederick A. Powell and Gerald R. Miller, "Social Approval and Disapproval Cues in Anxiety-Arousing Communications," *Speech Monagraphs* (June 1967), *XXXIV,* 152–159.

[22] C. William Colburn, "Fear-Arousing Appeals," in Howard H. Martin and Kenneth E. Anderson (Eds.), *Speech Communication: Analysis and Readings,* Allyn and Bacon, Boston, 1968, p. 220.

[23] Ibid., p. 223; Leventhal, p. 137 (cited in footnote 22).

[24] Gerald R. Miller, "Studies on the Use of Fear Appeals: A Summary and Analysis," *Central States Speech Journal* (May 1963), *XIV,* 117–124.

perhaps in the near future we can supply more precise prescriptions for the use of fear appeals.[25] But for now, if your audience perceives you as highly credible, you will change their attitudes more if you use a high fear appeal than if you use a low fear appeal. If your credibility is low, a high appeal may bring opposite results, so your fear appeal should not be strong.

The search for a universal fear appeal such as social disapproval has special applications to interpersonal and small group situations. It was noted earlier that the most effective transactions occur in these arenas. If social disapproval is universally fear arousing, then it follows that social disapproval expressed in interpersonal and small group settings can be a fearful thing. For example, if a good friend of yours strongly disapproves of something you have done, his rebuke could be quite distressing, and might prevent you from doing it again. Your friend is highly credible to you, therefore, his "high fear" appeal will motivate you to change. As distressing as personal criticism is, it may be an effective way to change a person's attitudes or behavior because it arouses fear. One does run the risk of "using too much fear." This is often the case when some parents constantly threaten or disapprove of their children or teachers constantly approach their students from a fear perspective. Constant threat or disapproval from a single source will probably, in the long run, become ineffective. A recipient of continual fear appeals from a given source will probably get to the point where he begins to refuse to accept the fear approach. One might reason, "You are always threatening or disapproving of me and I'm getting tired of it. I am simply going to refuse to listen to these appeals." Consequently, even though the research shows that in many cases high fear appeals and social disapproval are effective, one should use low fear and social approval at times.

One-Sided and Two-Sided Messages

Political candidates and soapbox orators are always faced with a basic decision when arguing for their favored postion on an issue. Will they be more effective if they present both sides of the issue, or should they ignore the arguments on the opposing side? Receivers who have not previously been exposed to the arguments prefer a two-sided

[25] Leventhal, pp. 159–181 (cited in footnote 22); Irving L. Janis, "Effects of Fear Arousal on Attitude Change: Recent Developments in Theory and Experimental Research," in Leonard Berkowitz (Ed.), *Advances in Experimental Social Psychology 3*, Academic Press, New York, 1967, pp. 166–224.

presentation.[26] Presenting both sides and refuting the opposite side seems to be the most effective technique under most conditions. If the receivers are poorly educated, and initially in favor of your position, however, you can generate more attitude change with a one-sided presentation.[27] But, these same receivers might be exposed to the opposing arguments later; for safety, you should try to counter those future arguments. As a persuader, you have less to lose if you "cover your flanks" by presenting a two-sided message. That way, you establish your own position and make the receivers negatively predisposed to the opposing views.[28]

Conclusion Drawing

In the final stages of your persuasive arguments, should you explicitly state your conclusion or let the audience draw their own? The vast majority of the evidence indicates that you should state your conclusion for the audience. By giving an explicit final statement to your position, you lessen the chance of receiver confusion. You not only need to lead the horse to water, you also have to push his head under to make sure he drinks.[29] So, when concluding your message, make your stand explicitly clear to the receivers.

MESSAGE ORGANIZATION

In organizing your message, there are two basic and entirely different considerations. First, how does your overall message fit within the context of the communication situation? If there is more than one speaker, are you the first speaker, last speaker, or in an intermediate position? Second, regardless of the specific communication event, how is your own message organized internally?

External Organization: Order of Presentation

If two sides of an issue are presented, does speaking first or last give you an advantage? In a trial, for example, does the prosecution

[26] Jonathan L. Freedman and David O. Sears, "Selective Exposure," in Leonard Berkowitz (Ed.), *Advances in Experimental Social Psychology 2,* Academic Press, New York, 1965, p. 85.

[27] C. I. Hovland, A. A. Lumsdaine, and F. D. Sheffield, *Experiments in Mass Communication,* Princeton University Press, Princeton, 1949; For a summary, see Arthur R. Cohen, *Attitude Change and Social Influence,* Basic Books, New York, 1964, p. 3; and McGuire, pp. 210–211 (cited in footnote 6).

[28] Note the discussion of innoculation effects in Chapter 12.

[29] McGuire, p. 209 (cited in footnote 6).

have an advantage because it presents evidence and arguments before the defense does? Early research on this question led to the formation of the *law of primacy*. It appeared that the source who spoke first could already have persuaded the audience to his side and an equal amount of argument from the other side would have less of an effect.[30] Subsequent research, however, demonstrated that sometimes there is a *recency* effect (the one who goes last has an advantage); and often times there is neither a primacy nor recency effect.[31] It does appear that if the initial source can get the receivers to make a public commitment (take a stand supporting his position in front of other people), then the opposing side is at a disadvantage.[32] Making a public commitment seems to reinforce the stand one takes on an issue and makes him less receptive to opposing arguments. But, in the usual situation where both sides of an issue are being presented, there is no opportunity for the first speaker to elicit a public commitment. For all practical purposes, we conclude that the law of primacy is not general. Speaking first does not give you an inherent advantage so you need not be too concerned about your speaking order.

Internal Organization

Many persons ponder over how to organize the arguments within their speech. Should one put his strongest argument last so it leads to a climax, or should he present his strongest argument first? Presenting your most important argument first has the advantage of arousing interest; but, it might also alienate the audience. Saving your best argument until the end can give a sense of building to a conclusion, but the listeners may be bored by that time. While the research shows that neither arrangement is consistently superior to the other, if you have three or more arguments, do not put the strongest argument in the middle.[33] Put your strongest argument either at the beginning or end.

As a source, you will get a better response to your message if you develop a need for your solution before you actually present the solution. Salesmen have recognized this principle for a long time. You have to "whet the appetite" before supplying the "food for thought." One of

[30] F. H. Lund, "The Psychology of Belief, IV, The Law of Primacy in Persuasion," *Journal of Abnormal and Social Psychology* (1925), *XX*, 183–191.

[31] C. I. Hovland (Ed.), *The Order of Presentation to Persuasion,* Yale University Press, New Haven, 1957; McGuire, p. 215 (cited in footnote 6); Cohen, pp. 9–11 (cited in footnote 27).

[32] Cohen, p. 10 (cited in footnote 27). See also Chapters 12 and 13 for a consideration of the role of commitment in persuasion.

[33] McGuire, p. 214 (cited in footnote 6); Bettinghaus, p. 153 (cited in footnote 11).

the most influential public speaking textbooks gives these steps to use in persuading an audience: (1) get their attention, (2) show the need, (3) satisfy the need with a solution, (4) visualize the results of the solution for them, and (5) try to get action from them on the solution.[34] The utility of such a scheme has been demonstrated many times. You will get better results by creating a need and then satisfying it instead of using the reverse order.[35]

RELATED MESSAGE VARIABLES

There are numerous other message variables. For example, the style of the language probably has some impact on how a message is received. "Birds of a feather flock together" gives a much different impression than saying "Ornithological species of identical plummage habitually congregate in the closest possible proximity." If appropriate to the situation, the use of metaphor can enhance the effectiveness of the speech. In one study, for example, the phrases "wiretapping is a one-way window," "the phone is a confession box," and similar methaphorical language enhanced the effectiveness of a persuasive speech on wiretapping.[36]

When presenting an argument, one has a choice of "opinionated" or "nonopinionated" language. Saying, "I believe that the United States should withdraw its troops from Viet Nam," is nonopinionated language usage, while "only a warmonger would oppose the withdrawal of United States troops from Viet Nam" is opinionated. An opinionated statement not only states your position, but rejects the positions of those who disagree with you.[37] If your audience is neutral on the issue, you can change their attitudes more by using opinionated arguments. If, however, the audience members are opposed to your position, using opinionated language is less effective than nonopinionated language. When the audience has views that oppose your own, "coming on

[34] Alan H. Monroe and Douglas Ehninger, *Principles of Speech Communication,* Scott, Foresman, Glenview, 1969, pp. 258–277.

[35] Cohen, p. 12 (cited in footnote 27); Paul F. Secord and Carl W. Backman, *Social Psychology,* McGraw-Hill, New York, 1964, p. 144.

[36] Nelson Lamar Reinsch, Jr., "An Investigation of the Effects of the Metaphor and Simile in Persuasive Discourse," *Speech Monographs* (June 1971), *XXXVIII* #2, 142–145.

[37] R. Samuel Mehrly and James C. McCroskey, "Opinionated Statements and Attitude Intensity as Predictors of Attitude Change and Source Credibility, *Speech Monographs* (March 1970), *XXXVII,* 47.

strong'' and using opinionated language will only serve to alienate them and cause less attitude shift than a milder approach.[38]

Message variables may receive more extensive study in the future. Since the message is the binding element in a communication transaction, its central role should be pursued further. At this point, one might say a source is more effective if (1) the receivers think he has adapted his message to them, (2) he advocates a position not totally at odds with them, (3) uses evidence, (4) uses a high fear appeal if he is highly credible and a low fear appeal if he is not, (5) presents two-sided messages, (6) draws conclusions rather than leaving that to the audience, (7) creates a need for a solution before presenting one, (8) uses appropriate language, and (9) uses opinionated language only when he is communicating with people who either already agree with him or have no strong opinion.

Keep in mind that the research findings on the impact of message variables were found mostly within the public speaking arena. As we stated, however, many of the principles can be applied to the other arenas of the personal communication process. Regardless of the communication arena, whenever someone is encoding messages, the message variables are operable. Verbal messages, whether planned in advance or entirely spontaneous, can be analyzed. An awareness of the encoding choices we make and an understanding of the effects of message elements will aid us in all our personal communication transactions.

Exercises

1. Give two speeches that contain the same content to the class. In one speech, follow the advice given in this chapter for message construction, and in the other, disregard the suggestions. Which speech was better received? Why?
2. Collect sample public speeches that had differing degrees of success. Analyze the types of appeals they contained. What inferences can you draw about the relationship between a message and its effects?

[38] The effects of credibility and use of opinionated language has been examined in Gerald R. Miller and Jon Lobe, "Opinionated Language, Open-and-Closed-Mindedness and Response to Persuasive Communications," *Journal of Communication* (1967), *XVII*, 333–341; Gerald R. Miller and John Basehart, "Source Trustworthiness, Opinionated Statements, and Response to Persuasive Communication," *Speech Monographs* (1969), *XXXVI*, 1–7.

3. Look at political campaign speeches from the perspective of message discrepancy. Do the most successful speeches advocate major or minor changes in the receiver's attitudes?
4. Have a salesman make his sales presentation to the class or to some representatives of the class. What sequence of internal organization does he use? Does he try to stimulate the need before he presents the solution? Also, notice what other variables in the situation seem to affect his success.
5. As a class, list the characteristic elements of "emotional" and "logical" messages. Then select some speeches that you all classify as either emotional or logical. If you are all able to agree, then compare the speeches sentence by sentence and note the defining characteristics of each type of appeal.
6. As an observer, try to classify message variables that acquaintances use in interpersonal transactions. Can you find examples of fear appeals, message adaptation, use of evidence, and the other variables mentioned in this chapter? Do you find message variables that have not been discussed in this chapter?

Suggested Readings

Erwin P. Bettinghaus, *Message Preparation: The Nature of Proof,* Bobbs-Merrill, Indianapolis, 1966.

Theodore Clevenger, Jr., *Audience Analysis,* Bobbs-Merrill, Indianapolis, 1966.

Paul D. Holtzman, *The Psychology of Speaker's Audiences,* Scott, Foresman, Glenview, 1970.

Patrick O. Marsh, *Persuasive Speaking: Theory, Models, Practice,* Harper and Row, New York, 1967.

Glen E. Mills, *Message Preparation: Analysis and Structure,* Bobbs-Merrill, Indianapolis, 1966.

Alan H. Monroe and Douglas Ehninger, *Principles of Speech Communication,* Sixth Brief Edition, Scott, Foresman, Glenview, 1969.

Chapter *11* ▶
Processing Messages: The Role of Decoding

Objectives

On completion of this chapter you should be able to:
1. Discuss selected personality variables that have been used to explain the decoding process.
2. Briefly summarize the theory of ego-involvement and specify how it attempts to explain decoding.
3. State the underlying assumption of all the consistency theories.
4. Explain, by the use of the consistency theory models, the tension that exists in some communication transactions.
5. List the possible ways one can reduce psychological inconsistency.

Communication can be viewed from various perspectives. For example, we have just finished looking at the source and the message as two important constituent elements. Regardless of the particular vantage point one takes, a third constituent element of the process is *always* present. That element is the receiver or decoder. The receiver is the core of the process, because all the other elements depend on his perceptions and interpretations. Therefore, understanding the way receivers decode messages is crucial to knowledge of the communication process.

PERSONALITY VARIABLES

Numerous theories have been advanced to explain how a person interprets incoming messages and reacts to them. Early theorists looked at receiver personality variables as the primary determinants of how a message is received. Personality variables are those aspects of the self that do not change from one situation to another. An "attitude" is not considered a personality variable because it varies from topic to topic and is often easily changed. But a person's intelligence, self-esteem, and sex, to name only a few, are personality variables. They are qualities a person brings to *every* communication encounter. Theoretically, these qualities should have some effect on the way a person decodes messages.

Intelligence

Generally, an intelligent person should be less moved by a persuasive message than a person of low intelligence. The more intelligent person should be more critical of a message than the less intelligent person; therefore, the more intelligent person should be harder to persuade. The research demonstrates that if the message that the "intelligent" and "unintelligent" persons receive contains unsupported generalizations or irrelevant arguments, the intelligent person, because of his critical abilities, is less influenced. On the other hand, if the persuasive message relies on impressive arguments with abundant support, highly intelligent receivers will be influenced more.[1] Therefore, contrary to expectations, there appears to be no consistent relationship between intelligence and the ease by which a person can be persuaded. Intelligence as a personality trait is not a good predictor of a person's susceptibility to persuasion.[2]

Self-Esteem

A person's attitude about himself, his self-esteem, appears to be related to persuasibility. As we would predict, individuals who have low self-esteem or confidence are easier to sway than those who are highly

[1] Paul F. Secord and Carl W. Backman, *Social Psychology*, McGraw-Hill, New York, 1964, p. 169.
[2] Carl I. Hovland and Irving L. Janis, "General Persuasibility," in Howard H. Martin and Kenneth E. Andersen (Eds.), *Speech Communication*, Allyn and Bacon, Boston, 1968, p. 252.

confident. Not only are low self-esteem persons easier to persuade, but they tend to conform more to the demands of others.[3] The low self-esteem person conforms more and is easier to persuade because he has little confidence in his own personal opinions. He readily discards his own opinions when presented with conflicting opinions from others. This is especially true if he perceives the source to have high self-esteem.

A person with high self-esteem has greater confidence in his personal opinions and is not as threatened when confronted with conflicting opinions. As a result, he is less susceptible to persuasion. You can probably observe the effects of self-esteem among your acquaintances. People who have great confidence in their own abilities are not as susceptible to changes of attitude as are those who are unsure of themselves.

Sex

The sex of a message receiver affects persuasibility. In general, it appears that women are more easily persuaded than men. The research shows that among first grade children, there are no persuasibility differences between boys and girls. But by the time they have reached adolescence, girls are easier to persuade than boys.[4]

One explanation of this finding is that our society expects and teaches females to be submissive and nonaggressive while males are expected to be self-assertive. An alternate explanation is that women pay more attention to verbal messages, and are, therefore, more susceptible to persuasive messages.[5] Or, it may be that the issues used in these studies were more important to men than women.[6] Regardless of the specific explanation of the greater persuasibility of females, the finding seems to hold in a variety of circumstances. As the women's liberation movement progresses, these current research findings will probably become more inaccurate. The notion of women as submissive and nonaggressive is becoming rapidly outdated.

Numerous other searches for personality factors associated with per-

[3] Secord and Backman, p. 170 (cited in footnote 1); Hovland and Janis, p. 248 (cited in footnote 2), a complex persuasive message alters the results and when such a message is used, no relationships are found between self-esteem and persuasibility; William J. McGuire, "The Nature of Attitude and Attitude Change," Gardner Lindzey and Elliot Aronson (Eds.), *Handbook of Social Psychology, III,* Addison Wesley, Reading, 1969, p. 250.

[4] Hovland and Janis, p. 252 (cited in footnote 2).

[5] McGuire, p. 251 (cited in footnote 3).

[6] Kenneth E. Andersen, *Persuasion,* Allyn and Bacon, Boston, 1971, p. 92.

suasibility have been conducted. Attempts have been made to relate "neurotic defensiveness," "ability to fantasize," and "isolation from others" to persuasibility, but they have not been successful. Only weak associations between these and other selected personality traits and persuasibility have been observed.[7] If better measures of personality variables were available, perhaps persuasibility would be found to be related to them. For example, it is reasonable to assume that if parents force their young children to agree with them, these children later in life will be easier to persuade than children who are encouraged to develop their own opinions and make their own decisions. The research dealing with parental control and persuasibility has, however, been plagued with problems of measuring the degree of parental control. Therefore, a reasonable proposition relating another personality trait to persuasibility goes unproven.

Dogmatism

Dogmatism, not usually considered a personality variable, has a lot in common with those traits. A person's dogmatism, his degree of rigidity or flexibility in approaching people, is supposedly a stable trait. If a person is dogmatic in his hatred of Jews he is unyielding to other views and carries his position from situation to situation. Regardless of the people present or the evidence presented to show why he should not hate Jews, he is "closed-minded" on the issue. Conversely, it is assumed that an "open-minded" person is not dogmatic; his views are subject to change.

One's degree of dogmatism can, under certain circumstances, affect his persuasibility. The dogmatic person puts a great trust into people who have authority over him. As a result, dogmatic people tend to be highly susceptible to persuasion attempts from sources they perceive as authoritative. A lowly dogmatic person is not as authority oriented. He listens more closely to the substances of a message; as a result, he is not necessarily persuaded by sources he perceives as authoritative. In summary, a highly dogmatic person is generally more difficult to persuade because his thinking is closed on most issues. He is, however, vulnerable to authoritative sources. A lowly dogmatic person is generally easier to persuade because he is willing to listen to new positions.[8] The lowly dogmatic person, however, must be convinced by the

[7] Hovland and Janis, pp. 250–251 (cited in footnote 2).

[8] Milton Rokeach, *The Open and Closed Mind,* Basic Books, New York, 1960; Applications of dogmatism to communication can be found in Erwin P. Bettinghaus, *Persuasive Communication,* Holt, Rinehart and Winston, New York, 1968.

substance of a message. Just because an authority says something is no indication that the lowly dogmatic person will agree with it.

Studies that have tried to predict a decoder's persuasibility based on his degree of dogmatism have had some problems showing consistent findings. While some research demonstrates a relationship between dogmatism and persuasion, other studies do not. Thus, dogmatism cannot be relied on too heavily as an explanatory variable of persuasion. Although it sounds reasonable to state that highly dogmatic receivers are difficult to persuade unless confronted with a source they perceive as authoritative and that lowly dogmatic receivers listen to the substance of a message, the research evidence is not conclusive.

Personality Traits versus A Functional Approach

One of the difficulties of trying to predict persuasibility from personality traits is that the notion behind "traits" is that they do not vary from one communication situation to the next. To expect to find relationships between traits and persuasibility that are always true regardless of the communication context is asking too much. A single trait of a receiver surely cannot be a completely accurate guide to his decoding process. The interrelationship of numerous elements in a communication situation makes the examination of a single personality variable an incomplete approach. In every communication transaction, all the elements are bound together.

Some of the more contemporary theories of the decoding process try to account for more than receiver personality trait elements of a communication transaction. Ego-involvement theory, for example, tries to make predictions about a receiver's responses that depend on the receiver's strength of feeling about a specific topic. Consistency theories try to account for a decoder's responses by examining the receiver's feelings about the message, source, other people present, and their feelings about the message. Both of these approaches try to account for many elements of the communication situation.

THE THEORY OF EGO-INVOLVEMENT

Ego-involvement is the label given to "a person's strength of feeling on an issue." Ego-involvement theory assumes that if you know how strong or intense a person's feelings are on a topic, you will be able to predict how he will react to persuasive messages on that topic. If you personally have an intense attitude about a topic, or if the topic is important to you, you are said to be highly ego-involved in it. Basically, the theory predicts that highly ego-involved persons are more difficult to persuade than lowly involved individuals.[9]

To predict the effects of high and low involvement, you must know a person's reactions to various positions on a controversial issue. Each of us (1) has his own position on an issue, (2) finds some of the other stands on the issue acceptable, and (3) rejects some of the other stands on the issue. If, for example, you favor school integration, you will find Supreme Court decisions that support integration acceptable. But you will reject the position taken by a segregationist. The range of positions you will accept on a given topic is called your "latitude of acceptance," while the range of positions you will not accept on that topic is labeled your "latitude of rejection." A persuasive message that advocates a position that falls within your latitude of acceptance is actually perceived by you as being closer to your own position than it really is. Conversely, a message that advocates a position that is within your latitude of rejection is actually perceived as being more distant from your own position than it really is.[10]

If you are highly involved in an issue, the theory predicts that you will have a larger latitude of rejection than if you are lowly involved. Therefore, when you are exposed to a persuasive message that deals with a topic on which you are highly involved, the chances that you will reject the position of the message are increased. Lowly involved receivers have a large latitude of acceptance and a small latitude of rejection. Thus, when you are lowly involved in a topic, a message position has a better chance of being accepted. Therefore, in general, a person who is highly involved in an issue is less susceptible to persuasion than a lowly involved person. Put simply, if a topic is important to you, you are less likely to have your opinion changed than if you are lowly involved in it.

Clearly, a person's ego-involvement in an issue seems to influence the amount of attitude change he will undergo when presented a mes-

[9] The basic notion of ego-involvement can be found in Muzafer Sherif and Carl I. Hovland, *Social Judgment,* Yale University Press, New Haven, 1961; C. W. Sherif, M. Sherif, and R. E. Nebergall, *Attitude and Attitude Change,* W. B. Saunders, Philadelphia, 1965; and Carolyn W. Sherif and Muzafer Sherif (Eds.), *Attitude Ego-Involvement and Change,* John Wiley, New York, 1967; For excellent summaries of the theory and subsequent research see Chester A. Insko, *Theories of Attitude Change,* Appleton-Century-Crofts, New York, 1967; and Charles A. Kiesler, Barry E. Collins, and Norman Miller, *Attitude Change: A Critical Analysis of Theoretical Approaches,* John Wiley, New York, 1969.

[10] This phenomenon is called assimilation-contrast.

sage position with which he disagrees.[11] Furthermore, level of ego-involvement affects the ability of two persons to reach agreement when they are in disagreement, and it influences one's desire to communicate with someone who holds a different position on the issue.[12] Recent evidence indicates that ego-involvement theory may have some weaknesses, but it still offers a unique perspective on how decoders react to persuasive messages.[13]

COGNITIVE CONSISTENCY THEORIES

The cognitive consistency theories also look at many elements in a specific communication transaction in order to predict a receiver's response.[14] All of the consistency theories view the decoder as only one part of a particular communication event.

The basic assumption underlying psychological consistency theories is that each of us tries to maintain a state of internal balance. *We strive to maintain internal consistency among our personal beliefs, feelings, and actions*.[15] Several theories that rely on this basic assumption have been introduced. They all have different names, but each is based on the assumption that a person needs internal, psychological balance. Terms that are commonly applied to a balanced state of mind are "consistency," "balance," "congruence," and "consonance." Each of the various theories is unique, but they all assume that a person is more comfortable in a balanced state of mind than in an imbalanced state of mind. Some of the theorists believe that balance "automatically follows" any awareness of imbalance or inconsistency. Others argue

[11] Kenneth K. Sereno, "Ego-Involvement, High Source Credibility, and Response to a Belief-Discrepant Communication," *Speech Monographs* (1968), *XXXV*, 478–481.

[12] Kenneth K. Sereno and C. David Mortensen, "The Effects of Ego-Involved Attitudes on Conflict Negotiation in Dyads," *Speech Monographs* (1969), *XXXVI*, 8–12; C. David Mortensen and Kenneth K. Sereno, "The Influence of Ego-Involvement and Discrepancy on Perceptions of Communication," *Speech Monographs* (1970), *XXXVIII*, 127–134.

[13] William W. Wilmot, "A Test of The Construct and Predictive Validity of Three Measures of Ego-Involvement," *Speech Monographs* (August 1971), *XXXVIII*, 217–227. and William W. Wilmot, "Ego-Involvement: A Confusing Variable in Speech Communication Research," *Quarterly Journal of Speech* (December 1971), *LVII*, 429–436.

[14] In fact, one could easily classify ego-involvement as a consistency theory. Ego-involvement, like all the consistency theories, states that man is basically a rational being.

[15] William J. McGuire, "The Current Status of Cognitive Consistency Theories," in Shel Feldman (Ed.), *Cognitive Consistency: Motivation Antecedents and Behavioral Consequences,* Academic Press, New York, 1966, p. 1.

that balance, instead of following automatically, is reached purposefully as a result of a "drive" that is as basic as the drive to reduce hunger.[16]

A great deal of research has been generated by these theories. We will briefly review some of the theories in an attempt to describe how they explain the ways in which receivers decode messages.

Heider's Balance Theory

The first consistency theory which was systematically developed was Heider's Balance Theory.[17] Heider developed a P-O-X model in which P stands for one person, O stands for another person, and X represents an object or issue (see Figure 1).

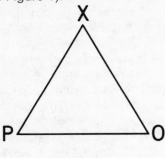

Figure 1

Basically, Heider's notion was that if person P likes person O and person O likes object X, person P will tend to like object X, also (Figure 2). The theory considers P's attitudes toward O and X and it considers O's attitudes toward X. As you can see in Figure 2, if P's attitude toward O is favorable, it is represented by a plus sign (+). If P's attitude toward O is unfavorable, it is represented by a minus sign (−). The same is true with respect to P's attitude toward the object or issue X. If P's attitude is favorable, it is represented with a +; but if it is negative, it is represented with a −. O's attitude toward the object or issue X is represented in the same manner. For clarity, we will briefly review the eight possible + and − combinations among the P-O-X relationships. (Notice that *anytime* you have three +'s or two −'s, the P-O-X relationship will be balanced. If you have three −'s or two +'s, the P-O-X

---

[16] Herbert W. Simons, "Persuasion and Attitude Change," in Larry L. Barker and Robert J. Kibler (Eds.), *Speech Communication Behavior: Perspectives and Principles,* Prentice-Hall, Englewood Cliffs, 1971, p. 238.

[17] Fritz Heider, "Attitudes and Cognitive Organization," *Journal of Psychology* (1946), *21,* 107–112.

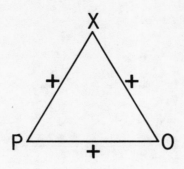

Figure 2

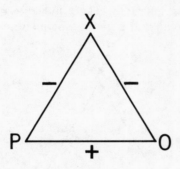

Figure 3

relationship will be unbalanced). As you examine the figures, imagine that you are discussing a recent movie with your instructor in this course. Let P represent you, let O represent your instructor, and let X represent the movie.

The situation represented in Figure 2 is balanced. You (P) like your instructor (O), and you liked the movie (X). Your instructor (O) liked the movie (X), too.

The situation represented in Figure 3 is also balanced. You like your instructor, but you disliked the movie. Your instructor, however, disliked the movie, also. There is balance because someone you like disliked something that you disliked.

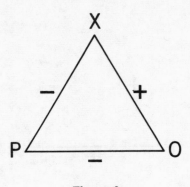

Figure 4

In the situation represented by Figure 4, you dislike your instructor and the movie. Your instructor liked the movie. Since you dislike your instructor, you remain in balance because he liked something you disliked.

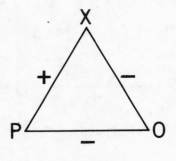

Figure 5

The situation represented in Figure 5 is similar to that in Figure 4. The instructor you dislike did not like the movie you liked. Therefore, no imbalance is created.

We do not always exist in a state of balance. Figure 6 represents a situation that is unbalanced. It is unbalanced because you dislike your instructor and he disliked something that you also disliked. We are more comfortable when people we dislike think differently about issues than we do.

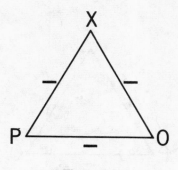

Figure 6

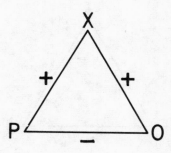

Figure 7

The relationship represented in Figure 7 is also unbalanced. You liked the movie, but so did the instructor you dislike.

The situation pictured in Figure 8 is unbalanced because the instructor you like disagrees with you about the movie—you liked it and he disliked it. We are uncomfortable when someone we think highly of disagrees with us.

The situation represented in Figure 9 is unbalanced for the same reasons as Figure 8. We want to agree with people toward whom we feel favorable.

In summary, Heider stated that in interpersonal relations we are in a state of balance if people we like have the same attitudes we do about objects or issues. Also, we are in a state of balance if people we dislike have different attitudes than we do about those objects and issues.

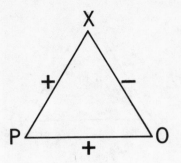

Figure 8

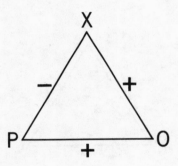

Figure 9

Symmetry Theory

Newcomb, in his symmetry theory, applied the Heider balance theory more directly to communication encounters.[18] His model contains A, B, and X elements. A and B are two communicators and X is an object or topic of the message. Newcomb was concerned with the direct relationship that exists between the two individuals (A and B) and their individual perceptions of matters treated in a communication.[19] He extended Heider's theory by developing the notion of "strain toward

---

[18] Theodore M. Newcomb, "An Approach to the Study of Communicative Acts," *Psychological Review* (1953), *60,* 393–404.

[19] Howard H. Martin and Kenneth E. Andersen, *Speech Communication: Analysis and Readings,* Allyn and Bacon, Boston, 1968, pp. 12–13.

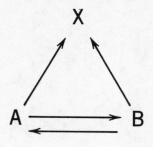

Figure 10

symmetry." Such "strain" leads to a similarity of attitudes when two people communicate about an object or issue.[20] Figure 10 represents Newcomb's basic model.

If a person (A) is attracted to another person (B), he wants to be like that other person. If A and B disagree about an object or issue (X), there will be a strain to bring their attitudes closer together (symmetry). The amount of the strain depends on (from A's viewpoint) the intensity of A's attitude toward X and the amount of attraction A has for B. As the intensity of A's attitude toward X increases or the amount of attraction A has for B increases, the potential amount of strain will increase. Also, the probability of A communicating with B increases and the likelihood of attitude change occurring increases. Thus, A and B's attitudes about X will be more similar after a communicative act than they were before. This kind of symmetry strain is to be expected if A and B are to remain in balanced states of mind when they are communicating with each other.

Congruity Principle

The principle of congruity is a refinement of Heider and Newcomb's theories.[21] It deals with the *direction* and *amount* of attitude change that will result from an unbalanced communication encounter. The basic model (Figure 11) is similar to the others we have discussed except its labels are P-S-O. P is the person whose attitude is subject to change, S is the source of a communication to person P, and O is the object or issue of S's message.

[20] Robert B. Zajonc, "The Concepts of Balance, Congruity, and Dissonance," in Kenneth K. Sereno and C. David Mortensen (Eds.), *Foundations of Communication Theory,* Harper and Row, New York, 1970, p. 185.
[21] Charles E. Osgood, George J. Suci, and Percy H. Tannenbaum, *The Measurement of Meaning,* University of Illinois Press, Urbana, 1967.

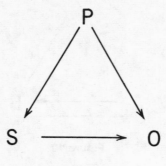

Figure 11

The same variations with +'s and −'s, which were discussed in Heider's theory, apply to this model. In this model we are most concerned with S's message (S→O). Degrees of relationships, which are more refined than simple +'s and −'s, are specified in this theory. As a source's message changes in position, P's attitudes toward the source and toward the message topic will change.

The amount of P's attitude changes toward the source and message topic are dependent on the strength of his initial (pretransaction) attitudes toward the two. For example, consider yourself to be person P and imagine that person S is the President of the United States. The President (S) is the source of a message about foreign policy (O). You greatly admire the President and are slightly opposed to our foreign policy. The congruity principle would say that when the President (S) makes a statement favoring our foreign policy (O), both your attitude toward the President (S) and your attitude toward foreign policy (O) will change. Your attitude toward the President will become less favorable because he is speaking in favor of a policy you oppose. At the same time, your attitude toward foreign policy will become more favorable after the President speaks than it was before because someone you admire spoke in favor of a policy you oppose. According to the congruity principle, although your attitude toward the President and toward foreign policy will both change, the amounts of change will not be equal. Since your attitude against foreign policy is not as strong as your attitude of admiration for the President, your attitude toward foreign policy will change more than your attitude toward the President will. Basically, then, the congruity principle says that to achieve a balanced situation, both of person P's attitudes have to change, with the more intense or strongest attitude changing the least.

The congruity principle contains many intricate details for calculating the strength of and degree of change of attitudes. This simplified explanation, however, should provide you with a basic understanding of how the theory works and how it differs from the other consistency theories that have been presented.

Dissonance Theory

The consistency theory that has generated the most systematic research is dissonance theory. This theory is similar to the others presented because it rests on the same assumption of a personal need for a balanced state of mind. It differs from the others, however, in two important ways. First of all, it is a post-decision theory. Put simply, dissonance or imbalance is created *as a result of making decisions or choices* in which one alternative is selected at the expense of another alternative. Secondly, it is a "drive" theory, in that consonance (balance) is something one *actively seeks*. Attitude change following an imbalanced situation does not automatically follow, one actively strives for it.

According to the theory, dissonance occurs when the obverse of one element follows from the other. For example, (1) you like to smoke, but (2) smoking causes lung cancer. The undesirable (lung cancer) follows from the desirable (smoking). Two elements in such direct opposition, when realized, create dissonance. Dissonance theory then describes what happens *after* dissonance is created. The underlying notions of the theory are:

(1) The existence of dissonance creates tension and we will be motivated to reduce that psychological tension (drive to reduce imbalance);
(2) When dissonance exists, we try to reduce it and we avoid situations which would increase it (selective exposure);
(3) The greater the dissonance, the greater the tension to reduce it;
(4) The amount of dissonance depends on (a) the importance of elements, and (b) the relationship between them.

The two elements can be perceived as irrelevant to each other (no dissonance), consistent with each other (no dissonance), or inconsistent with each other (dissonance).

Given that we prefer a balanced frame of mind, what do we do with messages in order to (1) retain balance or (2) regain balance if an imbalance is created? Chapter 7 described how we have a tendency to selectively attend, perceive, retain, and perhaps expose ourselves to messages. Each of these selectivity notions is related to the consistency theories. We prefer a state of balance and thus we have a tendency to perceive things in such a way that our balance is not disturbed. If our internal balance is disturbed, however, how do we rectify the imbalance? Dissonance theory gives us a description of possible alternative behaviors in which we can engage following the creation of imbalance. For example, when we are exposed to a communication that is disturbing, we may (1) criticize the source of the message; (2) decide that our disagreement with the source is not very important; (3) bolster our position by seeking additional information or persons who support it; (4) misperceive the source's position (selective perception); (5) compartmentalize (convince ourselves that the inconsistent positions are not relevant to each other); (6) attempt to persuade the source that his position is wrong; or (7) change our attitudes so they are consistent with the source's.[22] And there are other alternatives. For example, we can (1) repress the inconsistent message (put it out of our mind, refuse to think about it) or (2) bear it (consider the inconsistency a virtue).[23] This list of possible alternative behaviors should help you understand the difficulty of actually changing another person's mind about a particular issue. All of us protect ourselves when we decode messages. Even if we do come to grips with conflicting messages and actually alter our attitudes, there is good chance that we will not alter our actual behaviors.[24]

These ideas should be valuable to you as a communication source. You need to understand the difficulty of (1) actually "communicating" your position to recipients and (2) successfully changing their attitudes and behaviors. What can you do as a speaker to guide your receivers to select the desired response? How can you actually get receivers to listen to *your* position and evaluate it without thinking less of you, or diminishing the importance of your ideas? Unfortunately, we cannot give you a set of answers to resolve these communication problems. The biggest weakness of all the consistency theories is that although they specify possible ways of reducing imbalance, they do not help us predict which method of reduction a given receiver(s) will select. The alternative methods of reduction are convenient for the person experiencing imbalance, but they make it difficult for the communicator.

Although we cannot specify exactly which method or combination of methods to reduce dissonance a given receiver will select at a certain time, there are some variables that can help us make several educated

[22] Simons, p. 239 (cited in footnote 16).
[23] McGuire, pp. 10–11 (cited in footnote 15).
[24] For a treatment of behavior modification, see Chapter 12.

guesses. Let us examine a specific dissonance-arousing situation to illustrate what information could help determine which method of dissonance reduction might be used. A college professor, for example, when making out an examination, decides on a correct answer for each question. Dissonance is created for him when a student later argues that the professor's answer to a question is wrong. The professor can choose any of the possible methods of dissonance reduction. If you have a poor grade point average, he can easily choose the "criticize the source" method of reduction. He can simply reason to himself, "You are not a good student so how could you be intelligent enough to know what the most correct answer is? As a matter of fact, I'm surprised you even took the exam." The dissonance is reduced and you do not get an extra point on the examination.

If the exam question was not worth many points, the professor may select the second alternative method of dissonance reduction, which is to "decide that the disagreement is not very important." He can, in this case, easily reason to himself, "One point won't make much difference to this student anyhow. Rather than open myself up to criticism from the rest of the students and many hours of work grading all the exams over, I will just forget about it." He then says to you, "Well, one point won't affect your final grade anyway." Your protest that there is an important principle involved will go unheeded.

If, however, he perceives you as a credible student and the question is worth a significant number of points, he may select the method of "bolstering his position by seeking additional information or persons who support it." In this instance he may talk with other professors or students who he suspects would answer the question as he did. You lose again.

On the other hand, the professor might, although unintentionally, misperceive your message. If he greatly distorts your message, he may conclude that you want him to discard the entire exam and let the class take a new one. If he perceives your message in this way, it will be easy for him to act as if he disagrees with you and do nothing about it. But in this particular professor-student example, this is not a very likely alternative method of imbalance reduction. Also, in his case, it is not likely that he would select the method of "convincing himself that your position and his are not relevant to each other."

The professor may decide to "try to convince you that your position is wrong" in order to reduce his tension. This method of dissonance reduction would be quite likely if he did not perceive you as very bright or if he felt that you were extremely threatened by disagreeing with a professor. Then, once you are defeated in the argument, his dissonance will be reduced because "The student admitted I was right all along."

It may well be that if you are a good student, and the professor respects you and is not afraid of the additional work of rescoring the exams, he will "change his atttiude so it is consistent with the source's." In this case, he will agree with you and rescore the examination for the entire class.

While you certainly hope he will rescore the exam, he still has other options available to reduce the dissonance. He may simply "repress your message" by refusing to think about it. Or, he may decide to simply "bear the tension and consider it a virtue." He can reason, "Perhaps I was wrong, but I am a professor and I will prove that I can play the professorial role by not doing anything about it. Professors must appear to be perfect and not 'buckle in' to student wishes."

As a student whose score is affected, you certainly hope he will be convinced by your arguments and rescore the examination. You surely realize by now, however, that given certain conditions some other method of reducing the dissonance may be more desirable or easier for him. As we indicated, predicting which method or methods of reduction the professor will use is difficult, but there are many relevant variables that can help you make the prediction. For example, your credibility as perceived by the professor, the method in which you approach the professor, the professor's attitude toward the role of professor, the importance of the exam, the worth of the question, and others. In any given dissonance-arousing communication transaction, your ability to predict which method of reduction the other person will select depends on your understanding of the total context of the situation.

For further insight into the way people reduce tension, think about your own behavior in response to dissonance. What do you do with information that conflicts with your present opinions? Do you derogate the source? Do you repress the information? Do you bolster your present position? Exactly what *do* you do?

The decoding process is obviously very complex. The "trait" approach to understanding a decoder's reaction by looking at personality variables has not been very fruitful. Ego-involvement theory and the various consistency theories consider more elements than do the trait approaches in trying to account for the complexity of the communication process. Although the theories give us some insights into the decoding process, the process still remains a mystery. The most important future advances in understanding communication will occur as theorists continue to focus on the role of decoding.

Exercises

1. Observe people in everyday situations and try to collect statements they make that reflect "common sense" explanations of the decoding process. For example, you may overhear a conversation in a restaurant where someone says, "There is just no way to communicate with him, he is not intelligent enough to understand." In this case, intelligence is taken as the decoding determiner. Compare in class the lists you have collected.
2. Draw the basic Heider balance diagram and supply specific situations to illustrate the balancing operation.
3. Recall specific communication situations where you think the decoder may have been in a state of imbalance. What mode of reduction did he use to restore psychological balance?
4. Analyze the list of alternatives that can be chosen to reduce dissonance. What situational variables can you think of that will guide or affect a person in his selection of dissonance-reduction alternatives? For example, what nonverbal cues might make it more probable that a decoder will derogate or criticize the source as the decoder attempts to reduce dissonance? What situational factors will increase the likelihood of "repressing the information?" Most importantly, what situational factors will increase the likelihood of a decoder actually changing his attitudes in order to reduce dissonance? Discuss your thoughts in class.
5. You have been asked to speak to a group of people about a controversial topic. You believe that most of the audience members can be classified as highly dogmatic. How will the belief that many of the people are highly dogmatic affect how you prepare the message? What things would you do differently if the audience was composed of lowly dogmatic individuals?
6. Make a list of controversial topics and try to assess your degree of ego-involvement in them. Do you feel threatened when someone argues against your position on an issue you feel strongly about? How do you respond to a similar situation when a lowly involving issue for you is attacked?

Suggested Readings

George A. Borden, *An Introduction to Human—Communication Theory,* Wm. C. Brown, Dubuque, 1971.

Arthur R. Cohen, *Attitude Change and Social Influence,* Basic Books, New York, 1964.

Gary Cronkhite, *Persuasion: Speech and Behavioral Change,* Bobbs-Merrill, New York, 1969.

Martin Fishbein (Ed.), *Readings in Attitude Theory and Measurement,* John Wiley, New York, 1967.

Charles A. Kiesler, Barry E. Collins, and Norman Miller, *Attitude Change —A Critical Analysis of Theoretical Approaches,* John Wiley, New York, 1969.

Gerald R. Miller, *Speech Communication—A Behavioral Approach,* Bobbs-Merrill, Indianapolis, 1966.

Part IV ▶

The Effects of Oral Communication

Chapter *12* ▶

Receiver
Modification: The
Impact on Decoders

Objectives

On completion of this chapter you should be able to:
1. Discuss the effectiveness of "brainwashing" techniques.
2. Specify the relationship between attitudes and behaviors.
3. Know the limits to the amount of attitude change one can secure with a persuasive message.
4. Understand in which communication arena the most attitude change occurs.
5. Know the conditions necessary for attitude changes to be sustained for a long time.
6. List some factors that build resistance to persuasive attempts.

Many popular works of fiction portray a future world in which we are all controlled by those who hold power. *Brave New World* and *1984* (which isn't too long from now) both show a bleak future.[1] The control of communication systems will, according to these views, assist those in power to manipulate us according to their own whims. Once the "hidden persuaders" gain more influence they will be able to manipulate us totally.[2] For example, the advertising and political campaign

[1] Aldous Huxley, *Brave New World*, Bantam Books, New York, 1958; George Orwell, *Nineteen Eighty-Four*, Signet Books, New York, 1949.
[2] Vance Packard, *The Hidden Persuaders*, David McKay, New York, 1957.

people are already persuading us to buy unnecessary products and vote for unworthy political candidates. In short, given an increase in technology and a more thorough understanding of human behavior, those in power can have guaranteed communication effectiveness.

In *Walden Two*, B. F. Skinner paints a rosier picture.[3] The fuller understanding of human behavior will be used to build a Utopia, a sort of heaven on earth. The science of human behavior will not be used to manipulate us for someone's selfish ends; it will be used for social progress. If the principles of human behavior are applied by men of good will, true social equality and happiness will be achieved.

All the above views, whether Utopian or anti-Utopian, overestimate the effects of persuasive attempts.[4] We now know that just because a source wants to achieve a certain response does not mean that the receivers will oblige. This chapter deals with the behavior and attitude changes that occur as a result of communication. Even though, as we have often noted, we are all encoders and decoders, this chapter will focus only on effects on decoders. Chapter 13 focuses on the changes that occur as a result of encoding. Whether encoding or decoding, most of the changes that occur in a transaction are behavioral and attitudinal.

CHANGES IN BEHAVIOR AND ATTITUDE

Behavior Change

Following the Korean War, many Americans were extremely afraid of the Chinese Communists' "brainwashing" techniques. Amercan servicemen in prisoner of war camps had engaged in behavior that was very embarrassing to the United States. Some had signed confessions of war crimes, others had totally denounced the United States, and still others became declared communists. It appeared that the Chinese had mastered a technique for washing patriotism right out of the soldiers' minds.

The techniques of brainwashing revolved around complete control of the prisoners' environment. The prisoners were not allowed to have leadership in their groups, they received only the letters from home that contained bad news, and they were constantly spied on. The small

[3] B. F. Skinner, *Walden Two,* MacMillan, New York, 1948.
[4] A similar treatment of persuasive effects can be found in Howard H. Martin and Kenneth E. Andersen (Eds.), *Speech Communication: Analysis and Readings,* Allyn and Bacon, Boston, 1968, pp. 230–243.

groups that previously had given the men support were broken apart so that an individual could not receive reinforcement from his friends. And, obviously, the Chinese camp leaders had total control of the rewards and punishments.

In fact, however, the Chinese did not master "brainwashing." Few servicemen were converted to the communist ideology. What meager success the Chinese did achieve was not long lasting. While many prisoners did help the enemy in some small ways, only three refused to return to the United States when given the chance. The Chinese did not develop any "diabolical, new, or irresistable" persuasive techniques.[5] As soon as the soldiers were released from the total environmental control, the program lost its effects. From the standpoint of all the effort involved, the Chinese indoctrination program was a failure.

As the Chinese indoctrination program demonstrates, just because a person's behavior is altered does not necessarily mean that his values are changed. Engaging in certain behavior in order to avoid punishment means that one is only complying for the moment. *Compliance* will occur only so long as one is in the situation where others can control the rewards or punishments he receives. Once out of their control (for instance, when the prisoners came home), compliance ends. Some Army privates in basic training and people who compulsively try to say the "right" thing, are only complying to the demands of the immediate situation. Such people do not necessarily alter their attitudes so that they are consistent with their immediate behavior. The attitudes are simply disguised.[6]

Behavioral changes can, however, lead to changes in attitudes. Some people believe that our attitudes are a consequence of our behavior rather than our behavior a consequence of our attitudes.[7] If the new behavior "is repeated, if it is approved by one's reference groups, and

---

[5] See Edgar H. Schein, "Brainwashing," in Warren G. Benis, et al. (Eds.), *Interpersonal Dynamics: Essays and Readings on Human Interaction,* Dorsey Press, Homewood, 1968, pp. 406–426; Edgar Schein, "The Chinese Indoctrination Program for Prisoners of War," *Psychiatry* (May 1956), *19,* 149–172; J. A. C. Brown, *Techniques of Persuasion: From Propaganda to Brainwashing,* Penguin Books, Baltimore, 1963, pp. 244–293.

[6] Herbert C. Kelman, "Processes of Opinion Change," *Public Opinion Quarterly* (1961), *25,* 57–78.

[7] Daryl J. Eeon, "Attitudes as Self-Descriptions: Another Look at The Attitude-Behavior Link," in Anthony G. Greenwald, Timothy C. Brock and Thomas M. Ostrom (Eds.), *Psychological Foundations of Attitudes,* Academic Press, New York, 1968; Herbert W. Simons, "Persuasion and Attitude Change," in Larry L. Barker and Robert J. Kibler (Eds.), *Speech Communication Behavior,* Prentice-Hall, Englewood Cliffs, 1971, p. 246; Chester A. Insko, *Theories of Attitude Change,* Appleton-Century-Crofts, New York, 1967, p. 348.

if it is sanctioned by the social environment generally,"[8] then attitude change will likely follow. For example, a student who goes to college is usually more liberal when he graduates than he was as an entering freshman. The college environment rewards liberal political behavior such as volunteering for community action, working for open admission policies, or just stating that you are a liberal. As a consequence, attitudes tend to conform to the liberal college environment. Usually, on leaving college, individuals begin to become more conservative because most environments are more conservative than a college environment. If a person stays in a liberal environment, however, liberal attitudes will persist.[9] Support from a reference group maintains our attitudes.

It can be argued from the perspective of balance theory that in order to retain a state of balance, a person's attitude should correspond with his behavior. If, however, one can justify his behavior, imbalance is not created. The Army private in basic training can easily engage in behavior that does not represent his actual attitudes. He knows he is forced to shine boots and march. Since he has support from his fellow privates for his hidden negative attitudes, his attitudes will probably not change.

Thus, it is apparent that environmental or context variables are crucial considerations in maintaining or changing attitudes and behaviors. If one receives support from his environment, he will be able to justify retaining or changing attitudes or behaviors, whichever the case might be. Also, the hierarchy of a person's beliefs (how his beliefs compare in importance) is a big determinant of the effects of persuasion attempts. In short, some attitudes and behaviors are easier to change than others. In order to understand the effects of persuasion attempts, one needs to consider the importance of all these environmental and context variables.

Attitude Change

Attitudes, our predispositions for and against objects and issues, are subject to change. When attitudes change, behavior can also change to reflect them. If you are persuaded by a political campaigner, your

[8] Bernard C. Hennessy, *Public Opinion,* Wadsworth Publishing, Belmont, 1965, p. 341.
[9] Theodore M. Newcomb, "Persistence and Regression of Changed Attitudes; Long Range Studies," in Edwin P. Hollander and Raymond G. Hunt (Eds.), *Current Perspectives in Social Psychology,* 2nd Ed., Oxford University Press, New York, 1967, pp. 384–392.

change in attitude may be reflected by your voting behavior. If you "have a bad attitude" toward a particular course you are taking, it is likely that you will skip it once in a while. In that case, skipping class is a behavioral response corresponding to your attitude.

Attitude change can occur for a variety of reasons. One theorist, Herbert Kelman, writes that compliance, identification, and internalization are the three basic processes of social influence.[10] *Compliance* occurs when you adopt behaviors or attitudes because of rewards and punishments applied to you. You comply for the moment, but you do not alter your basic attitudes. This was the case in the prisoners of war examples.

Identifying with a person will produce attitude changes. If someone you admire holds a certain opinion, you may, in an attempt to be like that person, adopt attitudes similar to his. The student who respects the professor, the son who identifies with his father, and the parishioner who admires his minister all are influenced by their "idols." *Identification*, then, is the second process of social influence.[11] In these cases, one actually changes attitudes and behaviors by adopting the attitudes and behaviors of the "idol" figures. Such change, however, is based on identification rather than an actual intellectual agreement. Often when one is separated from his idol for a long period of time, his attitudes and behaviors will change back so they are more like the person's original attitudes and behaviors.

Even if one does not idolize the source of a message, he will accept attempts to influence him if the course of action advocated is in agreement with his basic values. When one internalizes the message substance and integrates it with his existing values, then he has been influenced at a deep level. *Internalization* occurs when one adopts a particular attitude because he is truly convinced by it. You hold certain values, a speaker shows how those values can be fulfilled by adopting a certain new or different attitude, and you adopt it. The alteration of your behavior or attitude is in line with basic values you already hold.[12] Such changes are long lasting as they are based on intellectual agreement instead of on compliance with a power figure or identification with an idol.

[10] Kelman, pp. 57–78 (cited in footnote 6).

[11] Charisma, discussed in Chapter 9, can be seen as a very specialized form of extreme identification. One identifies so closely with a leader that he has ultimate "faith" in him and becomes a disciple.

[12] This process can be seen as a special case of balance theory mentioned in Chapter 11. The incoming message is consonant with your preexisting beliefs, causes no imbalance, and is not rejected.

These three processes of social influence illustrate that attitudes and behaviors are not always directly related. Most of the research on communication effects, however, assumes that alteration of a person's attitude will automatically affect his behavior. Obviously, this assumption is subject to question. LaPiere reported in 1934 that he traveled with a Chinese couple for 10,000 miles in the United States. They patronized several motels, hotels, and restaurants. They were refused service only once. However, when a questionnaire was sent to these same establishments, over 90 percent of them said they would not accept members of the Chinese race as guests.[13]

From one point of view, the LaPiere study demonstrates the lack of correspondence between attitudes and behaviors. The establishment owners did one thing and said another. An alternate view is that "offering service" and "completing a questionnaire" are both *behaviors,* but the thresholds for the two behaviors are different. It is more difficult to refuse a well-dressed Chinese couple in a face-to-face encounter than it is to refuse the Chinese race on a questionnaire.[14] The demands of each situation are such that different behaviors emerge. Therefore, "we will not find a high correlation between attitude and behavior if situational pressures substantially contribute to the observed behavior—and they almost always do."[15] One may have a particular attitude that is not represented by a behavior because of situational pressures.

Because we cannot control other people's behavior all the time, we try to influence them by changing their predispositions to respond (attitudes). Persuasive messages are directed to attitudes in attempts to eventually alter behavior. The success of these attempts is greatly influenced by the communication arena in which they occur.

Effects Within Communication Arenas

Mass Media Arena

The effects of communication are usually exaggerated.[16] The mass media do not lead us like lemmings into the arms of the powerful manipulator; they play a relatively minor role in changing our attitudes. For instance, the televised debates between Nixon and Kennedy in the

[13] R. T. LaPiere, "Attitudes vs. Action," Social Forces (1934), *13,* 230–237.

[14] D. T. Campbell, "Social Attitudes and Other Acquired Behavioral Dispositions," in S. Koch (Ed.), *Psychology: A Study of a Science,* McGraw-Hill, New York, 1963, pp. 94–172.

[15] Charles A. Kiesler, Barry E. Collins, and Norman Miller, *Attitude Change: A Critical Analysis of Theoretical Approaches,* John Wiley, New York, 1969, p. 29.

[16] Simons, p. 246 (cited in footnote 7).

1960 presidential race had little influence on votes. The debates served primarily to stimulate the undecided Democratic voters to go to the polls and vote Democratic. Very few voters changed their choice of candidates as a result of the debates.[17] When one looks at most political campaigns, the media are "relatively ineffective" in converting voters from one party to another. Although the mass media may influence how we generally view events, the process occurs over a period of time and between political campaigns.[18]

The effectiveness of the mass media has been highly acclaimed in the field of advertising. Just hire a public relations firm and the masses will be thronging to the stores to buy your product, or so it is believed. Even as early as World War II, the media were believed to have a tremendous impact. For example, Kate Smith sold 39 million dollars in war bonds. Look at the size of her audience, however, and you will discover she only persuaded between 2 and 4 percent of her listeners. Cigarette ads only had to influence 0.5% of all adults in order to generate $60 million in sales.[19] The impressive results of media advertising are due to the size of the audience rather than the powerful effects of the media. Furthermore, even though the media may change your attitudes on relatively unimportant matters, they will not have that same impact on issues vital to your life. It is certainly easier to convince you to use a different toothpaste than it is to alter your religious beliefs.[20] But, even on unimportant items, the media effectiveness is a result of a tremendously large audience.

The mass media have limited effects partially because receivers are becoming more difficult to persuade. As the techniques of mass persuasion have become more sophisticated, so have the audiences.[21] Audience members know that the source is trying to persuade them, so they resist more. Another reason for the limited effects of the media is that the media must compete with other sources of communication. The media simply have no control over the counter messages you may

[17] Martin and Andersen, p. 307 (cited in footnote 4).

[18] William J. McGuire, "The Nature of Attitudes and Attitude Change," in Gardner Lindzey and Elliot Aronson (Eds.), *The Handbook of Social Psychology*, III, Addison Wesley, Reading, 1969, pp. 227–235.

[19] Raymond A. Bauer, "The Obstinate Audience: The Influence Process from the Point of View of Social Communication," in Hollander and Hunt, pp. 403–404 (cited in footnote 9).

[20] Joseph T. Klapper, "The Social Effects of Mass Communication," in Wilbur Schramm (Ed.), *The Science of Human Communication*, Basic Books, New York, 1963, p. 76.

[21] Raymond A. Bauer, "Limits of Persuasion," in Martin and Andersen (Eds.), p. 270 (cited in footnote 4).

get. For example, while you sit watching the television set, others around you may laugh at the message. The laughter affects the way you react to it. Or, when a political candidate appears on the screen, your friend sits and criticizes the person's position of the issue. Your friend's criticism will have an affect on your reaction to the political candidate.

Messages received in mass media and in interpersonal contexts have different effects. The research on the diffusion of innovations aptly demonstrates the differences. Whenever a new idea or product appears, its adoption follows certain steps. The diffusion of a new idea, whether it is a new farm practice or medical drug, follows a parallel development. One becomes aware of the innovation through the media, but subsequent interpersonal communication has more of an impact on the actual decision to reject or adopt the innovation.[22] Personal influence and the media are *both* important in the decision process, but personal influence is clearly more important.

Thus, the alleged effects of the mass media in changing attitudes and behaviors are generally exaggerated. To lead you to believe, however, that the effects of the media are unimportant or nonexistent is incorrect. The media play a vital role in *reinforcing existing* attitudes and behaviors. You lead a typical life, for example, and media programs usually support the notion that the typical life is desirable. A college education is a good thing, parents are to be respected, athletics admired, brushing your teeth is socially and hygienically necessary, a person should vote, and so on. Rarely are these habitual life style behaviors challenged by the media. As a result, one questions the desirability of these habitual behaviors much less frequently than if the media portrayed them as undesirable. Thus, the typical life remains in vogue. The media play a large role in reinforcing these and other existing attitudes and behaviors.

Public Speaking Arena

The research findings on the long-range effects of public speaking are meager. Most of the research has been conducted in experimental settings where only short-term effects are observed. There have not been, to our knowledge, any controlled empirical studies focusing on the long-range impact of a public speech.[23] It is difficult to assess the

[22] McGuire, pp. 234–235 (cited in footnote 18); Elihu Katz, "Communication Research and the Image of Society: Convergence of Two Traditions," in Alfred G. Smith (Ed.), *Communication and Culture,* Holt, Rinehart and Winston, New York, 1966, p. 555.

[23] The effects of a public speech on the speaker are developed in Chapter 13.

effects of a public speech because (1) given present technology, most speeches of import are criticized and analyzed immediately, and (2) the role that interpersonal and small group transactions have on the reception of the public speech has not been studied. If the direct effects of a speech could be isolated from other public opinions following it and from interpersonal networks relating to it, then some assessment of the effectiveness of public speaking could be made. A message delivered as a public speech has effects similar to a message delivered through the media. The long-range impact of a single speech on an audience appears to be small.

Small Group Arena

Small groups can be the agents for considerable change of attitude and behavior. When one joins groups he engages in numerous transactions with others. The sheer number of transactions will cause some change in attitudes over time. Trace group members' attitudes when a group forms to see how all the group members tend to become more alike. The process of going to college puts us into groups with others, and our attitudes change. On graduation from college, as we join different groups, our attitudes undergo further changes. As noted in Chapter 2, all work groups and social groups exert influence on their members to conform to their norms.

The small group and interpersonal arenas share one common factor. It is within these arenas that (1) the largest shifts of attitudes and behaviors occur, and (2) the effects of mass media or public speaking messages are altered. One's attitudes and behaviors are primarily formed and maintained in the small group and interpersonal arenas.

Interpersonal Arena

Even in the small group and interpersonal arenas, it takes considerable time for marked attitude changes to occur. Changes in attitude are usually not one-shot affairs; they require continued transactions over an extended period of time.

Within the interpersonal arena, some theorists contend that we communicate *especially* to produce attitude changes. Newcomb's "strain toward symmetry," discussed in Chapter 11, says that when we have an acquaintance we like, if he holds an attitude different from ours we will be motivated to communicate with him to alter his attitude. Whatever the explanation given for it, interpersonal influence is vitally important in securing small amounts of attitude change from a receiver. Interpersonal networks permeate our very existence. And, as noted in Chapter 8, your perception of yourself arises from communication with others. While one specific interpersonal encounter may not alter your life, the continuing transactions you form and maintain do affect both your attitudes and behaviors.

Intrapersonal Arena

In the intrapersonal arena, it is difficult to specify what changes occur. Measurement and observation of attitude and behavioral changes in response to internal messages are almost impossible. It does appear that radical changes, such as religious conversions, occur in the intrapersonal arena. One is stimulated by transactions in the other arena and then, by communicating with oneself, manages to undergo a drastic change in basic attitudes. The pressure of inconsistency becomes so great that only a radical realignment of attitudes can produce a reconciliation of conflicts.

Conversion is, however, a very rare happening. In the usual case, intrapersonal communication produces relatively small amounts of change. For example, free movies (dreams) can cause one to examine his life or question his decisions. Rarely, however, do they cause drastic realignment of basic attitudes. "Inner speech," talking silently to oneself, can help one resolve to do things differently, but it usually does not cause major changes in attitudes or behavior.

Whatever the respective communication arena, communication has, at any one point in time, limited effects. Sudden changes in attitude occur very rarely.[24] The effects of communication are usually limited and gradual and depend on several context variables.

THE PERSISTENCE OF EFFECTS

If one does manage to alter the receivers' attitudes or modify their behavior, how enduring can he expect these changes to be? Just because you cause attitudes to shift immediately during the presentation of a message does not necessarily mean the change will be long lasting. Research on the "sleeper effect" demonstrates that some receivers initially experience large changes in attitudes when they are exposed to a message from a highly credible source. These initial changes, however, decrease over time. The receiver's attitudes regress back toward their initial position. Apparently, the receivers stop associating the source of the message with the content. They retain parts of the message, but, three weeks to a month later, forget where they heard it and who said it. To sustain initial attitude changes, therefore,

[24] Hennessy, p. 340 (cited in footnote 8).

one needs to remind the receivers of the source. If people are reminded who it was that made the statements about a certain issue, the credibility effects will reappear. The highly credible source will again enjoy more attitude change than the lowly credible source.[25]

If you are planning a persuasive campaign and are using sources that are perceived as highly credible by most of the receivers, it will be wise to remind the receivers periodically who the source was and the relevance of the message to them. The persistence of the attitude changes can also be lengthened with proper social support. As with behavior changes, if a person changes his attitude and then does not receive continuing support for his new opinion, it will likely regress.[26] One of the reasons that organizations have newsletters is to provide continuing support for members' attitudes. Professional, hobby, and social clubs all have activities designed to keep the members involved and integrated into the organization's philosophy. The continuing support for attitudes, therefore, reinforces them.

RESISTING PERSUASIVE ATTEMPTS

Although we are interested in changing attitudes, we also want to know how to resist persuasive attempts. There are many factors that contribute to resisting persuasion.

Any personality trait, such as those discussed in Chapter 11, can interfere with persuasion and be a form of resistance. For example, raising a person's self-esteem will make him more resistant to persuasive attempts.[27] Or, if a person's attitude serves some deep-seated belief, it will be resistant to change. If a person feels unworthy, a belief that members of another race are inferior may heighten his sense of worth. If so, the attitude will be highly resistant to change.[28]

All the factors that contribute to "stability of attitude" can inhibit attitude or behavior change.[29] Selective exposure, perception, atten-

[25] See Carl I. Hovland, Irving L. Janis, and Harold H. Kelley, *Communication and Persuasion,* Yale University Press, New Haven, 1953, pp. 254–259; and McGuire, pp. 254–256 (cited in footnote 18).

[26] Leon Festinger, "Behavioral Support for Opinion Change," in Lee Richardson (Ed.), *Dimensions of Communication,* Appleton-Century-Crofts, New York, 1969, p. 116.

[27] McGuire, p. 258 (cited in footnote 18).

[28] An interesting typology of the functions of attitudes can be found in Daniel Katz, "The Functional Approach to the Study of Attitudes," *Public Opinion Quarterly* (1960), 24, 163–204.

[29] Goodwin Wilson, "Resistance to Change," in Warren G. Bennis, Kenneth D. Benne, and Robert Chin (Eds.), *The Planning of Change,* Holt, Rinehart and Winston, New York, 1969, p. 488.

tion, and retention are all phenomena that maintain attitude stability and retard attitude change. Attempts to retain psychological balance can also reduce one's susceptibility to change. For example, it is not uncommon to see a receiver misinterpret the content of a message or distort the purpose of a communicator in order to dismiss the influence attempt. When the encyclopedia salesman comes to the door, if you perceive of him as dishonest, his chances of influence are greatly lessened. Or, if you are in favor of integration and label all those who favor segregation as racists, you will not be very susceptible to their messages. All of these processes, and more, are ways that one resists influence.

The more committed one is to a belief, the more difficult it is to change it. If you are highly ego-involved on an issue (the issue is extremely important to you), then the possibilities of influencing you are slight. A person who is an atheist, and whose approach to life comes from this central belief, is not very receptive to proreligion messages. Likewise, a person who identifies strongly with a religion and has found it helpful in a crisis is not easily swayed from those attitudes.

Any act of public commitment will reduce one's susceptibility to persuasion. Internally thinking about an attitude, publicly stating a belief, and acting on the basis of the belief, all tend to make the initial attitude more resistant to change.[30] Further resistance can be induced by making additional commitments to the belief or attitude. For example, after a professor records a grade of "B" for you in a course, he will be much more resistant to your arguments that you deserve an "A" grade than he would have been had you talked with him before he recorded the grade. The "act of recording" serves as a type of formal commitment and makes him resistant to change. If, after he recorded the grade, he told other people that he gave you a grade of "B," he will be even more resistant to your attempts to get him to change his mind. As a result of publicly stating his belief, he has become more resistant to your persuasive attempts.

One can also resist persuasion by actively arguing against the persuasive message. McGuire's inoculation theory suggests that just as a vaccine inoculates one against future germs and viruses, attitude inoculation can protect one from future persuasive attempts. A medical vaccine stimulates body defenses against a disease, but it is not strong enough to actually give the person the disease. Similarly, weakened versions of arguments will serve to stimulate one's defenses against

---

[30] McGuire, p. 261 (cited in footnote 18); The effects of encoding messages are treated in Chapter 13.

them, but the weak arguments will not be strong enough to sway one to that position.[31]

Using "germ-free" topics (statements about good health practices that most people in our culture accept), McGuire and his colleagues tested the strength of attitude inoculation. People received statements such as "Everyone should brush his teeth after every meal." These statements were then attacked with weak arguments. The people were asked to refute these weak arguments. At a later date, the statements were again attacked with stronger arguments. The people who had earlier received the weak arguments were better able to resist the strong arguments that came later. Those who had not received the weak arguments did not develop defenses and were swayed by the strong arguments. McGuire's research shows that people can build defenses that inoculate them against future attacks on beliefs.

If you are a parent and wish your child to be able to resist future persuasive attempts, you can "inoculate" him. One of the authors of this book maintains that "Thank you, no" is a more polite response than "No, thank you" when one is declining an offer from someone else. He wanted his young daughter, Johnna, to use the more polite statement. Anticipating that she would come in contact with people who would try to "correct" her to say "No, thank you," he tried a minitest of inoculation theory by inoculating her against the "No, thank you" position. As a result, she is able to say "Thank you, no" with a clear conscience and not be swayed by majority opinion.

The process of attitude and behavior change is usually slow. Few persons are dramatically converted to a new political party or to a new way of life overnight. Even the small changes that might occur can be resisted because of personality traits, commitment, or practice at refuting counter arguments. In short, persuasion is a slow process. Our behavior and attitudes change slowly as we transact with other individuals.

Exercises

1. Write down some of the attitudes you now hold, such as your attitude toward (1) the need to believe in God, (2) your major department in school, and (3) your parents. At the end of the term or school year, pick the same issues and once again jot down your

[31] William J. McGuire, "Inducing Resistance to Persuasion," in Leonard Berkowitz (Ed.), *Advances in Experimental Social Psychology, 1,* Academic Press, New York, 1964, pp. 191–229; McGuire, pp. 263–265 (cited in footnote 18).

attitudes. Compare the lists. What alterations occurred? Can you specify what caused the changes that did occur?

2. In small groups, draw up lists of behaviors that represent attitudes. Are there certain behaviors from which one can easily infer an attitude and are there other behaviors that have multiple meanings?

3. Engage a person in a discussion on the "brainwashing" techniques of the Communist Chinese. Do you find a large number of people who still believe the Chinese program was extremely successful?

4. Try an experiment on a friend. Pick two topics that he feels equally strong about (he may not feel strongly about them, just so the feelings are about equal in strength). On one topic, over a period of time, try to change his attitude. On the second topic, "inoculate" him and then have a third friend try to change his attitude over a period of time using the same techniques you used to change the first attitude. Compare the results.

5. With a group of friends not enrolled in this class, attend a public speech or watch a television show that contains controversial material. What communication transactions occur among the friends during and after the presentations that alter its impact?

6. List examples you have seen in the past few days where a person's attitude and behavior are (1) consistent and (2) inconsistent. Specify the situational pressures in the two cases that might account for the differences.

Suggested Readings

J. A. C. Brown, *Techniques of Persuasion: From Propaganda to Brainwashing,* Penguin Books, Baltimore, 1963.

Chester A. Insko, *Theories of Attitude Change,* Appleton-Century-Crofts, New York, 1967.

Joseph T. Klapper, *The Effects of Mass Communication,* The Free Press, New York, 1960.

William J. McGuire, "The Nature of Attitudes and Attitude Change," in Gardner Lindzey and Elliot Aronson (Eds.), *The Handbook of Social Psychology,* 2nd Ed., *III,* Addison-Wesley, Reading, 1969.

Walter Weiss, "Effects of the Mass Media of Communication," in Gardner Lindzey and Elliot Aronson (Eds.), *The Handbook of Social Psychology,* 2nd Ed., *V,* Addison-Wesley, Reading, 1969.

Chapter *13* ▶

Source Modification: The Impact on Encoders

Objectives

On completion of this chapter you should be able to:
1. Observe how a person is affected by the messages he encodes.
2. Understand the significance of feedback in encoding effects.
3. Generate attitude change in people by inducing them to actively participate in encoding behavior.
4. Understand how commitment, both verbal and nonverbal, affect a communication source.
5. Help people understand opinion differences by having them engage in role playing.
6. Understand the concept of self-persuasion.
7. Speculate about and appreciate the effects that your own messages have on you as a sender.

We have repeatedly said that communication is a transactional process and that all participants encode and decode messages simultaneously. In Chapter 12 we looked at communication transactions as they affect decoders. In this chapter, we examine communication transactions as they affect encoders, or, how the act of constructing a message affects the encoder of the message.

ENCODING FOR SELF-UNDERSTANDING

Think about a time when you were experiencing a very personal problem. You may have revealed your innermost fears or concerns to a friend. You probably did most of the talking while your friend sat and listened. What impact did this communication transaction have on you as an encoder? Did you feel better after sharing the problem with someone? Later, how did you feel about the friend with whom you shared your problem? Did you feel closer to him because he knew about your problem? Or did you feel threatened by him and angry with yourself for revealing yourself? There are several possible combinations of reactions that may have developed as a result of the encounter, but there were reactions. *You changed* as a result of being a source in the situation.

It is not unusual for a personable instructor to have the opportunity to help students with their personal problems. The instructor might just listen while the student talks about the problem. Often, when the student finishes sharing his problem, he realizes that it is not as severe as he originally thought. By keeping his concern "locked up" inside, the severity of the problem grew and grew to the point of unreality. After sharing it, however, he was able to regain a sense of perspective and take a more objective view of his problem.

In some cases, the opposite happens. After sharing the problem, one realizes that it is more crucial than he originally thought. In these instances, the person with the problem was probably not very concerned at the outset of the conversation. This lack of concern can be as unrealistic as "overconcern." In any case, all of us have had this type of experiences. In such situations, we are changed because of our encoding. We are changed both in our assessment of the problem and in our feelings toward the person with whom we communicated.

As well as putting old thoughts in a new light, encoding can produce totally new thoughts. Often one's best ideas emerge in the heat of an argument. The expresson of thoughts creates new thoughts. This view of language and thought highlights the fact that we are susceptible to change as a *direct result* of our own encoding behavior.[1] Whatever the explanation, it is clear that our messages affect us as well as our receivers.

It has been said, ". . . the good listener is the best physician for those who are ill in thought and feeling."[2] This statement emphasizes

[1] See Chapter 5 for an explication of the various views of the relation among language and thought.

[2] Wendell Johnson, *Your Most Enchanted Listener,* Harper and Brothers, New York, 1956, p. 20.

the point made in Chapter 8. From a source's perspective, responses to his encoding can be extremely important. The person who is "ill in thought and feeling" needs someone to listen to his message. Or, stated differently, the lack of an available receiver can affect an encoder. We have said or heard someone else say, "If he just could have found somebody to talk to." Or we may have thought, "If I could just find someone who understands—someone who will listen to me." Such thoughts reveal that at times we need to be sources so that we can benefit from the effects that encoding has on us as sources. Such effects can help us fulfill our interpersonal needs of affection and inclusion as well as help us "straighten our thinking." One can argue that communication participants have an *ethical obligation* to be attentive to other's encoding. We should be willing to listen to others—"lend our ears and minds to our fellow man." Such a view supports the notion that people can gain self-understanding and fulfill their interpersonal needs through the encoding process.

Nondirective therapy in psychiatry is based on the assumption that people need the opportunity to encode. They need to "get it off of their chests." Psychiatrists often say very little to their clients—they just listen well. A person can feel comfortable sharing with them because they are professional people. They are objective listeners who can decode messages and a person need not fear that the psychiatrist will reveal the content of the transaction to others.

This type of client-centered therapy is similar to communication patterns in student-centered classrooms. Instead of being information centered with a lecture format, some instructors prefer to have the students do the major portion of the encoding. The rationale for the student-centered approach is that as encoders, the students will find the subject more meaningful to them, personally.

By giving people the opportunity to be encoders, self-understanding can result. A person can reveal his thoughts, create new thoughts, and get to know himself better by engaging in encoding behavior.

Making Additional Commitments While Encoding

The encoding act, because it involves a commitment, can have beneficial results. Alcoholics Anonymous operates on the principle that once an alcoholic can admit publicly and to himself that he has a drinking problem, he can begin to overcome his weakness. The same principle is used in weight watching organizations. If a person with a weight problem will encode messages in which he admits his problem, he can often begin to solve the problem. Some communities have organized smoking groups for the same reasons. If a person wants to stop smoking and can be induced to encode messages accordingly, he stands a better chance of controlling his urge to smoke. The statement, "If I can just get him to say (admit) it." is applicable to this principle. The notion, "Now I feel better—at least I've said it." logically follows.

Once an encoder has admitted a problem and has committed himself to a course of action, he tends to remain on that course and thinks in a manner that will sustain his decision.[3] An initial commitment leads to thoughts and actions that strengthen that commitment. The very act of becoming a source by encoding a message indicates a strong commitment on the part of a source. We find it difficult to abandon the feeling of, "I gave my word."[4]

This same principle (inducing one to admit a problem and thereby commit himself) can be used in situations in which the message is primarily nonverbal. Take, for example, religious crusades. People are encouraged to "come forward" and "kneel at the altar" as a demonstration of their commitment to a new way of life. Becoming a source of a nonverbal message (walking to the front of the room) can have a dramatic, emotional impact on a person.

The Varied Effects of Encoding

Encoding can lead to learning and attitude change as well as self-understanding. One can be affected by the encoding process even if the messages he encodes are originally other people's messages. It has been speculated that a message decoder may experience encoding effects simply by relating a communication experience to other people. If the receiver "later repeats to others some of the arguments and conclusions which he recalls from a persuasive communication he may elicit social approval or disapproval which could facilitate or interfere with acceptance."[5] This simply means that if you are talking with someone or listening to a speech being delivered by someone, your acceptance or rejection of the statements will be affected by the way

[3] Edward E. Jones and Harold B. Gerard, *Foundations of Social Psychology,* John Wiley, New York, 1967, p. 418.

[4] Kenneth E. Andersen, *Persuasion: Theory and Practice,* Allyn and Bacon, Boston, 1971, p. 255.

[5] Carl I. Hovland, Irving L. Janis, and Harold H. Kelley, *Communication and Persuasion,* Yale University Press, New Haven, 1953, p. 232.

people react to you when you later describe the communication encounter to them.

Examples of these "message-relating" effects are readily available. For example, the parents of a college student who has recently become "liberalized" in his political thinking may be appalled by the son's new way of thinking. If, however, on relating their son's new notions to their friends, they find that their friends react favorably toward the son's position, they, too, will be more favorably disposed to their son's statements. If their friends react negatively, it will serve to reinforce the parent's initial rejection. As a result of this reinforcement, the parents will be even more strongly convinced that their son has serious problems.

Research shows that getting a receiver to actively participate as a verbal source can affect how much he learns or remembers. "Experimental evidence indicates that one of the effects of overt verbalization is to increase the rate of learning verbal material. . . ."[6] You can, as a student, test this notion. If this research is correct, you can get better test scores if you study "out loud" and verbalize while you read. One study revealed that if a source gets his receivers to recite or repeat material verbally, there will be an increase in their ability to recall the information.[7] This indicates that when dealing with informational material, a source can enhance his effectiveness by getting his audience members to become verbal sources. Research also indicates that in terms of attitude change, receivers who are required to read messages orally are more influenced by the messages than receivers who read the messages silently.[8] Again, verbal encoding enhances message effectiveness. These same researchers found that people who had to participate in the creation of messages were more influenced by the messages than people who simply read messages that were already created.[9] Thus, getting one to play the role of encoder enhances the possibility of changing his attitudes. Support for this principle is demonstrated in the behavior of different types of active sources. Salesmen, for example, become convinced by their own sales talks and political speakers tend to be swayed by their own improvised arguments.[10]

[6] Ibid., p. 217.

[7] Carl I. Hovland, A. A. Lumsdaine, and F. D. Sheffeld, *Experiments in Mass Communication,* Princeton University Press, 1949, pp. 223 ff.

[8] I. L. Janis and B. T. King, "The Influence of Role Playing on Opinion Change," *Journal of Abnormal and Social Psychology* (1954), XLIX, 211–218.

[9] B. T. King and I. L. Janis, "Comparison of the Effectiveness of Improvised Versus Non-Improvised Role Playing in Producing Opinion Change," *Human Relations* (1956), IX, 177–186.

[10] Hovland, Janis, and Kelley, p. 218 (cited in footnote 5).

ENCODING TO UNDERSTAND OTHERS

Role Playing

An extension of message impact on encoders can be seen in role-playing situations. In such instances, people are asked to "play the role" of another person and encode messages from the other person's point of view. Role-playing situations are unique in that people are being asked to encode messages from another's point of view instead of publicly state beliefs they already hold. Role-playing research suggests that an individual will experience attitude change if he is induced to verbally express arguments that he does not necessarily believe. The role playing causes him to actively rehearse counterarguments. Such rehearsal can be convincing because, perhaps for the first time, he is exposed to a new set of arguments. Furthermore, when you verbalize arguments to others, you pay greater attention to the content of the arguments. This, alone, increases the chances that one will think about the "other side" and be influenced by it.[11]

Self-Persuasion

The area of self-persuasion is directly related to role playing. In a role-playing situation, a person may play the role of five or six different people who hold views at odds with the role player. In the self-persuasion situation, however, a person is asked to publicly encode a message that is noticeably different from his personal beliefs. For example, if a person is against labor unions, he might be asked to prepare and deliver a message that argues in favor of labor unions. The basic assumptions is that if a person argues publicly against what he truly believes, he will change his attitudes so that they are more in line with his public statements. Obviously, several variables are in operation in such a situation. For example, the type of feedback the encoder perceives will have an effect on how much attitude change he experiences. Also relevant is the amount of choice the encoder had in deciding to deliver the message in which he does not believe. Another consideration is the susceptability of the audience to the advocated position. That is, prior to hearing the message are they in agreement with the advocated position? Do they disagree with the position? Are they undecided? In other words, what is the potential impact of the message going to be? The research, which is much too extensive and

[11] Hovland, Janis, and Kelley, pp. 218–230 (cited in footnote 5).

complex to explain here, leads us to conclude that in general, when a person publicly advocates a position he does not believe, he will be persuaded by his own message.[12]

Practical application of the self-persuasion principle can be found in the classroom setting. A common teaching technique is to ask students to encode, either orally or in written form, the potential payoffs of taking a particular course. For example, the instructor might say, "Forget for a moment all of the bad rumors you have heard about this course and discuss some reasons why you think this course will be beneficial to you." This technique of inducing students to become sources of messages that are inconsistent with their attitudes appears to be an effective way of changing their attitudes in the desired direction. Evidence on the effectiveness of this technique is advanced in an early research report by Myers. He found that during World War I some soldiers were extremely critical of the Army. The Army, rather than changing Army ways, placed the men in a public speaking course. In the course, they were required to develop and deliver speeches that were favorable to the Army way of life. He found that after a while they began to believe what they were saying and acted accordingly.[13]

ENCODING EFFECTS AND REWARDS

The effects that result from encoding messages are, in part, determined by the *rewards* a person receives for encoding a message. This is directly related to the notion of positive feedback. Based on how a source perceives the feedback to his encoding behavior, his future thinking and behavior will be affected. The feedback will affect his personality and self-image to a significant degree. Also, if the feedback he perceives is positive, he will hold his expressed position more firmly. If the feedback, however, is perceived as negative, he will be susceptible to attitude change.[14]

Similarly, if a person conforms outwardly to social pressure and expresses an opinion because he feels he is compelled to, he will

[12] For excellent treatments of much of this research, see Gerald R. Miller, "Counter-attitudinal Advocacy: A Current Appraisal," in C. David Mortensen and Kenneth K. Sereno (Eds.), *Advances in Communication Research,* Harper and Row, New York, 1972; and Edward M. Bodaken, "Choice and Perceived Audience Attitude As Determinants of Cognitive Dissonance and Subsequent Attitude Change Following Counter-attitudinal Advocacy," unpublished Ph.D. thesis, Michigan State University, 1970.

[13] G. C. Myers, "Control of Conduct by Suggestion: An Experiment in Americanization," *Journal of Applied Psychology* (1921), 5, 26–31.

[14] Andersen, pp. 248–252 (cited in footnote 4).

begin to believe what he is saying if he is made to feel he is saying it well.[15] Thus, when one encodes ideas because he feels they will be socially acceptable, he will actually internalize and believe them if he perceives the experience of expressing them as rewarding.

In the self-persuasion situation (getting one to express views he definitely does not believe), the element of reward works differently. In such a situation a person is more likely to begin believing the opposing views if the amount of reward he receives is just sufficient to induce him to make the statement.[16] If he recevies more reward than is necessary to get him to perform the "counterattitudinal" encoding behavior, he will not need to change his attitude. The reason for this is simply that if a person is given a large reward, he has sufficient justification for publicly stating something in which he does not believe. If he were given the opportunity, he would probably do the same thing again because he stands to gain significant reward. If the initial reward, however, is small, what justification does one have for encoding beliefs he does not believe? Without the necessary reward justification, he will likely change his attitudes so that he can justify his "lies" by reasoning, "Maybe I really do believe what I said." Again, the amount of choice the sender had in deciding whether or not he would encode the message with which he disagreed must be considered. If he perceived he had a free-choice situation, the smaller the reward he received, the more he will change his attitude. This basic conclusion stems from dissonance theory, discussed in Chapter 11.

The effect of reward on encoding can be extended further by equating it with success. A source will probably abandon a project if he feels that the responses to his encoding indicate he will not be successful in achieving his goals. A political campaigner, for example, will probably abandon his campaign efforts if the responses to his encoding behavior indicate failure. Presidential candidates' withdrawals from presidential campaigns support this point. The responses to a person's encoding do have long-term effects on a person's future behavior.

EAVESDROPPING

By now, you should agree that many of the effects which take place in communication transactions happen to the persons constructing the messages. Another way to look at an encoder in communication is to think of him as his own listener. That is, a source is a receiver of his

---

[15] Hovland, Janis, and Kelley, p. 229 (cited in footnote 5).
[16] Andersen, p. 256 (cited in footnote 4).

own messages. Wendell Johnson provides us with insight into this view of senders when he says

"If we would understand a man by his words it is best that we listen to what he says when he is either in trouble or in love. For if we do, and if we are quiet and attentive, we will notice that no matter how fully he may be taken over by the illusion that it is to us he speaks, he talks at such times most surely to himself."[17]

Johnson develops his point further by stating that every source is his own most captive listener. If one ponders these ideas, he is led to listen to others "in a spirit of eavesdropping." That is, listen to others as though you are "listening in" while they are talking to themselves.

". . . in the spirit of eavesdropping, we can hardly help noticing that people talking about themselves and their private desperations are saying the most fantastic things to us, to themselves, that is. They are saying so much that is just not true, and much that is questionable at best, and they are saying it all as though it were to be taken for granted as wholly true, listening all the while quite unwonderingly to themselves saying these things."[18]

One of the main points Johnson makes with his "eavesdropping" analysis is that one should listen well to himself. He contends that we need communicators, especially those in positions of power, who are "capable of speaking to themselves in public with wholesome effects on themselves and on the people who listen to them."[19] One cannot help but be fascinated with the insight Johnson provides with this analysis of communication effects on senders.

It is very common for a person to discuss "a friend's" personal problem with another friend, when, in fact, the "friend" to whom he is referring is himself. Such behavior indicates that each of us realizes that by encoding messages to others, we can effect changes in ourselves. Not all of our messages are attempts to change other receiver's attitudes. Some of our messages are designed specifically for ourselves as receivers of our own messages.

Do the messages that we encode have effects on us as encoders? The answer is obviously yes. Encoding can lead to self-understanding or the understanding of others. The question that remains is, "If we were better receivers of our own messages, could we improve in our attempts to understand ourselves and others?" Again, the obvious

[17] Johnson, pp. 24–25 (cited in footnote 2).
[18] Johnson, pp. 23–24 (cited in footnote 2).
[19] Johnson, pp. 27–29 (cited in footnote 2).

answer is yes. However, to conquer the ability to listen to ourselves is a difficult task. We can gain insight into the entire procedure if we try to observe other sources from an eavesdropping perspective. Such insight may help us pay better attention to our own messages.

Exercises

1. As a class, discuss experiences that you as individual class members have had in relating personal problems to friends. Discuss what happened to your own perception of the problem as you shared it. Discuss the impact that sharing the problem with the friend had on your relationship with the friend.
2. Describe to a friend a recent conversation you have had with someone else. How does the friend respond to your description of the previous transaction? What did the impact of his response to your description have on your own thinking about the conversation?
3. The next time you have a friendly argument with your parents or with a friend, stop the argument and switch roles. Have the person with whom you are in conflict argue from your position and you argue from the other person's position. What effect does this role playing have on (a) the content of the conflict, (b) the understanding of the other person? Discuss your experience in class.
4. "Eavesdrop" on yourself. Listen to the messages you send to others as if they were intended for yourself. That is to say, be a receiver of your own messages. Deliver a brief speech to your class in which you discuss the insights you gained about yourself.

Suggested Readings

Kenneth E. Andersen, *Persuasion: Theory and Practice,* Allyn and Bacon, Boston, 1971.
Carl I. Hovland, Irving L. Janis, and Harold H. Kelley, *Communication and Persuasion,* Yale University Press, New Haven, 1953.
Wendell Johnson, *Your Most Enchanted Listener,* Harper and Row, New York, 1956.
Gerald R. Miller, "Counterattitudinal Advocacy: A Current Appraisal," in C. David Mortensen and Kenneth K. Sereno (Eds.), *Advances In Communication Research,* Harper and Row, New York, 1972.

Chapter *14* ▶ | *Personal Modification: The Impact of Self-Disclosure*

Objectives

On completion of this chapter you should be able to:
1. Define intrapersonal and interpersonal self-disclosure.
2. Discuss how one's self-image influences his communication behavior.
3. List some of the benefits of self-disclosure.
4. Specify the risks of self-disclosure.
5. Discuss the pressures in society that work against self-disclosure.
6. Evaluate the necessity for adjusting to various roles in life.

Chapter 1 states that human communication is, by its very nature, a personal process because one can never separate his own opinions and beliefs from his perception of communication events. The person-ableness of a communication transaction can also be discussed in terms of the amount of openness and honesty the participants allow. When participants are concentrating on openness and honesty, they are engaging in self-disclosure.

INTRAPERSONAL SELF-DISCLOSURE

When one is open and honest with himself, he is engaging in intrapersonal self-disclosure. Each of us, in order to build realistic views of ourselves, must engage in this type of disclosure. Effective interpersonal communication begins with an accurate understanding of the self—an accurate self-concept.[1] Although we realize that one can never have a *completely* accurate self-concept, intrapersonal self-disclosure can assist us in developing a maximum amount of self-understanding.

Better understanding of the self is beneficial. For example, through intrapersonal self-disclosure you can become a self-actualized person,[2] one who functions fully, communicates effectively with others, and adjusts to changing situations. In fact, people in personal distress can often be helped if they are assisted in self-disclosure so they have a more accurate self-concept. If a personal problem is caused by one's view of himself, then changing his self-concept may solve the problem.[3] Once his self-perception is accurate, he can begin to see why others react to him the way they do. In short, a more accurate self-perception built through self-disclosure leads to an understanding of communication events.

Whether we accurately understand ourselves or not, we project our self-image in our communication transactions.[4] The way we address others, both verbally and nonverbally, reflects our apparent self-image. We all have met the "know-it-all" who gives us the impression that he has all the answers and never has any doubt. His projected self-image greatly affects others. Because he reveals an inflated self-image, he will repel many people. They will not trust him and will react negatively to him. Similarly, some people project deflated self-images. An acquaintance of the authors always begins his statements by saying "You will think this is a dumb idea, but . . . ." He consistently projects an unfavorable self-image. He has some creative ideas, but, because of his incorrect self-image, he and others do not appreciate their worth.

Regardless of your self-concept, you must each be willing to engage in intrapersonal self-disclosure. If you improve the accuracy of your

[1] John W. Keltner, *Interpersonal Speech-Communication: Elements and Structures,* Wadsworth, Belmont, 1970, p. 43.

[2] C. N. Cofer and M. H. Appley, *Motivation: Theory and Research,* John Wiley, 1964, p. 663.

[3] William C. Schutz, *Joy: Expanding Human Awareness,* Grove Press, New York, 1967, p. 248.

[4] Erving Goffman, *Presentation of the Self in Everyday Life,* Doubleday Anchor Books, Garden City, 1959, p. 242.

view of yourself, you will better understand why others react to you the way they do.

INTERPERSONAL SELF-DISCLOSURE

When two or more individuals are open and honest with each other, they are engaging in interpersonal self-disclosure. Each individual discloses himself to the other. Such disclosure permits free and spontaneous communication to develop. As a result, the people, over time, will come to know one another better.

It is important to note that the increased knowledge gained through interpersonal self-disclosure may actually produce impasses in a relationship. Conflict between two people might develop because the disclosure process allows important differences of opinion to emerge. Interestingly, these conflicts can produce growth in personal relationships. As the impasses or conflicts are resolved, growth in the relationship is fostered.[5]

As growth is fostered in an interpersonal relationship, a person's respect for the other person increases. Each person sincerely has the other person's interests at heart and wants to preserve the integrity and autonomy of the other. This type of "healthy" relationship can only develop, however, if each partner has given the other partner the opportunity to get to know him.[6] The basic necessity for healthy interpersonal relationships is that the participants know each other as *distinct individuals*.[7]

Those who create an atmosphere of interpersonal self-disclosure will be able to communicate at optimum effectiveness. The more we know about each other, the more effective and efficient will be our communication attempts.[8]

Reflect for a moment about some of your own interpersonal relationships. Do you have any relationships where the integrity and autonomy of the other person are as important to you as your own integrity and autonomy? If you do, you and the other person are engaging in self-disclosure. By letting the other person know you as a distinct individual, you have fulfilled a prerequisite to a healthy interpersonal relationship.

[5] Sidney Jourard, *Personal Adjustment,* 2nd. Ed., Macmillan, New York, 1963, pp. 341–342.
[6] Ibid., p. 356.
[7] Ibid., p. 312.
[8] Keltner, pp. 53–57 (cited in footnote 1).

BENEFITS OF SELF-DISCLOSURE

Personal growth depends on both intrapersonal and interpersonal disclosure.[9] For personal growth, one needs to know himself and to have healthy interpersonal relationships with others.

A person can be compared to a turtle who "makes progress only when his neck is out." His neck is out only when he is being open and honest. A person who is open and honest with himself and others has the "courage to be." Such an individual is considered to have a healthy personality. He states his feelings, beliefs, and goals, and accepts the consequences that follow.[10] He knows himself and is free to let others get to know him; as a result, he will probably have the opportunity to get to know them through their self-disclosure.

Thus, the main benefit of self-disclosure is personal growth. This growth will be a general increased satisfaction with life. The characteristics of personal growth are the development of meaningful interpersonal relationships and intrapersonal understanding.

If one is going to receive the benefits of disclosure, he must realize that self-disclosure is a **process**. It must be incorporated into one's daily behavior. We cannot just "disclose" ourselves once and then forget about it. Disclosure, as an act, is prerequisite to personal growth; but disclosure, as a process, is necessary for continued growth.

RISKS OF SELF-DISCLOSURE

Although self-disclosure sounds easy, it is not. For true self-disclosure to exist, one must communicate "personal, private" information. The information is "personal" because it is of such a nature that another cannot acquire it unless you disclose it. The information is "private" because you will not disclose it to just anyone who might inquire about it.[11] Each of us is reluctant to disclose "personal, private" information because of the risks involved in any act of disclosure.

While self-disclosure is not as dangerous as some make it out to be, it does entail risk. For one to become open and disclose his thoughts and feelings to others, he must **truly believe** that he will be in no danger

[9] O. Hobart Mowrer, *The New Group Therapy,* Van Nostrand, Princeton, 1964, p. 64.
[10] Jourard, p. 11 (cited in footnote 5).
[11] Samuel A. Culbert, "The Interpersonal Process of Self-Disclosure: It Takes Two to See One," *Explorations in Applied Behavioral Science,* NTL Institute for Applied Behavioral Science, Washington, D.C., (1967), *3,* 2.

if he allows himself to become defenseless and unguarded.[12] If one believes there is danger, he will fail to disclose.

There are factors that make us fear both intrapersonal and interpersonal self-disclosure. Among these factors are a fear of intimacy, a fear of self-knowledge, and a fear of responsibility.[13] Each of us has the three basic interpersonal needs of affection, inclusion, and control. If we feel that we have not successfully fulfilled any of these needs, we will probably fear both intrapersonal and interpersonal self-disclosure. For example, if we have not realized satisfactory fulfillment of our need for affection, we will probably fear the risk of too much or too little "intimacy" involved in any self-disclosure. By the same token, if we have not fulfilled our need for inclusion, we will not feel we have successfully learned to deal with our environment. If this is the case, we will probably fear the knowledge about ourselves that will be revealed in either intrapersonal or interpersonal self-disclosure. Also, if we have been unable to realize a satisfactory level of control, we will fear the responsibility for revealing or receiving personal, private information.

Another risk involved in self-disclosure is that one may not receive positive feedback to his behavior. Because positive feedback helps one fulfill his interpersonal needs, if it is not received at certain times, a person will feel diminished.[14] As noted in Chapter 8, *all* interpersonal communication is potentially threatening to a person who needs, but fears he may not receive, certain responses to his messages. Since all interpersonal communication is potentially threatening to some people, it is easy to understand why most of us feel that there is risk involved in self-disclosing personal, private information.

There are additional risks in self-disclosure. It is a simple fact, for example, that when a man openly and honestly discloses himself to another, "then the mystery that he was decreases enormously."[15] As one permits his personal "mystery" to dissolve, he, figuratively speaking, stands naked. Fears of such exposure are real and are not to be shunned. It is quite reasonable for one to assume that another person may think less of him if the other person is allowed to see him "naked." Although one might inappropriately reason, "Well, if that person doesn't

[12] Sidney M. Jourard, "Toward A Psychology of Transcendent Behavior," in Herbert A. Otto (Ed.), *Explorations in Human Potentialities,* Charles C Thomas, Springfield, 1966, p. 366.

[13] Gerard Egan, *Encounter: Group Processes for Interpersonal Growth,* Brooks/Cole Publishing, Belmont, 1970, p. 191. (Egan, however, restricts these fears to the intrapersonal level.)

[14] Ibid., pp. 242–263.

[15] Sidney M. Jourard, *The Transparent Self: Self-Disclosure and Well-Being,* Van Nostrand, Princeton, 1964, p. 3.

like me after he recognizes my weaknesses then he isn't worth knowing in the first place," the risks involved in self-disclosure are still real.

Furthermore, the "reverse halo-effect" is a risk in self-disclosure.[16] Put simply, we fear that if a person is exposed to *one* of our "weaknesses" he will generalize from that one weakness and think we have *many* weaknesses. Earlier, we discussed the notion that if one sees a person as highly credible on one topic, he will probably see him as highly credible on several topics. This "generalizing of credibility" across topics is called a "halo-effect." The fear of a "reverse halo-effect" is the fear that, "If I demonstrate one weakness, people will think that I have several weaknesses." Such a fear is understandable because many of us operate on a reverse halo-effect principle. Take, for example, when you dislike someone. You may say things such as, "I sure feel sorry for his children," or "I'd sure hate to be his wife," or "I bet he's terrible to his parents." You assume his behavior with you is similar to the way he reacts to others. Disclosing a weakness to someone may open the way for their general rejection of you. The reverse halo-effect is definitely a risk in self-disclosure.

Self-disclosure, then, always entails a certain degree of risk. These risks lead to fears that are understandable, predictable, and justifiable. But because self-disclosure is necessary for personal development, one cannot let the fears of disclosure constantly thwart his attempts to reveal himself. Never disclosing to others becomes an unbreakable cycle. A continuous flight from self-disclosure is a flight from responsibility as well as from the anxiety and work involved in constructive personal change.[17]

SOCIAL NORMS WORKING AGAINST SELF-DISCLOSURE

Our society, perhaps in an attempt to protect individuals from the risks of self-disclosure, releases two forces that deter self-disclosure between people. First, there is a cultural ban against intimate self-disclosure; second, there is a norm that says one should accept the "lie" as a way of life.

One of the reasons for the cultural ban against self-disclosure is that we consider it inappropriate to openly express feelings toward others. We are expected to display "respect for others."[18] Although each of us probably agrees with the social norm of respecting others, it is unfor-

[16] Egan, pp. 211–212 (cited in footnote 13).
[17] Egan, p. 209 (cited in footnote 13).
[18] Egan, p. 146 (cited in footnote 13).

tunate that pressures to display respect often inhibit our expression of feelings. Have you ever wanted to tell someone whom you have just met for the first time that you find them extremely attractive? Many observers would interpret such an honest expression as a lack of respect. Some receivers of such an expression, in an attempt to maintain their personal "dignity," would not be able to cope with the situation. Overtly, they may interpret the expression as weird or rude.

The cultural ban against intimate disclosure is placed most heavily on the male segment of society. The masculine ideal says, "Little boys don't cry."[19] Extended, the masculine ideal implies that men who self-disclose are weak. One need not observe human behavior very long to discover that men are not expected to self-disclose, but to "take charge." They must be strong and know where they are going in life. Only "sissys" or weak-willed males are expected to express emotions.

It is not important whether society is right or wrong for placing a cultural ban against intimate self-disclosure. The fact is, such a ban exists; as a result, most of us are inhibited in our disclosure efforts. When coupled with the intrapersonal and interpersonal risks, the social ban is difficult for many of us to overcome.

The second social force against self-disclosure is the cultivation of the "lie" as a way of life.[20] It often appears that if one is going to succeed or "get ahead" in life he must take advantage of every situation. This belief forces us even further away from a willingness to self-disclose. If one is open and honest, he may have to sacrifice some success. Being open and honest, it is believed, is not a very effective way of "manipulating" people. For manipulation purposes, one should "appear" open and honest, but actual openness and honesty may thwart materialistic success.

There are several possible explanations for the existence of these social forces against self-disclosure, but explanations seem incomplete. The forces are real, however, and they do make many of us incapable of engaging in any expression of honest emotions. *We, for the most part, live in emotional bondage.*

The existence of emotional bondage is evident in the recent, rapid development of sensitivity laboratories. These are places where people can go for a few days, or a weekend, to talk honestly and openly with others. Many contemporary churches and several business organizations have developed short programs for their members or employees to have the opportunity to experience honest interpersonal communication with others through sensitivity sessions. Courses in "group

[19] Egan, p. 200 (cited in footnote 13).
[20] Egan, p. 199 (cited in footnote 13).

dynamics" are popular on many college campuses. Typically, such courses consist of sensitivity exercises—exercises designed to help students "open up," be honest, and become aware of others' needs.

"Emotional bondage" is a product of the risks involved in self-disclosure and of the social forces that deter such disclosure. There are several ways to alleviate the "emotional bondage" problem. Communication channels in our modern organizations can be developed to eliminate part of the problem. Most large bureaucratic structures prevent honest and open communication. For example, many contend that formal education, as a large bureaucratic structure, is overloaded in the area of intellect and impoverished in the area of emotion. The development of our emotions is "left to the crowd compellers, the press, radio, TV, churches, and the commercial exploiters with their lying advertisements. Our leading schoolmasters who deal with emotions are our pop heroes and film stars."[21] Although we may reject this statement as being exaggerated, there is some truth in this indictment of formal education. In most cases, the system simply does not allow for the development of expression of honest emotions.

The same criticism can be made against other contemporary organizations. The structure of business organizations often precludes the expression of anything except task messages. Academic departments in colleges and universities are normally oriented around and only sensitive to task completion. Contemporary churches are often perceived as opposed to emotional expression, too. The administrative structures of these organizations are so tightly organized in the name of efficiency that we, as members, are discouraged in our efforts to express open emotions. Without the opportunity to express feelings during "working" hours the need for sensitivity laboratories to help us escape "emotional bondage" will continue to grow.

Opportunities for honest and open interpersonal communication could be incorporated, at least to some extent, within the tightly organized structures in our society. It is doubtful, however, that opportunities for open expression will be developed because of the social forces against self-disclosure. Recently, one of the authors of this book visited his oldest daughter's teacher. During the discussion he asked the teacher if she ever let the students engage in open, interpersonal communication in the classroom. He asked her if she ever just let the students talk with each other—relate to each other about themselves, their concerns, and their impressions. The teacher's response was, "No, we can't permit that type of freedom in the classroom with such

---

[21] A. S. Neill, "Can I Come to Summerhill? I Hate My School," *Psychology Today* (1968), *I*, 37.

young children. You see, they're too self-oriented. They are not very good listeners. All they would want to do is talk about their own problems rather than giving the other children the opportunity to relate, too. They are simply too young to relate to each other." When she finished speaking, the author sat there for a moment and then said, "You know, your description of these 'youngsters' is a fairly accurate description of our adult world." He went on to say, "One of the biggest problems facing our society today is that most of us are self-oriented. We cannot, because we rarely have the opportunity, relate to others. We do not open ourselves to others—perhaps because we would not know how to handle it if they opened themselves to us. Maybe part of our problem is that we have never been given the opportunity or necessary encouragement to try to relate. As a result, the only time many of us can now relate in an honest and open manner is in a planned, controlled environment."

What do you think? Are seven-year-old children old enough to relate to each other? We think so—age may be a totally irrelevant consideration. One must be given the opportunity and encouragement to be open and honest before he can learn how to be open and honest. One must be given the opportunity and encouragement to face the fears of open and honest disclosure before he can handle those fears. This same criticism applies to most of the organizational structures in our social system as a whole—not just in some school systems. Thus, society has a built-in communication problem. And, it may be that we are self-oriented because we have not had the opportunity to be others-oriented. If openness and honesty are not encouraged, it is unlikely they will come about.

SELF-DISCLOSURE AND ROLES

The basic ingredient in self-disclosure is open and honest communication. Many of us seem to think that if something is "honest," it is "honest." Or, we often act as if something is either right or wrong—if it is not right, it is wrong. "Rightness," "openness," "truthfulness," and "goodness" are only a few of the many concepts we have a tendency to think of as being absolute. It either is or it is not—it is either black or white.

If one operates from this "absolute" position, then any type of role behavior is dishonest when viewed from a self-disclosure perspective. From this perspective, one cannot perform various roles. For example, he must be the same whether he is speaking as a parent's son, as a woman's fiance, as a teacher's student, or as a student seeking a campus political position. Viewing honesty and openness from such an absolute perspective means that a person has to "be himself"; he cannot have more than one role.

One basic fact that cannot be ignored is that as we proceed through life, each of us has several roles to live. To deny that we must live various roles is to assume that there is only one "real" you. And, any deviation from that one, honest you is the real you wearing a costume. Is that true? Is there only one real you? We do not think so. Who is to say that the "you" interacting with a professor really isn't "you?" It is you. It is you in that role at that time and you are *real*. The "you" in this situation, is not the same "you" as the "you" at a Friday beer party. The person is the same, but the "yous" are different—they are, however, *all real*. We all have to adjust to various situations; therefore, we cannot show constant behavior regardless of the circumstances.

The person who convinces himself that he can and should project a constant, "honest" image in all situations will run into difficulty. The difficulty will be both intrapersonal and interpersonal. We must have a large repertoire of *honest roles*. Notice, we said "honest roles." Roles are not necessarily dishonest. One must decide what is the most desirable and effective way he can communicate in each situation. One who attempts to sustain a single, consistent role in all situations and with all people will perform stereotyped behavior. As a result, he will probably be ineffective both as a person and as a communicator.[22]

More importantly, the person who insists on defying the necessity of making role adjustments is often selfish and inconsiderate. We say "selfish" because his major concern is his own personal goal of consistency. We say "inconsiderate" because his refusal to modify his behavior patterns can hurt some people very deeply. For example, the son who rejects the religious tenets taught by his parents is being both selfish and inconsiderate when he informs his ailing mother that her beliefs are wrong.[23]

Reasoned Self-Disclosure

It is possible for a person to engage in intrapersonal and interpersonal self-disclosure while performing various honest roles. There is, however, a fine line between necessary, honest roles and unnecessary, deceitful roles. Vast inconsistency in all roles leads to a total lack of

[22] For similar treatment, see Keltner, p. 50–58 (cited in footnote 1).
[23] The question of totally consistent behavior was also examined in Chapter 4.

disclosure. "No disclosure" becomes total dishonesty and it is more undesirable than the extreme of "absolute consistency" in all roles.

"Reasoned self-disclosure" is both possible and desirable. In order to disclose in an open and honest manner, it is not necessary to totally ignore situational constraints. *In reasoned self-disclosure, one is concerned with the other person as well as himself.* He does not let his own honesty and openness destroy the integrity and autonomy of the other person. Reasoned disclosure can help us overcome the unnecessary, vastly inconsistent role differences we have erected for ourselves. At the same time, such disclosure can help us determine the minor role adjustments we should maintain.

Both the "absolute disclosure" approach and the "no disclosure" approach to dealing with people can be extremely inhumane. The receiver of our messages must be considered. One does not have the right to hurt others in the name of absolute honesty. There are instances when such unreasoned disclosure ("honesty for honesty's sake"), has destroyed beautiful relationships. On the other hand, there are other instances when honesty may have saved a deteriorating relationship. There is no magic formula for establishing a reasoned self-disclosure atmosphere. One thing is definite, however; when such an atmosphere exists, it is beautiful.

Most of us, hopefully, will develop the "reasoned self-disclosure" approach to dealing with people. It is with such an approach that we get to know ourselves and others, and let others get to know us. The development of healthy interpersonal communication relationships results. In such relationships, *concern for both the self and the others involved is central*.

SELF-DISCLOSURE AND LIFE

A person can sensitize himself to be concerned for himself and others. This sensitization can lead to reasoned self-disclosure. The result will be personal growth.

The sensitivity a person gains from reasoned self-disclosure can help him be open to experiences as well as open to himself and others. Are you sensitive to experiences in general? Are you, for example, sensitive to each day? Can you recall what you did yesterday? Last week? Can you remember a typical day of two weeks ago and list the specific things you did?

Most of us would be hard pressed to recall much about two days ago—let alone two weeks ago. Why is this so? Is not each day important? Evidently not. Many of us go through day after day without *really* experiencing life—without *really* being able to say, "I'm glad I lived this day—it was certainly worthwhile." Why don't we experience every day? Or, in the words of a playwright, "Why must we live for the days of glory—why can't we live the days between?" That is an extremely profound question. The "days of glory" are the graduation days, the marriage days, the birthdays, the Christmas days, the New Years days, the job promotion days, the new car days, and the pledge days, to name only a few. Although the list of "days of glory" can be rather lengthy, the vast majority of the days of life are the "days between"—the normal days, the yesterdays, and the todays. Do you *live* the "days between," or do you *exist* during the "days between" and *live for* the "days of glory?" Unfortunately, most of us do the latter.

A poet once compared a normal day of life to a common rock laying on the shoulder of the road. He was walking down a normal road on a normal day and he, as usual, kicked normal pebbles off the shoulder of the normal road into the normal ditch. As he started to kick another pebble, he stopped for a moment, picked it up, and examined it closely. As he looked at it in the sunlight, he noticed that the normal pebble had some small pieces of sparkling mica embedded in it. He also noticed that it contained some pretty fragments of pink feldspar diffused in shiny, white quartz and black tourmaline. This normal pebble was actually very beautiful when it was examined carefully. He speculated about all of the other normal pebbles and reasoned that each of them was probably as pretty as the one he had examined— each was unique and beautiful in its own way.

A normal pebble can easily be compared to a normal day. Each normal day is unique, worthwhile, and potentially stimulating if it is carefully examined and experienced. Inherent in the careful examination and experiencing of a normal day is the awareness of self, of others, of objects, and of happenings. One can live each day as a "day of glory" if he consciously tries. Such attempts will lead one to become more aware of, and thereby, more open to all that happens around him. One of our acquaintances who is familiar with the normal day theme consciously tries to sensitize himself to living each normal day. He always carries a small, normal pebble in his pocket to remind himself of the potential beauty of a normal day. Each evening, when he removes the pebble from his pocket, he asks himself, "What was it about today, that (1) made it truly worth living and (2) made it a special rather than a normal day?" More often than not, the uniqueness and worth of the day centers around open and honest interpersonal experiences with others.

We cannot guarantee that disclosure with self and others will solve all of a person's personal problems. We can predict, however, that open and honest self-disclosure will help one become excited about himself, others, and living. Intrapersonal and interpersonal self-disclosure represent the epitome of good communication transactions. Such communication experiences render communication central to life. Understanding human communication behavior should help one be a more effective participant in meaningful interpersonal relationships. These relationships are formed and maintained through interpersonal communication.

The personal communication process is just that; it is personal. The essence of communication is people touching other people's lives, trying to share meanings. Communication, whether it is intrapersonal, interpersonal, small group, public speaking, or mass communication influences and is influenced by us all. The transaction of ideas and feelings binds us all together through the personal process called "communication."

Exercises

1. Make a list of conditions that must be met before you feel you can engage in open and honest intrapersonal self-disclosure. Discuss the list with the class.
2. List the general characteristics that you believe a person must have before you feel free to engage in intrapersonal self-disclosure with him. Discuss the list with the class.
3. List the roles that you play during a normal day. Try to determine what necessary behavioral adjustments you make as you move from one role to another. What unnecessary behavioral adjustments do you make as you switch roles? Discuss these adjustments with the class.
4. Pick an issue such as "water pollution." Tell the class what you predict is the thinking of one of the persons sitting next to you about the issue. Give reasons for why you think the person would feel in that way about the issue. Next, have the person reveal his thinking on the issue.

Suggested Readings

Gerard Egan, *Encounter: Group Processes for Interpersonal growth,* Brooks/Cole, Belmont, 1970.

Gerard Egan, *Encounter Groups: Basic Readings,* Brooks/Cole, Belmont, 1971.

Sidney M. Jourard, *Disclosing Man to Himself,* Van Nostrand, Princeton, 1968.

Sidney M. Jourard, *The Transparent Self,* Van Nostrand, Princeton, 1964.

O. H. Mowrer, *The New Group Therapy,* Van Nostrand, Princeton, 1964.

Herbert A. Otto (Ed.), *Explorations in Human Potentialities,* Charles C Thomas, Springfield, 1966.

Anselm Strauss, *Mirrors and Masks: The Search for Identity,* Free Press, Glencoe, 1959.

Index

Abdicrat person, defined, 27
Adaptation, 157—159
Addington, D. W., 101
Affection, and credibility, 149
  and feedback, 129
  need for, 25—26
Alexander, H. G., 83, 89, 92
Allen, J. P., 86
Andersen, K. E., 28, 47, 69, 112, 114, 118,
    120, 123, 140, 145, 151, 173, 182, 198,
    210, 213
Appeals, emotional, 161—162
  fear, 163—165
  logical, 161—162
  types of, 160—166
Appley, M. H., 218
Aristotelian model, 47—48
Aristotle, 47, 67, 144, 146, 148, 161
Arnold, C. C., 157
Arnold, W. E., 119
Aronson, E., 21, 23, 133, 153—154, 160,
    173
Asch, S. E., 34
Attention, defined, 112
  selective, see Selective attention
Attitude, changes in, 196—198
Auer, J. J., 69
Autistic thought, 88
Autocrat person, defined, 27—28
Axioms of communication, 99—105
Ayers, H. J., 134

Backman, C. W., 172, 173
Baird, A. C., 150
Barker, L., 21, 24, 41, 178, 195
Barnlund, D. C., 22, 39, 51—53, 99, 114,
    129

Barnlund model, 51—53, 61
Basehart, J., 169
Bateson, G., 20, 25, 38, 102
Bauer, R. A., 199
Beavin, J. H., 55, 99—105
Becker, S. L., 150
Behavior, changes in, 194—196
Benne, K. D., 203
Bennis, W. G., 124, 128—129, 195, 203
Berkowitz, L., 122—123, 163—166
Berlo, D. K., 49, 50, 92, 127, 145—147
Berlo model, 49
Bettinghaus, E. P., 150, 161—162, 174
Bevan, W., 118
Birdwhistle, R. L., 97, 102, 106
Blau, P., 151
Bodaken, E. M., 36, 213
Body orientation and nonverbal communica-
    tion, 108
Bombard, A., 132
Bordon, G. A., 139, 140, 143
Bormann, E. G., 29, 33, 35—36
Boulding, K. E., 45
Bradbury, R., 7—17
Brainwashing, 194—195
Brave New World (Huxley), 193
Brembeck, W. L., 69
Broadbent, D. E., 112
Brock, T. C., 195
Bronfenbrenner, U., 119
Brooks, R. D., 142
Brooks, W. D., 19, 38, 140
Brown, J., 195
Brown, R., 83—85, 88—89
Brownfield, C. A., 129—130, 132
Bruner, J. S., 114
Burke, K., 49

Campbell, D. T., 198
Campbell, J. H., 96, 114
Carmichael, L., 116
Carroll, J. B., 82, 85, 89, 92
Cartwright, D., 29—31, 34, 36, 121
Charisma, defined, 149—151
Chin, R., 203
Chomsky, N., 86—87
Clevenger, Jr., T., 151
Cliques, 29
Cofer, C. N., 218
Cognitive consistency theories, 177—188
Cohen, A. R., 166—168
Cohesion, 31—32
   defined, 31
Colburn, C. W., 164
Collins, B. E., 38, 176, 198
Commitment, and persuasibility, 204
Communication, axioms of, 99—105
   defined, 5—7
   as interaction, 4—6, 17, 41
   interpersonal, 22—29, 57, 201—202
   intrapersonal, 20—22, 57—58, 202
   and mental illness, 102—103
   models of, 47—61
   as personal, 3—7, 17—20
   as a process, 4—7, 17, 55
   punctuation of, 104
   as static event, 4
   as transactional, 4—7, 17, 39—42, 53—59
Complementary transaction, 104—105
Compliance, cause of, 197
Conceptualization, process of, 45—47
Conclusion drawing, 166
Condon, Jr., J. C., 90
Conformity, 34—35
Congruity principle, 183—185
Conklin, F., 101
Connotation, 92—93
Control, and credibility, 149
   defined, 131, 149
   need for, 27—28
Cottingham, D. R., 163
Credibility, and affectation, 149
   and control, 149
   defined, 140
   dimensions of, 144—151
   dynamics of, 140—144
   enhancing, 151—154
   and evidence usage, 163

and feedback, 129
from an interpersonal perspective, 148—
   149
from a mass perspective, 149—151
from a public speaking perspective, 144—
   148
and message adaptation, 159
and message discrepancy, 160
and persuasibility, 204
posttransactional, 142—143, 153—154
pretransactional, 142, 152—153
transactional, 142, 153—154
Crossman, R., 75
Cues, behavioral nonverbal, 20, 52, 57, 97
   behavioral verbal, 20, 52—53, 57, 97
   private, 20, 52, 97
   public, 20, 52, 97—99
Culbert, S. A., 220

Dance, E. X., 20—21, 28, 87
de Bono, E., 114—115
De Fleur, M. L., 46
Democrat person, defined, 28
Denotation, 92—93
Dissonance theory, 185—188
Distance and nonverbal communication, 107
Dobb, L. W., 106
Dogmatism, 174—175
Double bind theory, 102—103
Dunham, R. E., 152

Eavesdropping, 214—215
Eeon, D. J., 195
Egan, G., 221—223
Ego-involvement, 175—177
Ehninger, D., 168
Encoding, effects of, 210—211, 213—214
   rewards of, 213—214
Ethics, application to communication, 73—75
   approahes to, 71—73
   historical perspective of, 66—68
   individual code of, 71
   situational code of, 72—73
   universal code of, 71—72
   views of, 68—70
Ethos, 161
   defined, 48
   see Credibility
Evidence, use of, 162—163
Ewbank, H. L., 69

Exposure, selective, *see* Selective exposure
Eye contact, 107—108

Feedback, and affection, 129
  costs of, 134—135
  defined, 128
  effects of, 133—134
  in mass communication, 41
    nature of, 28, 39, 54—55, 126—128
    need for, 24, 128—132
    in public speaking, 39
    sources of, 132—133
Feldman, S., 177
Feshback, S., 163
Festinger, L., 31—32, 203
Fidelity (of communication), defined, 50
Fishman, J. A., 89
Fletcher, J. F., 72
Fodor, J. A., 87
Fotheringham, W. C., 140
Freedman, J. L., 122, 166
Freeley, A. J., 169

Gardiner, J. C., 134
General semantics, *see* Semantics
Gerard, H. B., 210
Giffin, K., 151
Goffman, E., 23, 99, 100, 102—103, 218
Goodman, C. C., 114
Golden, B. W., 154
Gordon, G. N., 91
Gorgias (Plato), 67
Graphic model, defined, 44
Greenwald, A. G., 195
Gregg, R. B., 143
Groups, assumptions about, 30
  concepts about, 31—37
  defined, 29
  obstacles, 37—38
  socioemotional, 31—32
  task, 31—32
  types of, 30—31
  model of, 59
Grove, T. G., 143
Guetzkow, H., 38

Haiman, F. S., 153
Haley, J., 103
Hall, E., 100
Hassling, J., 150
Harrison, R., 96
Harvey, I. G., 152

Hayakawa, S. I., 90—91
Heider, F., 178
Heider's balance theory, 178—181
Hepler, H. W., 96, 114
Hennessy, B. C., 113, 195—196, 202
Heraclitus, 4
Hewgill, M. A., 164
Hogan, H. P., 116
Hollander, E. P., 196, 199
Holtzman, P. D., 152
Hovland, C. I., 144—145, 148, 166—167,
  172—176, 203, 210—214
Howell, W. S., 69
Hunt, R. G., 196, 199
Huxley, A., 193

Identification, 197
Inclusion, and feedback, 129
  need for, 26—27
Individual code (of ethics), 71—72
Information theory model, 50—51
Inoculation theory, 204—205
Insko, C. A., 176, 195
Intelligence, and persuasibility, 172
Internalization, 197
Interpersonal communication, defined, 22—
  29
  effects on behavior, 24, 201—202
  model of, 57
Interpersonal needs, 25—29, 31, 38. *See
  also* Affection; Control; and Inclusion
Intrapersonal communication, defined, 20—
  22
  effects on behavior, 21, 202
  model of, 57—58

Jackson, D. D., 55, 99—105
Janis, I. L., 144—145, 148, 163, 172—174,
  203, 210—214
Jenkins, J. J., 87
Johnson, W., 208, 215
Jones, E. E., 210
Jourard, S., 219—221

Kaplan, A., 62
Katz, B., 118
Katz, D., 203
Katz, E., 122
Kelley, H. H., 144—145, 148, 203, 210—214
Kelman, H. C., 195, 197
Keltner, J. W., 39, 218—219, 226
Kibler, R. J., 178, 195

Kiesler, C. A., 176, 198
King, B. T., 211
Kirk, J. T., 123, 199
Knower, F. H., 150
Koehler, J. W., 119
Kramer, E., 101
Kuhn, T. S., 45

Language, acquisition, 84—89
  characteristics of, 84
  dynamics of, 93—94
  nature of, 81—84
  and thought, 88—89
La Piere, R. T., 198
Law of primacy, 167
Lazarsfeld, P. F., 54, 122
Leadership and charisma, 150
  functions, 37
  traits, 36—37
Leavitt, H. J., 129, 133—134
Lee, I. J., 75, 92
Leeper, R. R., 81
Lefford, A., 161
Lemert, J. B., 145, 147
Lenneberg, E. H., 87
Leventhal, H., 164—165
A Lie Is Always A Lie (Grossman), 74—75
Lindzey, G., 121, 123, 160, 173
Lobe, J., 169
Logan, W., 81, 94
Logos, 161
  defined, 48
Lumsdaine, A. A., 166, 211
Lund, F. H., 167

McCauliff, M. L., 134
McCroskey, J. C., 119—120, 147—148, 152,
  162—163, 168
MacDonald, J. B., 81
McGuird, W. J., 121—122, 160—162, 166—
  167, 173, 177, 186, 198, 200, 203—
  205
MacLean, Jr., M. S., 28, 53—55, 114
McNeill, D., 82
Machiavelli, N., 68
Mandlebaum, D. G., 97
Manic-depressive, 102
Marsh, P. D., 157
Martin, H., 28, 47, 123, 182, 198
Mass communication, 40—42

changes in views of, 46
  and credibility, 149—151
  effects on behavior, 198—200
  model of, 54
Meaning, 91—94
Mehrly, R. S., 168
Mental illness, and communication, 102—103
Menzel, H., 54
Mertz, R. J., 147
Message adaptation, 157—159
Message discrepancy, 159—160
Message organization, 166—168
Message style, 168
Miller, G. A., 87
Miller, G. R., 5—6, 44, 70, 141, 159, 161—
  162, 164, 169, 213
Miller, N., 176, 198
Mills, J., 153
Models, defined, 44, 47
  Aristotelian model, 48
  Barnlund model, 48
  Berlo model, 50
  functions of, 61—62
  historical insights, 47—49
  Shannon and Weaver model, 51
  Westley and MacLean models, 53—54
  Wenburg and Wilmot models, 56, 58, 60
Monroe, A. H., 168
Mortensen, C. D., 22, 28, 51, 177, 183, 213
Mowrer, O. H., 220
Mueller, R. A., 129, 133—134
Myers, G. C., 213

Nebergall, R. E., 176
Neill, A. S., 224
Newcomb, T. M., 182—183, 186
1984 (Orwell), 193
Nilsen, T. R., 70
Nonverbal codes, 105—106
Norms, alteration of, 35—36
  defined, 33
  formal, 33
  informal, 33
  and pressures, 33—35

Ogden, C. K., 90
One-sided and two-sided messages, 165—166
Operant conditioning, 85—87
Opinionated language, 168
Orwell, G., 193

Osgood, C. E., 183
Ostrom, T. M., 195
Overpersonal person, defined, 25—26
Oversocial person, defined, 26—27

Packard, V., 193
Pathos, 161
  defined, 48
Paulson, S. F., 162
Pearce, W. B., 101
Perception, selective, *see* Selective perception
Perceptual noise, 51
Personal person, defined, 25—26
Personality variables, 172—175
Persuasibility, and commitment, 204
  and intelligence, 172
  and self-esteem, 172—173
  and sex, 173—174
Plato, 66—67
Powell, F. A., 164
Precker, J. A., 122
Public speaking, 38—40
  admonitions for, 69
  characteristics of, 39
  effects on behavior, 200—201
  historical view of, 48
  as part of Wenburg and Wilmot model, 58—61

Quintilian, 67

Recency effect, 167
Reinsch, Jr., N. L., 168
Retention, selective, *see* Selective retention
Reusch, J., 20, 25, 38, 97, 102, 130
Rewards, and persuasion, 213—214
The Rhetoric (Aristotle), 47, 67, 161
Richards, I. A., 90
Rokeach, M., 174
Role-playing, 212, 225—226
Rosenfield, L. W., 47
Royce, J. R., 82—83
Ruechelle, R. C., 162
Rycenga, J. A., 84

Sapir, E. A., 96—97
Saporta, S., 87, 89
Schacter, S., 35

Schein, E. H., 195
Schizophrenia, 102—103
Schramm, W., 123, 199
Schutz, W. C., 129, 131, 148
Schwartz, J., 84
Sears, D. O., 166
Secord, P. F., 118, 172—173
Seeleman, V., 118
Selective attention, 111—113
Selective exposure, 120—123, 185
Selective perception, advantages of, 120
  defined, 113
  and expectations, 118—120
  of language, 113
Selective perception, of objects, 114—118
  of persons, 118
Selective retention, 123—124
Self-disclosure, benefits of, 220
  interpersonal, 219
  intrapersonal, 218—219
  and life, 227—228
  reasoned, 226—227
  risks of, 220—222
  and roles, 225—226
  and social norms, 222—225
Self-esteem, and persuasibility, 172—173
Self-persuasion, 212—213
Semantics, 90—93
Sereno, K. K., 22, 28, 51, 177, 183, 213
Sex and persuasibility, 173—174
Shannon, C. E., 50—51
Sheffield, F. D., 166, 211
Shepherd, C. R., 32—33
Sherif, C. W., 176
Sherif, M., 176
Signs, 82—83
Siipola, E., 117
Simons, H. W., 178, 186, 195, 198
Situational code (of ethics), 72—73
Skinner, B. F., 84—85, 194
Smith, A. G., 89, 97, 112, 119, 127, 200
Smith, F., 87
Socialized thought, 88
Social person, defined, 26—27
Sophists, 66
A Sound of Thunder (Bradbury), 7—17
Source, defined, 140
Source credibility, *see* Credibility
Spatial relationship, 106—107
Statts, A. W., 86

Stevans, S. S., 6—7
Suci, G. J., 183
Sullivan, H. S., 132
Symbols, 82—84
   and referents, 90—91
Symmetrical transaction, 104—105
Symmetry theory, 182—183

Talbot, G. D., 119
Tannenbaum, P. H., 183
Teaching as a Subversive Activity, 46
Theatre, change in views of, 46
Toch, H., 114
Transaction, complementary, 104—105
   symmetrical, 104
Tustin, A., 127

Underpersonal person, defined, 25
Undersocial person, defined, 26—27
Universal code (of ethics), 71

Van Buren, P., 86
Van Bertalanffy, L., 83
Verbal Behavior (Skinner), 85
Vetter, H. J., 85
Vygotsky, L. S., 88—89, 92—93

Walden Two (Skinner), 194
Walter, A. A., 116
Watzlawick, P., 55, 99—105
Weaver, W., 50—51
Weber, M., 151
Webster, B., 153
Wenburg, J. R., 158—159
Wenburg and Wilmot model, 55—61
Weiss, W., 121, 123
Westley, B. H., 28, 53—55
Westley and MacLean model, 53—55, 61
Whorf, B. L., 89
Whorfian hypothesis, 89
Why Children Fail (Holt), 46
Widgery, R. N., 153
Wiener, N., 127
Wilmot, W. W., 177
Wilson, G., 203
Wilson, J. F., 157
Winckler, J. L., 151
Wiseman, G., 21, 24, 41

Zajonc, R. B., 183
Zander, A., 29—31, 34, 36